Sixth Sense

Also by Stuart Wilde

Sixth Sense

Including the Secrets of the Etheric Subtle Body

Stuart Wilde

Hay House, Inc.
Carlsbad, California • Sydney, Australia

Published and distributed in the United States by:
Hay House, Inc., P.O. Box 5100, Carlsbad, CA 92018-5100
(800) 654-5126 • (800) 650-5115 (fax)

Editorial: Jill Kramer, Anna Scott   *Design:* Jenny Richards
Diagrams: Valerie Komodikis

    The author of this book does not dispense medical advice or prescribe the use of any technique as a form of treatment for physical or medical problems without the advice of a physician, either directly or indirectly. The intent of the author is only to offer information of a general nature to help you in your quest for emotional and spiritual well-being. In the event you use any of the information in this book for yourself, which is your constitutional right, the author and the publisher assume no responsibility for your actions.

Library of Congress Cataloging-in-Publication Data

Wilde, Stuart.
        Sixth sense   :   including the secrets of the etheric subtle body /
    Stuart Wilde.
            p.   cm.
        Includes bibliographical references.
        ISBN 1-56170-501-2 (pbk.)
            1. Extrasensory perception. 2. Astral body.   I. Title.
    BF1321.W49   2000
    133.8—dc21   99-38060
                                                            CIP

ISBN 1-56170-501-2
03 02 01 00   8 7 6 5
1st printing, February 1999
5th printing, November 2000

Printed in the United States of America

CONTENTS

SCIENCE AND THE SIXTH SENSE

The sixth sense is a sacred energy—it taps you in to the state of all-knowing. And with that comes a special responsibility, hand-in-hand with a higher state of consciousness and more spiritual awareness. You seek to develop your sixth sense to make a greater connection with the Infinite Self and the eternal light within. The sixth sense also taps you in to the shaman's world of the nature-self. Of course, developing awareness helps keep you safe.

I think it is correct to say that the process is one of shining a light on your spiritual evolution as a human—empowering you with an esoteric inner power, a special power—one that was used by the initiates of old who knew how to access the ancient wisdom. They knew about shape-shifting, dimensions, and the technicalities of the chakras and the etheric web.

The subtle body (the *etheric*) is a key component in understanding the sixth sense, but most of the old information about the subtle body got lost over the eons. When it was rediscovered by Theosophists such as Madame Blavatsky and brought back from India, much of the information was misunderstood. The Theosophists did a magnificent job—almost all of our esoteric knowledge in the Western world was laid down by them. But it was the early days, and the later writers of the 1920s and '30s scrambled the information and inserted a lot of extra information, which I think confused people. It certainly confused *me*. I found that, at times, I could make no headway with it at all.

In the end, I decided that the only way we can properly rediscover the lost knowledge of the subtle body is to feel it out inside ourselves—a journey of trial and error. I imagine that the people who initially figured out acupuncture and the complexity of all the meridians must have worked in the same hit-or-miss way. They probably sat on the banks of the Yangtze one sunny afternoon, stuck a pin in their toe, felt it tickle their ear, and said, "Cool, this is where the meridian flows."

I'll talk more about the subtle body and the adjustments I made, then you can check it out for yourself—and perhaps add a whole new chapter to what is known so far. I see the process of unlocking the sixth sense as a major part of our human journey. It's the next step, for beyond the physical experience is the metaphysical one.

The story of metaphysics can be described in words and concepts, but in the end, all metaphysics is written in the oscillations and shifts of the subtle body. It is there, I believe, that the real *you* lies—it's where your true feelings and spiritual identity reside. I'll explain myself as I go. Suffice it to say that we have all moved on a lot in the last 20 to 30 years. We are now embracing a new sophistication in the technicality of perception and awareness, and especially the subtle body. Faculties such as remote viewing, which would have seemed impossible in the olden days, are now commonplace. Hopefully, we will lay down the definitive text that leads future generations in the right direction. Once you have the heightened sixth sense as a natural part of your life, you can help others. That's the bonus that comes from the time and effort we spend working on ourselves.

How I See the Sixth Sense

I see the sixth sense as a power that encapsulates a dimension of awareness, one that is outside space and time. It's like stepping through a doorway to another realm. Once you pass through, your life changes, and you move to a higher oscillation. In the olden days, rational folk saw the world of extrasensory perception as a Victorian parlor trick. Anything to do with mediumship, telepathy, psychic powers, and the sixth sense was ridiculed as being in the domain of the feeblcminded.

The modern world has been influenced by two main ideas—causal determinism and material realism. Isaac Newton established causal determinism, which says that the universe is made up of lots of balls—big ones and little ones—which orbit and bang into each other in a predetermined way, according to the laws of cause and effect. If you could work out all the mechanical laws that govern the way things move and clang together, you could work out everything. You would become godlike, and you'd know where all the little balls were at any given moment in time.

The other dominant concept, material realism, states that only the external world of matter—with its constituents, atoms, and so forth—is real, and that it is independent from the observer of that matter. Quantum theory has dealt a fatal blow to material realism.

In the old days, the Church was much more powerful than it is today. Scientists got into trouble if they contradicted the religious world-view. Galileo was hauled before the Inquisition for describing the motion of the planets. Previously, it had been decided that the earth was at the center of things and that the entire universe orbits around it.

Partly as a defense mechanism, the philosopher René Descartes divided reality into two parts, know as the concept of dualism. On the one part, he said, is the solid physical reality, the domain of scientists. The second part is mind or consciousness, which remains firmly in the domain of religion. That kept everyone happy because science and religion each had a kingdom to govern. History is riddled with some amazing ego trips. In fact, most of history is the story of ego trips if you think about it.

The Wave-Particle Nature of Reality

By the early 1900s, scientists had worked out that light is a wave phenomenon. They discovered this by noticing wave interference. When two boats pass close to each other on a lake, say, the wave set up by each boat travels outwards from the vessel until it meets the wave coming from the opposite direction. Then the two waves interact and cancel each other out. If you hold your first two fingers together, up to the light and about four inches from your eyes, you will notice faint black lines in the small spaces between your fingers. Those lines are waves caused by interference, as particles of light get in each other's way trying to squeeze between your fingers. You may have to adjust the distance between your fingers slightly to see the lines. If your fingers are pressed too firmly together, there is no gap for the light to pass through. And if they are slightly too far apart, you won't see the black lines because the light will pass between your fingers without creating interference.

Early this century, New Zealand physicist Ernest Rutherford described the way electrons orbit the nucleus of an atom, which he said was much like the planets going around the sun. The idea wasn't complete. It didn't explain why as the electrons emit light and lose energy, they would not descend into ever-smaller orbits and eventually crash into the nucleus—as orbiting hardware in space crashes to Earth from time to time.

German physicist Max Planck had already suggested that electrons emit energy in discrete packages that he called *quanta*. And Einstein went further to say that light also exists in quantum packages. Electrons orbiting a nucleus make quantum leaps from a higher orbit to a lower one, emitting energy as they do so. When they get to the lowest orbit and can go no farther, they become stable—which is why they don't crash into the nucleus. Here's how all this ties into the sixth sense.

When an electron makes a jump from one orbit to another, it doesn't travel the distance between the orbits. It just disappears from the higher orbit and simultaneously appears in a lower one. It momentarily leaves space-time and appears instantly somewhere else. Imagine our planet, the third from the sun, suddenly jumping to the orbit of Venus, the second planet from the sun—instantly, without crossing the vast distance between the two planetary orbits. Luckily for us, it can't happen, because quantum leaps don't apply to large objects such as planets.

So science, then, had instances of particles emitting energy and jumping from one place to another without passing through the space in between. Gradually it was discovered that all matter and light comprise both a particle and a wave at the same time, which is known as the *wave-particle duality*. Erwin Schrödinger wrote out the mathematical equation of the wave, and quantum mechanics was born.

The wave-particle nature of our reality caused a few headaches. Our reality at a quantum level is spread out in a hazy-wave. Only when we observe a particle does it disappear from its location somewhere in the hazy-wave and suddenly reappear as a particle at an exact spot in space-time. The hazy-wave could be said to be the transcendent, soft, yin-state of a reality. Once we collapse the hazy-wave by observation, a solid yang particle appears at a particular spot in space-time, which is our definitive yang-state of reality. In passing, I came to wonder if our hazy-wave etheric isn't just the yin-wave version of our yang, solid-particle physical bodies. Perhaps the reason most people don't see the etheric is because they don't know it's there, so they can't make it real by observing it.

For thousands of years, psychics and mystics have known that thoughts and ideas jump. When thoughts jump, we call it *telepathy*. Science proved, first, that electrons jump. Then it proved irrefutably that photons (light particles) interact at a distance. This phenomenon is termed *nonlocality*—meaning, of course, not local, but at a distance.

Alain Aspect, a French physicist, confirmed that when two quantum particles are correlated and fired in opposite directions, if you observe and measure one—thus collapsing its wave function—it automatically collapses the wave function of the other particle, no matter how far apart the two might be at the time. This would require information to travel from one particle to another faster than the speed of light. If there were such an information transfer that said, "My field has been collapsed, so please collapse your field," it would contradict one of the basic tenets of science. Einstein's Law of Relativity doesn't absolutely preclude a particle moving faster than light, and scientists have suggested a hypothetical particle, called a *tachyon*, named after the Latin word for "speed," that might travel faster than light. What is precluded by relativity is information moving faster than light. Paul Davies also points out in *About Time* that a particle can move faster than light, provided it never moves at a speed slower than light. Davies says, ". . . nothing can cross the light barrier, by going either up or down in speed."

The faster-than-light conundrum posed a problem for Alain Aspect. However, he went on to prove conclusively that no signal, at light-speed or slower, passes from one particle to another. He did this by inserting a switching mechanism in the experiment that clicked on and off, changing the polarization of one of the particles every billionth of a second. This was faster than the speed of light could travel to let the other particle know. Yet, still, the distant particle changed to match its partner as expected. Aspect thus eliminated the possibility of information traveling by a local signal from one particle to another.

Mystics would say that the space or distance between the particles is an illusion, that there is no time and so no space, and that everything is connected. Others have suggested that there is an ether, which is outside our space-time continuum, through which information can travel faster than light-speed. The third possibility is that the human mind can collapse a wave function at a distance, as well as the wave in its immediate vicinity. This would mean that human consciousness is also nonlocal, outside space-time, and therefore transcendental.

Of course, psychics have known all along that the transcendental nature of the mind allows one to tap into information at a distance. But the idea is more accepted now that science has proven it. I think psychics and mystics are still considered a bit dippy, but gradually the true nature of our human reality and the power of the mind will be better understood. Then a scientist will write the equation that ties consciousness to matter, and he or she will win a Nobel prize for discovering something that's been known for thousands of years. Heaps of fun!

Roger Penrose, a famous Oxford University mathematician, has suggested that the universe needs consciousness in order to exist, and certainly the fact that consciousness can collapse a quantum field to establish a solid particle is a wondrous thing. Which of the above three explanations of nonlocality is correct? I don't know for certain. No one does. It could be all three, and/or some other explanation we are not aware of yet.

The idea that space-time is an illusion sounds odd. You can gaze off into the distance and see the gap between you and the horizon, say, and you can very well argue that it is not an illusion. Of course, you are right, but at a transcendental level, everything seems connected. So one law may exist for external reality and another for our internal reality.

Through my experiments in the trance state and my sightings up the near-death tube, I've seen glimpses of spirit worlds where there seemed to be distance, for I could look off in one direction or another and see things that appeared to be placed away from me. However, that spirit world had no horizon—none that I remember, anyway—and whatever I concentrated on in the distance came to me if I wanted it to. Also, I could concentrate on some object, seemingly in the distance, and see minute details of it that would not be normally visible at such a distance on Earth. I remember looking at a tree that I'd guess was five to ten miles away in Earth terms, yet as soon as I concentrated on it, I could see every vein on every leaf of the tree. That's probably the process of distance viewing. Most sophisticated folk nowadays accept that reality comes to us day to day, according to what we think and feel. Certainly, in that particular spirit world, things would come whizzing over to me if I wanted them to.

In the quantum hazy-wave state, reality is spread out. You can't say where a particle is; you can only calculate where it *probably* is. So the hazy-wave of itself has transcendent qualities. It seems to me that spirit worlds also have hazy-wave qualities. Things come to you, or appear, if you concentrate on them—as a physicist might concentrate on a particle and have it duly appear.

The second explanation of nonlocality—the ether explanation—has taken a lot of criticism over the years. It is not favored by science. In Victorian times, people thought that outer space was filled by ether. In 1887, Michelson and Morley performed a famous experiment to test the idea. Their premise was that, if the earth was traveling through an ether-filled outer space, then a resistance would develop in the direction of the earth's motion, much like a wave builds up at the front of a boat. Michelson and Morley felt that there would be a discernible difference in the speed of light, between readings taken in the direction of the earth's motion, and those taken in the other direction once the ether wave had passed. No difference was found, and ether was trashed as an idea.

However, what wasn't realized at the time was that the earth in itself is a wave field—and that the lack of ether could possibly be explained by the fact that the earth's wave-field interfered with the ether's field, thus canceling it out. This might explain why Michelson and Morley didn't find ether. Since the advent of string theory and zero-point energy, the ether theory has made a small but inconclusive comeback, but the jury is still out on the ether idea.

From a sixth-sense/etheric point of view, ether or no-ether makes little difference. For although etheric and ether are derivatives of the same word, they are obviously not quite the same thing. Ether, of the outer-space variety—if it exists—would be invisible, whereas the human etheric, although hard to see, is definitely visible. Ether and the etheric may possibly be two versions of the same energy, in different forms, just as ice and steam are both forms of water. For centuries, clairvoyants have claimed to see the etheric, and everyone can feel the etheric even if they are not able to explain it to themselves technically in etheric terms. To say it doesn't exist is a bit daft. Eventually science will catch up and tell us that the etheric field of the human body/personality is definitely there.

The point of this book is to show you ways to discover the etheric for yourself. All the mathematics in the world can't beat a good subjective experience, in my view. To feel the etheric, you have to become quite sensitive. The transition comes about when you see your life in grander terms. There has to be a desire in you to reach beyond the mundane to a special level of spirituality.

You have to remember that, in our society, everything we are taught as children and most of what we see and read in the media is specially designed to lull us into a docile acquiescence. Selling fear is a nationalized industry. If you want to disempower people, offer them a perpetual diet of scary problems that they have no power to fix. Keep all the real information hidden or obscured. Feed people loads of trivia, and hype endless, meaningless sporting events to keep them entertained, while you keep repeating that they have no power to run their own lives. Pass laws to make sure people are encumbered as much as possible, and take half of their money to make certain of that fact. Keep people insecure, and tell them that only the important men at the top have the power to protect them, heal them, provide for them, inform them, and so on. Welcome to our Bureaucratic Droneland. My mind, and probably yours as well, was programmed at a young and tender age by a very insidious and long-running mind-control mechanism that said we couldn't make it on our own. Piffle.

The Benefits of Awareness

I came to see my spiritual journey and the development of awareness as part of my escape. You may very well see it in the same way. In the worldly context, Bureaucratic Droneland is much like an invisible prisoner-of-war camp. I feel that there must be a place in God's plan for those of us who want to flee. I came to believe vehemently that perception is our passport out of the nightmare society being created for us, for perception carries us to another evolution, not one after death, but one that is right here in the world of the living. It's a world inside a world. I'm betting my bottom dollar that our level of awareness and the acuteness of our perception will be inexorably linked with the quality of our life's journey in years to come.

The philosopher Gurdjieff talked a lot about the *sleeping man,* a term he used to describe the consciousness of a bourgeois, mundane life. Gurdjieff said that one had to exercise the force of will in order to wake oneself up in this lifetime, otherwise one drifts through life, more or less in a sleep state, missing most of the good stuff.

I must say, watching people coming out of the subway, trotting off to work, or heading down the freeway at rush hour, you can see the kind of collective sleep state that Gurdjieff was talking about. I don't think it's people's fault for the most part—they are programmed that way. Anyway, it's comfortable to tick-tock along, following a familiar rhythm.

But if you've ever had the experience of finding that time has flown by—for example, that a week or a month or a year has gone by without you really being aware of it—then you will have slipped into Gurdjieff's

"Sleeping Man State." In the sleeping state, time flies.

Conversely, the spiritually awake, sixth-sense state is very much the observer's state—one of self-observation. Through introspection and observation, looking at and understanding yourself, you become more solid. Time slows down and reality gets thicker. By "thicker," I don't mean that it's heavier or harder to move through. What I mean is that it is *richer*. You are aware of more, time frames are suddenly broader, and your vista is more expansive.

The world of the sixth sense opens the energy centers in your subtle body and you take on more light. So you naturally go from stiff to pliant, from resistant to fluid, from hesitant to flowing. Once you open to more power and the all-knowing, you can perceive life in all its subtlety and vastness.

The natural sixth sense takes work to develop, and it involves discipline. That is because you have to engage the force of your will to get the ego to back off, and you know from experience that it is very strong. You can engage the force of will in a negative way, or you can use it positively, to wake yourself up. Ding! Ding!

Sometimes, of course, the universe-at-large figures a wake-up call for you. Something weird happens. Life whacks you in the head and wakes you up that way. But the slower, inner way is better—it saves you from any nasty shocks.

It is a marvelous thing to know that you have the courage, discipline, and follow-through to enliven your consciousness. In reaching for a higher state of awareness, a higher ability, and a greater spirituality, you come to a more profound sense of self. There's a lot of healing in that. Much of the dysfunction and emotional pain that people experience comes, initially, from a lack of self-knowledge. I've always believed that you don't necessarily have to fix the various aspects of your life to feel good—you usually only have to understand them.

The various tools, techniques, and disciplines laid out in these pages require a certain amount of diligence and concentration to reap the rewards of success. The new awareness comes in the form of an extrasensory perception. This comes from allowing reality to impact your subtle body, and allowing that impact to register as perceptions in your mind. It grants you a multifaceted awareness of what is going on around you. For example, in your relationships, you start to become aware of subtle or subliminal information that flows from you toward others, and the energy flowing from them to you. You start to know what others are thinking and feeling.

In your finances, you can use this same awareness, the sixth sense. It not only carries you to where financial opportunities lie, but it shows you the inner energy of things so it keeps you from suffering losses. You can also use it to tap in to that reservoir of ideas and creativity that may lie hidden deep within you. One half-decent idea can make you a million dollars. There are a lot of people out there whose successful ideas came to them in a vision, a dream, a meditation, or some flash of inspiration. Their ideas were not necessarily radical or way out. In fact, more often than not, successful ideas are not way out, because they have to be easily understood by people. Often, all it takes is to express an idea, or develop a product or service, in a way that it hasn't been done before.

So by developing a higher awareness, you get more in touch with the energy of life. You become more at peace with yourself, developing confidence and skills. You may suddenly realize that you have abilities that you never saw or understood before—because you weren't aware of them. Or, maybe you *were* very aware of them, but you've never been confident in expressing them. So the journey toward the sixth sense is wider, larger, and bigger generally than party tricks, fortune telling, and the ability to read the cards or whatever. It is really an emergent quality of your spiritual journey.

You may describe that journey in whatever religious, spiritual, or sacred terms you wish. In the end, the sixth sense flows down an etheric pathway, which directs you toward a greater, more colorful, inner-self. And that is reflected in a more enriched *outer* self.

When you look at it, life is a replica—an external manifestation—of your thoughts and feelings. When things happen that you don't understand, or when things fail to happen that you feel *ought* to happen, you're confused. But it's all explicable somewhere in your deepest, most subtle feelings and thoughts—in those impulses and motivations that lie hidden in the subconscious, below the threshold of normal waking perception. *There is always an answer in there somewhere.*

So by getting in touch with your intuition, your psychic ability, and the sixth sense—and I'm going to define these terms for you very carefully— what you are doing is giving notice to that spiritual, infinite part of you saying, "Hey, I want to know more. I want to see; I want to understand."

Rather than being a victim of circumstances, one who is just carried along, who allows life to happen to them, you are saying instead, "I want to generate my life. I want to be the controller of my destiny. I want to exert the force of my will so that life gives me those things I'm entitled to."

Think of it like this: Imagine if, through some magical power, you instantly know everything there is to know on Earth. You instantly become the most powerful person in the world. You know what everybody is thinking, how their destiny is about to unfold, how the stock market is going to perform, which horse is going to win the next race at Santa Anita. You suddenly become immensely powerful—and very, very rich.

The opposite of that is: Imagine that you know nothing. You can't remember your name or where you live or what day of the week it is. You have no idea how to buy food or how to maintain yourself. You are powerless. So, somewhere between knowing everything and nothing is where human consciousness orbits. If you develop and tap in to the sixth sense, you begin to tap in to knowledge, you gain a silent power, and life becomes less fearful. You flip to a higher orbit to journey beyond the karma of the day-to-day, for part of the karma we inherit here on Earth is the karma of ignorance. We just don't know enough about life and energy and what it all means, and we don't usually comprehend why things happen the way they do. With awareness, the world becomes a safer place.

Physical power, physical strength, political strength, and social clout are all fleeting. Physical power wanes, political parties come and go, today's glamour-puss is tomorrow's has-been. Real energy is indestructible. Real knowledge is perpetual. We are looking to the immense power and value of perception. I always feel over-awed by the heroic nature of the human journey. There is tremendous pathos in the nature of it as we journey from fear to love, from ignorance to knowledge, from powerlessness to being in control of our lives. I have a lot of compassion for the nature of this amazing journey—tough and painful as it sometimes is.

Over the last several hundred years, humanity has developed greatly. As our societies became richer and healthier and more clever, we came to rely very much on the intellect. Yet computers are taking over our left-brain function. So I'd imagine that, over time, our creative, intuitive right brains may develop much more quickly. The old inner knowing of tribal people will return as modern people engage that faculty within themselves. I often wonder if the scorn poured upon metaphysicians and the old ways isn't just a part of the attempt by the status quo to monopolize thinking and control us all.

It's not as if the sixth sense is rare. Almost everyone has had some kind of sixth-sense experience—strange happenings, prophetic dreams, or psychic and intuitive flashes. A moment before the phone rang, you heard somebody's name in your head; or you thought about a distant relative—and suddenly that person called. We have all been given an intuitive sixth sense; it's part of the compassion that the God Force has for us. We are all, at one level, little, scared, and often confused. And here plops in our laps a great gift. I feel we should try to make use of it. Why would we get more gifts if we haven't used the ones we've already been given? Training yourself to become more aware is a way of saying thank you. It opens you up for another dollop of loveliness, courtesy of the God Force. Coolisimo!

I believe that at a deep, inner, subconscious level—what Jung called the *collective unconscious*—we are all linked. Just as there is probably no space between distant particles, there is no space-time in consciousness either. It is obviously nonlocal. The separateness we feel from others is an illusion of the ego. At an inner level, we are as close to somebody who is 10,000 miles away as we are to the person next to us, or to the child in our arms, or even those who have made the transition from the Earth plane. In the realm of consciousness, we are all linked.

So the first shift in awareness is that your reality becomes spatially linked. Everything and everyone is closer to you, and you have the ability to push them away when you don't want them near you. Once you're in the world of the inner-self, you shift the shape of reality around to suit your needs. In the end, the idea that things are fixed is part of the illusion of the physical. They are and they aren't.

Logic, science, medicine, and research have greatly assisted our evolution as human beings on this planet, but an inner connection and perception is also vital.

Here's something interesting to think about: I doubt that there is a single self-made millionaire who didn't use their sixth sense to make those millions. Every scientist uses their sixth sense—to work out concepts prior to writing the formulas that might prove those concepts. We all *use* it, but many can't *admit* to it.

A lot of sixth-sense perception is the ability to imagine and intuit new ideas from old ones. For example, you could be writing a piece of music, just plink-plonking along with a few notes, and you might think, *That sounds like it might have commercial appeal.* At that point, you don't know it's going to sell 11 million copies. It's an intuitive guess, but you put it down on your music sheet because it feels right. Everything is energy—the marketplace of life, relationships, money, products, your actions, creativity, music—everything. And you can pick up information about that energy via the subtle senses.

You might meet someone who might be exactly the opposite of what your intellect thought you'd be attracted to. This person is tall and skinny with a big nose, and you were expecting someone of average height and muscular with a perfectly shaped nose. He or she may not be of the culture, nationality, or religion you were expecting, but there is something about them—it's a feeling. They've got energy. You *know*. Suddenly, there's your special mate in this lifetime.

We derive our security from logic. We plan and think, and we hope we have covered all the bases. But the insecurity of logic and left-brain thinking disempowers us. Logic operates in a linear way; it can't see around corners. At best, it can only make an educated guess. So it worries all the time. As soon as you fix one worry, along comes another in your mind. Logic allows you to fall prey to the forces of control—using your insecurity to keep you scared and weak. These forces mold you in the direction they want to go, selling you stuff as you dutifully trot along.

The only real security is in energy and the use of your subtle feelings. It's a logic that isn't logical, a part of the natural etheric power within you. It comes to you as impressions, extrasensory perceptions, and subtle feelings. It is the only way you will ever be certain. You know everything is well because your feelings tell you it is so. Once your feelings are well honed, they are almost never wrong.

People don't understand it, but I'm sure you do, and over time you'll find that it sets you free. Some worry about being ridiculed, and of course you don't want people seeing you as a complete space cadet. The answer is, don't tell people what you're doing. You are on a sacred journey to recapture a lost wisdom; you don't need anyone's permission or approval.

I must say, the subtle energies have certainly helped me a lot in my lifetime. As I developed more and more inner knowing, tapping in to other worlds helped me see life in a totally different way. A vision would come to me in trance, and it would send my life in one direction. Then, after a year or two, as that petered out, a new vision would guide me off in a slightly different direction. In addition, I'd learned a lot about people and the way they think and feel deep within. I'd be walking down the street and I'd look at a person, and bits of their life story would evolve in front of me. I'd understand them better.

But if I had to go and prove my perception, to substantiate it—or get on TV and argue about it—it would be lost. It's much too subtle. So why bother discussing it or defending the illogical? The power unfolds as a part of the epic grandeur of your journey. Strangely, it looks like a step backwards to the old shamanistic tribal ways, but it is, in fact, a step forward into the realm of the gods and a greater spirituality.

YOUR PSYCHIC POWERS, SPIRIT WORLDS, AND THE ALL-KNOWING

The Three Components of the Sixth Sense

L et us look at the various forms of the sixth sense and define them properly. When an ethereal quality such as the sixth sense is defined and broken out into its various components, it helps you understand it properly, which facilitates the task of linking you to the flow of extra-sensory information. The sixth sense divides into three main categories—and then there are a few subcategories. The main components are: the *psychic sixth sense,* the *intuitive sixth sense,* and the *all-knowing sixth sense.*

It is easy to work out. The psychic sixth sense is mostly the process whereby thoughts and information jump from one person to another—for example, the psychic reader picks up on the energy of the client's (or sitter's) mind. Snippets of their attitudes and thought patterns are in the etheric, and the psychic *sees* those thoughts in their mind's eye *(clairvoyance).* Sometimes the psychic reader *hears* words go off in their head describing aspects of the client's life *(clairaudience);* or they *feel* the ideas, emotions, and thought-forms of the sitter *(clairsentience).* Clairsentience is not in most dictionaries, but it's a term used in psychic parlance to describe non-local information picked up via one's feelings.

Most psychic energy is quite fleeting. That's because it is, in its most common form, telepathy. No one can yet pin down exactly how telepathy works, but it is something we all practice from time to time, often without being aware of it. It is especially strong between people who know each other well: spouses, family members, good friends, and so on. I imagine that the answer lies in the same subatomic wave-field that requires one particle to change if its partner alters itself in any way. Perhaps the emotion of close relationships sets up the same correlation as that described in Alain Aspect's experiments.

Whatever the explanation, telepathy isn't rare. How often have you been thinking about something totally in left field and the person next to you mentions the exact same idea? How can that happen? Well, a small part of it may be coincidence, but that doesn't explain how such thoughts seem to jump across from one person to another. If you added up how many times it occurs around the world, it's probably millions of times a day. Thoughts definitely jump, so either you got the thought from the person next to you, or they got it from you, or you both got it from someone else, such as a passerby. As I said, an electron that orbits the nucleus of an atom can jump from a higher orbit to a lower one. When it does so, it does not travel across the intervening space between the orbits. It just disappears from the higher orbit and simultaneously appears in the lower one. While it makes this maneuver, it exits in space-time, as we know it, and reappears in space-time in its new position. Thoughts must exist in a wave-field and act much like electrons. They seem to be able to perform the same kind of jumps.

Psychic readers may use a tool, such as tarot cards or a crystal, to help them focus, but the process is still one of picking up thoughts and feelings in the consciousness of another. That may be partly the action of feeling them out, but the psychic may also attract thoughts to make them jump across from the client's mind to their own mind. It's a pulling motion; the pull is established by the psychic's ability and their desire to know. It is also helped by the client, who will be projecting expectancy toward the psychic that says, "Tell me about myself." That is an outward-moving etheric direction, so it's easier for the psychic to pick up on it. That is not to belittle or put down the psychic's ability—it's just to define how it's done.

Then, of course, some of the psychic reader's perception comes out of common sense and understanding people. When you can really look at people and notice them, there is a whole bunch of things they tell you without ever opening their mouths. So the reader can see struggle written all over their client's face and says, "Your life has been hard, and you need a special person in your life to give you a bit of support and help, and you deserve a bit more money, don't you?" And the client goes, "Yes! Yes! How did you know that? Amazing!"

Intuition is slightly different from the three psychic faculties. It is often the sudden appearance of what was previously subliminal information from your subconscious mind. So you'll say, "I've got a gut feeling that this project will work." Where did that gut feeling come from?

As often as not, your intuition comes from subliminal information you've picked up about a situation as you've gone along. *Subliminal,* as you probably know, means "below the normal threshold of conscious awareness." Day by day we pick up so much more information than we are consciously aware of. That subliminal information is stored in the subconscious. So if you have an intuitive feeling about a project, say, you may have gotten that from the people involved. They might have silently told you about their attitude—so that subliminal information is stacked within you from the business meeting you attended. Later, your subconscious sorts out that hidden information, and in a quiet moment it pops into your mind as a hunch or a strange thought that doesn't seem to connect to your current stream of thinking. You seem to know things that, logically, your intellect shouldn't know. So intuition is accessing and retrieving information that is buried deep within. The way to enhance it is to constantly ask your subconscious to tell you what it knows that your intellect doesn't.

The third form of the sixth sense is the faculty of all-knowing. This one is the most interesting in my view, for through the crown chakra, you are linked to everything. The faculty of all-knowing doesn't mean that you will be *perpetually* all-knowing—it means that you receive flashes of all-knowing in your feelings, or more likely, through visions. How it differs from a psychic ability is that it isn't an emanation that comes off another person's energy necessarily. It's more like information spilling out of the global mind or beyond that to a transdimensional intelligence, to which we are fleetingly connected. The all-knowing usually operates when you're on your own, once you've developed serenity and silence in your life. It often deals with the spiritual aspects of life or various nuances of your journey. It is a teaching tool from a higher power.

As a young man, I got into meditation, and I studied consciousness, brain waves, and trance states. I practiced meditation every day, and eventually I found that I could enter a deep trance state and stay awake. After a few years, symbols and visions started to come to me—each was very poignant and alive with meaning. I came to see how much inner vision could assist one with one's journey through life.

Eventually, through repeated trance practice, I saw in my mind's eye the bottom of what looked like a tube. I was later to discover that it was the near-death tube that people report seeing during trauma surgery, often while clinically dead. At first, the tube seemed a long way off; gradually, over time, I got closer and closer to it. At the bottom of the tube at its entrance is a *singularity*. It's an area of extreme gravity a bit like a black hole in space, I'd imagine. The singularity is so tough to move through that it took me more than two years to cross the short distance between my point of perception and it. In my mind's eye, it looked like just a matter of yards. Finally, I was at the bottom of the tube looking up it. It has a bend in it, so you can't see all the way. Frustrated, I attempted to move my perception up the tube, and I messed with that method for more than nine months without great success. Then I decided that it might be better to try to pull whatever was at the end of the tube *toward* me, rather than trying to move my awareness up the tube in its direction. That technique worked instantly.

After that adjustment, I found myself looking into spirit worlds on a daily basis. Some were very beautiful, full of radiant light. On a number of occasions, I saw what I imagined was the light of God. I use the words "I imagine," as I have no idea what God really is, yet the light I saw was so full of wisdom and compassion and radiance, and it was so completely overwhelming, that I believed it must be the God Force. It was all the love that I could ever imagine and more. So much love and radiance, in fact, that I couldn't look at it for more than a few seconds at a time before it overcame me. And I was forced to leave.

During my sighting up the near-death tube, I learned quite a bit about those spirit worlds and the nature of those dimensions—the ones that I got to look at, anyway. There were horrid, hellish ones; and gray, dull ones in which people (spirits) looked drab and lost; and then there were the celestial dimensions. Some of the places I visited were just black, devoid of light; the void was neither pleasant nor unpleasant.

On one occasion while in trance, I asked to see what infinity looks like, and I found myself whisked off to some location, hovering in the middle of nowhere, and all around me was infinity. I realized that our human version of infinity is a bit limited; there's a point where our mind just can't quite grasp it. But in the all-knowing version, you can see that infinity has a characteristic: It has a kind of personality, and it's really special because it is so much more vast than you can imagine. And no matter how far you look, there is more. And beyond that, your feelings tell you, there is more still.

Infinity is so vast, in fact, that it's scary for a human. Well, it scared me, anyway. We're a bit too little to be messing with too much infinity—especially the real thing.

I have always felt while experimenting with sightings up the tube that I have been helped. Often I felt I was being directed to various dimensions, and other dimensions that I wanted to see were barred from me, probably for good reason. One conclusion I came to is that those spiritual worlds, which form a part of our after-death experience, are symmetrically placed as if in a mirror, to our Earthly world—meaning that they are opposite us, facing us. So their left is our right and vice versa.

Somehow between the Earth-plane, the near-death tube, and the other worlds, a rotation takes place. Maybe that happens at the point where the bend is in the near-death tube; anyway, the rotation reverses things left to right and right to left. Here is how this links to the sixth sense, spirit worlds, and the subconscious mind, but first let me tell you a clue I discovered about the mirror worlds and the mind that you might find rather interesting.

The Mirror Worlds of Reverse Speech and the Subconscious Mind

There is a phenomenon known as *reverse speech*. For those unfamiliar with it, it is the process of taking a piece of recorded dialogue like, say, a news broadcast, and playing it backwards. The leading proponent of reverse speech is an Australian broadcaster working in America named David Oates. What Oates and others have found is that, rather than the backward audiocassette being full of just gibberish, it often contains coherent messages. Oates claims that there is approximately one coherent word or message every 10 to 15 seconds on every recorded piece of dialogue.

David Oates says that the backward messages are thoughts, appearing as dialogue, that emanate from the subconscious mind of the speaker. In other words, the tape played backwards is what the speaker really thinks silently deep within.

Sometimes, reversals appear on musical recordings. I found a reversal in the Greenwood album that I worked on last year, *Voice of the Celtic Myth,* track 11, "Triumph of the Gods of Light" (see my home page: **www.powersource.com/wilde** for the reversal). Angel-like voices seem to sing, "We love you, love you." It is repeated twice.

What is fascinating about reverse speech is that more often than not, the backward dialogue relates to what is being said forwards. If the backward dialogue was totally unconnected to the subject matter being discussed, then one might say that it's just a coincidence that certain words in English sound coherent when played or written backwards. However, if you look at the words on this page, you'll soon see how few of them make any sense when spoken or written backwards. Then to get, for example, five or ten consecutive words to make sense, one after the next, is a very high linguistic improbability.

There is one reversal of Oates's that I heard that is quite astounding. A female bilingual translator is at a press conference; she is translating from English into one of the Chinese languages. The forward audio is in Chinese, while her subconscious reversal is spoken quite clearly in English. This rather discounts the idea that reverse speech is coincidentally coherent. It's impossible that, say, Mandarin or Cantonese played forwards, sound like a coherent comment in English when played backwards. Reverse speech really is an enigma. It may be a major breakthrough in our understanding of dimensions, reality, and the nature of consciousness.

In theory, it ought to be impossible, but the reversals are always in the exact voice and accent of the speaker, and usually the reversal refers to what is currently being said in the normal forward dialogue. An interesting example was found in Neil Armstrong's famous words as he stepped onto the surface of the moon. You'll remember that he said, "That's one small step for man, one giant leap for mankind." On the back of that, he is heard to say, "Man will space walk." This was a subconscious thought that reflected what he knew or felt was coming later in the space program. You can listen to it on David Oates's site: **www.reversespeech.com.**

How the subconscious imprints a magnetic tape backwards is beyond me; however, psychics such as Ted Serios have been proven to be able to imprint photographic film with their minds, so why not magnetic tape? What is hard to figure out about reverse speech is the strange, twisted, time-warp effect it demonstrates, whereby words at the end of a reverse sentence seem to be recorded on the tape before the words at the beginning of the same sentence. If the time line were normal, Armstrong should have been heard to say on the reverse, "Klaw ecaps lliw nam." The flip of the time line implies one of two things—either the subconscious is operating backwards in time, or somehow the subconscious can deliver a completed sentence all at once, with every word in place simultaneously. So in a four-word sentence, for example, all four words impregnate the audiocassette at exactly the same moment. If this scenario were correct, the subconscious would have to be timeless, as it would have to organized and project all four words from its memory onto the tape simultaneously.

Whatever the case, the backward dialogue is time-reversed to our normal forward dialogue, and it is opposite of our normal dialogue. Again, like the spirit worlds, it is placed symmetrically as if in a mirror. So that might be a major clue that could explain much paranormal phenomena, inner knowing, and the sixth sense. There seems to be a link between the mirror worlds of spirit and the mirror world of the subconscious.

This idea is not so daft, for when we look at something via normal sight, we perceive it the right way up; however, we know that that image reaches us upside down, twisted left to right. There is a mechanism in the brain that turns reality's images around for us, so we see the room we are in, for example, the right way up. However, perhaps information from our senses reaches the subconscious in its original upside-down, twisted right-to-left state, instead of our how our normal waking perception sees and perceives reality—which is when one is facing north, with left to the west and right to the east.

Why I have never before seen the link between the backward mirrorlike nature of reverse speech and the mirrorlike symmetry of the spirit worlds beats me. But the implication of it, if it is true, is quite awesome. It may lead us to a completely new understanding of psychic powers and the nonlocal nature of consciousness. I find that exciting.

If the subconscious is symmetrically aligned to the spirit worlds, then one could quite confidently argue that it is a part of those worlds, and that a part of us is perpetually in the spirit world via our subconscious—not just after death, but also while we are still alive.

I have always felt intuitively that a greater part of our identity and our conscious self is not present here on the Earth plane; that our waking consciousness is only one small tip of an infinite iceberg that holds our greater memory or Higher Self, as it is often called. I came to that conclusion in various ways. The most convincing of which is through the experiencing of a strange "blip" of consciousness that I have had on ever-increasing occasions, a phenomenon that many others have also reported, which I can only describe as "spreadoutness." I'd be walking along a street, and suddenly my mind seems to come to a halt. It feels like my brain electricity is diminished, or turned down suddenly. In those silent, blank seconds, I feel my consciousness momentarily timeless, and expanded into an infinite state—connected to all things, with all reality momentarily inside me and my mind—rather than outside, which is how we all normally see the world.

I think the mirrorlike effect of reverse speech means that the subconscious is in a nonlocal spirit dimension even while we are alive, so then you can easily see how psychic power, intuition, and the sixth sense become explainable. There is a correlation here that astounds me. On the one hand, we have our Earthly existence, then the near-death tube beyond which there is a mirror twist entering the nonlocal spirit worlds. And on the other hand, we have our intellect, then a mirror twist of reality in the brain, and beyond that, the nonlocal subconscious mind. Of course, it has been argued that it is all an anomaly of the brain and that there is no near-death tube or spirit worlds beyond it. But I would argue, saying that the near-death tube is only normally visible once the brain has stopped functioning, as in the case of flatline surgery cases. So it can't all just be an anomaly of the brain. Further, I am convinced, having understood the etheric and the out-of-body experience somewhat, and having seen those spirit worlds and the God Force, that they are real. I am also confident that there is a nonlocal spiritual reality to which we all belong.

Of course, part of the sixth sense's psychic power is explained by thoughts jumping from one person to another via the etheric. However, some of it must be explained because a large part of our consciousness, and therefore our evolution, is outside the intellectual 3-D world of our normal ego-based separate reality. Via the mirror world of the subconscious, we are all in the nonlocal, interconnected spirit worlds. In those spirit worlds, there is no Earthlike atmosphere through which words (sound) might travel, and all communication between conscious entities is via thought transfer. Telepathy is the only means of communication I ever came across. So if the subconscious is in the spirit world already, then we would have the same interconnectedness of spirit, and we would be in silent dialogue with each other all of the time.

Intuitively, I have known that to be a fact, and mystics have taught it as fact since the beginning of time. But I have never read a proper explanation anywhere in the sacred texts as to why we are in silent dialogue with each other or why we are interconnected. Certainly the God Force is everywhere, and we all have a spark of that God Force within us, so that explains what the mystics were trying to say. But it doesn't offer a complete technological answer. The fact that everything is linked and interconnected was one of the early and most impacting impressions I had up the near-death tube. But it is only now, through the technology of reverse speech, that we can come to a reasonable explanation of why there is an interconnection between us all.

If everyone's subconscious is placed in the timeless, mirrorlike dimensions of spirit, even while they are alive, then we all exist in those worlds right now. So Jung's idea of the collective unconscious and some of the ideas I have written about in *Whispering Winds of Change* regarding the global mind seem to be correct. In the mirror world of the subconscious, there is a global connection between us all. For that is how it is in the spirit worlds—the ones *I've* seen anyway.

Spirit Mediumship and Channeling

I don't think we can discuss the sixth sense without talking about spirit mediumship and channeling. It's hard to exactly slot those two aspects, as they don't strictly fit into any one of the three categories. Spirit mediumship seems like a form of psychic power, when it relates to talking to the spirits of people who have passed over. But, unlike the situation where the client is alive and in front of the psychic, you can't really pull information from a dead person's etheric. In fact, mediumship must be a part of the all-knowing, linked as we are through the mirror worlds of spirit and the subconscious. Suddenly, it all becomes explainable, and so I'd imagine that the medium is probably pulling information from the perpetual memory of a deceased person. The faculty of mediumship must rely somewhat on the spirit entity projecting information to the medium. When spirit mediumship is done well, it is awesomely impressive. But then again, sometimes it is mixed with a bunch of foolishness, and if mediums are not quite all there energywise, they make up bits as they go along. I've seen good mediums who were phenomenal, and I've seen others who fudged it as they went.

Mediumship, as they call the process of talking to the dead, began in America in the 19th century with the three Fox sisters. They lived in Hydesville, New York, and became famous for supposedly communicating with departed spirits via rapping sounds that occurred in their home. They claimed to be in contact with a traveling peddler who was murdered in the house and buried in the cellar. Fifty years later, a human skeleton was found behind one of the walls in the basement.

However, although mediumship began in America, it really took root in Britain and became quite an institution. In fact, there are still quite a number of spiritualist churches around Britain that hold regular services on Sundays. They are really quaint, and I enjoy going to them from time to time. They start with a few Christian prayers and sing the odd hymn, and then the medium gets up and does his or her stuff. On an energy level, the medium pulls the power up, from lower in their etheric up to the third eye. A part of it comes from the heart chakra, and the rest from the kundalini at the root chakra, although I imagine that some mediums might be a bit too shy to admit that. The medium also pulls energy from the ambience of the room that often has had previous spiritualist sessions in it. The memory or residues of those previous sessions form a part of the room's etheric identity. The medium also pulls energy from the congregation, making a solid connection with them. Then, of course, the subconscious-to-subconscious interplay of our shared mirror evolution might just explain everything.

Spiritualism has its place. It's big in Africa, and South America has a lot of mediums; in fact, there are mediums in every country of the world. The problem I have with mediumship is that the spirits of the dead—who are supposed to be talking, making predictions, giving advice, and so forth—seem to have such a limited knowledge of what is going on in the day-to-day world. They also seem to have a limited understanding of life.

After we're finished with this incarnation, we move out of the physical into a sidereal dimension, but the nearby spirit worlds are made up of thought-forms we are familiar with, so they are not very different from what we already know. Perhaps that is why the spirits of the departed seem to have such a limited knowledge of what is going on in our world, and they also seem to have a limited understanding of the nature of the universe and life. They'll tell you loads of very mundane stuff about how yer Granny is just hunky-dory in the spirit world, and that you'll meet a tall, dark stranger (hopefully not from the tax office), and things will be getting better for you, given a month or two or ten or whenever.

This information elevates people. I know it does; I've seen them react. Sometimes the medium is very accurate. They might be communicating with your deceased father, and they will tell you very personal things that only you and your dead relative could know. That helps convince people that the deceased are really alive in some other celestial dimension. Naturally, that comforts people a lot. It's a good thing, in my view.

I cannot say if the spirit medium is actually talking to your dead granny or not. The medium may be pulling information from the client's thought-forms—that is, from the memory they have of their grandmother. Just as easily, the medium might be telepathically communicating, one subconscious to another, with the spirit entity that has departed the Earth plane. Whether it is real or not doesn't matter much—as long as it's helpful and it pleases people and it does them a bit of good.

I must say, having trained as a spirit medium years ago, I became convinced of the presence of other entities at seances. *Seance* is a French word that comes originally from the Latin word *sedere,* "to sit." In a seance, you can feel the energy of the room change. A flood of symbols and words come to you, seemingly from nowhere, and suddenly you see a pig in your mind's eye and tell the person sitting with you, "I've got your dad here, and he's showing me his prize pig." Then the individual confirms that her dad was a pig farmer, and so on.

Here's what I think happens. I believe that when we incarnate into the Earth plane, we descend from a more rarefied spirit evolution—to enter into the feeling and thought-form of the wave-field dimension we call human. It's the world of atoms, and the Second Law of Thermodynamics, which requires everything to entropy, governs it. It's hard to figure out why we would enter the dimension of atoms, where we are bound to fall apart. The planet is very lovely, and there is a lot to learn, but life can be a bit harrowing, and death is a bit grim. Why are we messing with this stuff?

It is obviously part of our karma. Maybe we were awfully naughty someplace else, and something in our care fell apart, so we've been sent here to discover how falling apart feels. More likely, I imagine that we need this human experience, as it compacts us. It stuffs us into a finite body in a finite location in the confines of space-time. It's the particle state personified. It helps us to concentrate. I feel that in the act of concentrating on life, we become more spiritual. That's why I feel that the sixth sense is linked very much to spreading yourself out. I'll talk about that at length in later chapters. It's mostly understanding that you are moving past the mundane, reaching for the Infinite Self. In effect, you are saying, "Okay. I've done the coarse, boring, mundane world of atoms and entropy. Now I want my Infinite Self back. Thanks for the ride!"

I've heard it said that the spirit worlds are the spaces between atoms, and the physical universe, the atoms themselves. Looking up the near-death tube, I can't say if I was looking at the space between atoms or not, but I've had a nagging feeling for a long time that the galactic universe we see out there at night is, in fact, from one perspective, very, very small. Astronomers talk about parsecs and megaparsecs. A parsec is the distance traveled by light (approximately 300,000 kilometers a second) for 3.2616 years. A megaparsec is one million parsecs, or roughly 3,261,600 light-years, which is approximately the distance to the nearest large spiral galaxy, M31, in the constellation of Andromeda.

So the universe, on the one hand, is vast, but the distances aren't much different, in ratio, to the relative distance between the nucleus of an atom and the electrons that orbit around it. Quarks make up the nucleus, the nucleus and the electrons make up the atom, and atoms join together to form molecules, which, in turn, form cells. Maybe the galactic universe is just one tiny cell made up of all the stuff of the universe, and that small cell is in the kneecap, say, of a being that really is vast. So what looks vast to us is, in fact, minute when you get up with the big guys.

The other problem is that we have to look at everything through our personalities. Joe Blow, the dead pig farmer the medium is talking to, is a collection of memories that formed the personality of Joe. However, if you ever see the light of God up the near-death tube, you'll know that it melts your identity. It's as if your personality disappears, as you are inexorably drawn into the light. You don't care about holding on to your self; you are happy to join. You can see the same phenomena in a mild form as you travel the spiritual path. After a few years of meditation and introspection, you are a lot less the old stiff personality that made up the former "you"—you are now a different person, much more fluid and expansive. That sometimes gives rise to mild panic because you don't know who you are anymore. You may feel you're losing your grip, as the old solid structures of your previously more-confined life tend to melt and fall away. Perhaps how much we can lose ourselves, and how well we can embrace the scariness of that, defines our spiritual bigness.

When you are no longer Joe, the pig farmer, you drift up and out of this world into the nearest spirit dimension that suits your evolution so far. Gradually you become less and less Joe, and you drift farther up to a more rarefied dimension of angels and spirit entities—a dimension of a greater spiritual evolution. Some people are very set inside their own personality, religion, and life. They know what they know, and they are often solidly locked into the place where they live. Perhaps they haven't moved very far all of their life. They are in a cosmic play called "the mundane life of Joe, male, human, pig farmer."

But as you ponder your life, meditate, and discipline yourself, you become more open and infinite. And if you then travel around the world, you see that nothing is absolute—everything is fluid and shifting. It is cosmic in its most basic essence. You become less dogmatic. You become less and less certain that the world and perceptions of Joe Blow, the pig farmer from Little Rock, is what you are. You begin to see that you are multifaceted and global; you can live anywhere and adapt to anything, embracing many ideas and religions. Then you see that you are universal and not necessarily limited to planet Earth. You extend beyond it—beyond universal are all the other dimensions—which we call spirit worlds because we don't know what else to call them. Eventually you'll see that you are a multidimensional being—etheric and physical, straddled across an eternity. You are simultaneously finite and infinite, here and not here.

What you believe at death is what you see over there after death. People of a particular mind-set would enter a spirit dimension of that mind set, and no doubt they'd bump into other people/spirits that had the same mind-set. It would be easy for everyone to convince themselves that they were the only ones in heaven. For example, there are a lot of people who think that humans are the only living beings in the universe—an idea that will eventually be proved wrong, no doubt. But once a spirit has done enough time on a particular level of the spirit world, one that reflects what he or she was absolutely sure of at the time of death, then perhaps a shift takes place. It may be impelled by a spiritual boredom, whereby the spirit decides to travel onto higher ground. And, sooner or later, he or she finds that there are truly many mansions in the spirit worlds.

Through transcendence, your identity melts; but it doesn't disappear completely. So rather than being Joe Blow with a little bit of God Force within him, he becomes the God Force with a little bit of the memory of Joe Blow. It's slightly different, isn't it? On the one hand, you are a human personality with a bit of God Force knocking around within you; and on the other hand, you have melted into the divine light, and you are the God Force with a bit of the human personality within it. You are the God Force, Joe Blow-shaped. The emphasis is different, if you see what I mean.

I can feel that this process has been happening in my life, and I now feel less connected to the common aspirations of life on Earth. I have only a passing interest in the mundane, and that is very different from where I was, say, 20 years ago. I'm sure that if you've been on the path for any length of time, you'll have experienced the same thing I have. You changed: What you were, melted and became more. You are a human in the process of life, but you are aware that a large part of your evolution and your spiritual growth is happening elsewhere. You intuitively know that you are a part of many dimensions, not just the human one—a spiritual identity inside a body, rather than a body that has a spiritual identity, a soul, within it.

Channeling/Astral Entities

When talking about spirit worlds, I should also mention *channeling*. Channeling, really, is a modern term for *mediumship*. It's not far removed from *automatic writing,* either, in that the channel enters a meditative state, and a stream of consciousness issues forth. Sometimes that stream of consciousness takes on a personality, and so channels will say they are channeling a dead spirit. Again, it may be very possible, and then it's also highly probable that all or some of what is being channeled is coming from the channel's subconscious mind. You'll discover that the subconscious, once you get more in touch with it, really does feel like a very different person, separate from you.

The other possibility is that the channel is communicating with another entity—except that the psychic is not necessarily in touch with a Mayan priest from the Yucatan, but with a ghostlike entity from the astral plane that's in the room—and that entity has assumed the Mayan priest's identity to make itself sound more important and credible. The reason I became convinced that this is so—at times, anyway—is because I've had a lot of transdimensional experiences in other worlds. I'd hover over my entranced body and perform a few nippy etheric turns (I'll give you all those in chapter 9), and I'd see, or become aware of, astral entities, earthbound spirits, or thought-forms that looked like spirits—but most were phantoms, constructed from thought-forms deposited in the astral.

Here and there, from time to time, those astral entities would communicate. Then, dialogue, which didn't seem to be mine, would go off in my mind. I'd answer back and interact, and I came to realize that, first, the astral entities can't see you any more than you can see them and, second, that they are just stuck there in the astral, drifting around not doing anything much. Being in the vapid, lifeless world of the astral plane talking to a human who is full of life force must be quite alluring to them. I'm convinced that they know how to make it all sound fantastic and coherent. They know how to suck you in and how to get you to open up to them and trust them by telling you things that sound good—for example, that you've been chosen to bring the world the great secrets of the cosmos, that you are being granted special powers, and that your function is to tell the world of a great cataclysm that's about to unfold.

It's interesting that most UFO abductees report the same phenomena. They are told by the Grays (the little gray entities that we've all heard about by now) of great changes and cataclysms to come, and how important the abductee is in the scheme of things and so on. I'm sure it's easy for the terrified abductee to believe it all, but it has its ludicrous side. If the Grays really wanted to impart an urgent message to humanity, they could show up and tell us. Alternatively, they could abduct someone of influence, such as a major politician or a famous broadcaster. If delivering an important message is the agenda, why select people who don't necessarily have communication skills, who have no access to the media, who are ordinary folk with no special education or status, and who might have no real method of getting the important message out to people?

The astral entities, fairy worlds, and the Grays all feel the same to me. They sell you a grand story that may be convincing at first, but it's shot with holes if you look at it with a bit of skepticism. If you ever come across any astral entities, or if a character appears to you through automatic writing or the Ouija board and you find that you are communicating with an entity that claims great things, the way to handle it is this: Ask it questions, ones that will back it into a corner. Ask it to describe its world. When it claims great knowledge, ask it something technical, like what size a Planck length is (10^{-33} cm—named after Max Planck). Ask it how fast the earth is moving around the sun (30 kilometers per second). If the entity claims to be an Egyptian god, ask it who built the pyramid at Saqqara. Force the entity's hand by letting it know you are not gullible. If the channeled spirit claims to be a Mayan priest, then ask it about the Mayan calendar. They predicted the end of this particular age for A.D. December 2012, so that's something you'd imagine the priest ought to know. If your spirit entity is as thick as two planks, doesn't know Mayan from My Ass, and can't answer simple stuff that any bright 13-year-old would know, then you at least know what you've got. So don't get carried away. Most of it is a lot of "ooh" and "aah" and no facts—lots of inaccurate hogwash and no technical knowledge.

Communicating with spirits is an interesting form of research, but it does have its limitations. You could join a spiritualist group or train in a circle as a medium; or you can just get a piece of paper, relax, open up, and let your mind go blank. You may find that you start to experience automatic writing. It may be a communication from the spirit worlds, or it may come from your subconscious. It could also be a nearby spirit talking through your subconscious so that the information is partly from it and partly from you—a mixture.

The world of spirit mediums, Grays, astral entities, and psychic phenomena can be very confusing, and dippy folk can be easily led astray. But if you evaluate information and phenomena with a questioning mind, you'll soon sift out the little gems from the hogwash and the hype.

Next, I want to talk about the nature-self as part of your development. I'll show you a couple of subtle ideas that will help you develop the expanse of your mind. Once you're "open for business," there's a whole bunch of things you can do. Then I'll give you some special etheric exercises that will help kick-start you along.

SHAMANISM AND THE NATURE-SELF

As we moved out of a tribal, natural, right-brain state into a logical, ego-based, competitive state, the nature of our evolution changed.

Tribal people have to be aligned to the nature-self and the four elements or they don't survive. So they are naturally close to fire, earth, air, and water. The spirit of nature forms part of the atavistic power of their people: the spirit and vitality of their tribe, and its tribal knowledge or memory. In the same way, birds know when there is going to be an earthquake because they can feel the piezo-electrical changes in the earth's crust—they react to subtle shifts of energy as pressure drops, and so on. The nature-self carries us back to that same special type of ancient knowing. We listen and feel and keep ourselves safe.

Once science and intellect took over, the inner knowing atrophied and died because it wasn't quite so important. Now we can use a computer to calculate when the crops will grow; we don't have to feel it out. We can plot and track everything by satellite. So, for many, their nature-self died. We became more sterile.

The Wave-fields of the Nature-Self and the Animal Kingdoms

Embracing the nature-self is a vital part of returning you to the sixth sense. It's more than just spending time in the mountains or watching birds fly. It is an etheric action of entering into the spirit of nature—its evolution, its grand emotion—the one the rationalist says doesn't exist. It is leaving the finite world of the ego's mind-set and spreading yourself out, first via the collective human spirit, and then on through the animal kingdoms and beyond to the spirit of the four elements. It's the shaman taking on the identity of the panther, or transferring their consciousness into that of an eagle in flight to gain an overview of things below. Because a wave-field can spread out to a vast distance in a matter of seconds, it doesn't take much for you to join the etheric evolution of the nature-spirit of the planet and every living creature on it. It is part of how you spread yourself out. Because of the nonlocality of the sixth sense, spreading your consciousness out is very much the way to the opening of self.

Nature is the closest reservoir of natural energy available to us. The Taoist looked to nature to understand God. They saw behind its purely physical manifestation an invisible spirituality. In the simplicity of its order, they saw the God Force. The Native Americans have much to teach us in the same regard, for they look at the metaphysical reality of nature. So the coyote is not just a scruffy animal that wanders the mountains—it has a spirit, and it offers a teaching: coyote medicine. Each animal is observed and honored for the lessons and healing it provides. That's the humility of the nature-self, a far cry from those who want to shoot the animal and place it on a wall among other material trophies.

In the egocentricity of the modern era, humans became paramount, regarded as the only conscious beings on the planet. In returning to the nature-self, we see the error of this thinking. Just because animals don't talk doesn't mean they don't communicate and have consciousness. Certain higher species of animal have very complex social behavioral patterns and the rudiments of language. Domestic pets are more sophisticated than animals in the wild because of their interactions with humans. They soon develop "personality" that you can see as clear as day. To say that an animal doesn't have feelings and thoughts and that it doesn't communicate is silly.

The individual coyote in the wild may only have a limited awareness, but it belongs to the collective spirit of coyote—and that genetic, evolutionary line is complex. Biologist Rupert Sheldrake says that such a genetic line is surrounded by a field of information called a *morphic field*. In that field is the inherent memory and the characteristics of the coyote spirit, its group identity. The morphic field is "coyote shaped," if you like. It's more than just genetics. The field has the memory and traits of all the coyotes that there have ever been. I recently interviewed Rupert Sheldrake (RS) for my bimonthly newsletter, *Wilde Wizdom*. Here's an excerpt of what Rupert had to say to me (SW) about morphic fields:

> **RS:** A morphic field is a field concerned with a form or organization of behavior or structure. The fields that organize the growth of embryos and maintain the structure of bodies are called morphogenetic fields, from the Greek word *morphe*, meaning "form"; and *genesis*, meaning "coming into being." Other types of morphic fields organize distinctive behavior in animals and social groups, like flocks of birds, schools of fish, and there are also morphic fields for crystals and molecules in the realm of chemistry.
>
> For the human body, the morphic field is what organizes the body as the embryo, and it maintains its form and helps in healing and recovery from injury or disease. These fields have a kind of memory, through the process I call morphic resonance, which involves organisms tuning into all similar organisms of the same kind in the past. So each giraffe as it grows tunes into the actual forms of previous giraffes. So the form in its morphic field, that shapes the growing embryo, is a kind of average of previous giraffe forms.
>
> **SW:** Are we therefore linked to the memory of humans in the past via morphic resonance as well as DNA?
>
> **RS:** When we grow, we tune in to the memories of people in the past, most especially our ancestors. Genetics account for the inheritance of chemicals in the body through DNA and the proteins it codes for. But morphic fields are concerned with the organization of form and behavior. They are quite similar to the idea of the etheric body, and perhaps they're what people who see auras are seeing. . . ." (**http://www.sheldrake.org**)

So if Sheldrake and the Native Americans are right, the nature-spirit of an animal rests in the wave-field of its perpetual memory. So you would imagine that the field is eternal—as is, I believe, the inner metaphysical identity of a human. If the spirit field of an animal is eternal, it must be evolving. Nothing is stationary in our universe. To expect the coyote spirit to be stationary in its inner spiritual identity would be contradictory to what we observe as a quality of energy. Everything is moving toward entropy (heat death), or it's moving in the opposite direction (expansion).

An animal's etheric is hard to see, as it doesn't boom out like a human's, but it is there, nonetheless. As you watch an animal in the wild, a mammal, say, flip your mind into its heart. Reach out and hold its heart with your hand, and imagine its pulse, the rhythm of its life. Suddenly, you are *inside* nature, not just outside.

At some of my seminars, we'd take people riding and blindfold them. Eliminating the faculty of sight helped them understand the essence of the aliveness of the animal underneath them. We'd start the ride by placing two fingers on the horse's neck, over its jugular vein, listening to its heart. As you feel its heart beating, you project yourself mentally into the animal and join its life force for a moment. It's a very special and intimate feeling. You join the silent emotion that governs the animal's reality. A huge door swings open with a great "clunk."

If you have a small pet, pick it up, close your eyes, and listen to its heart. You'll learn something about your little mate that you never knew before. It will *talk* to you. You'll see that your relationship to it—the fact that you give it attention and concentrate on it—brings it inside your evolution. Its spirituality is inside yours. You come to understand that it relies on you for its spiritual growth. When you are not around, it returns to the collective animal spirit to which it belongs. As soon as you show up, it flips out of that collective spirit, individualizes, and hangs out with you. Flipping back and forth, it develops personality—the first step to an individualized soul. For *soul* is just the spiritual term we use for the traits and memories that make up the human personality.

The process of the spiritual evolution of animals is no different from that of humans. What are we, if not just animals that have advanced a bit more than others have? We are made from the dust of dead stars, and that dust found its way into the primordial soup that existed on the earth in the early days. Everything alive today came from that soup in one way or another. Who's to say that one branch of evolution is more special than another?

Paul Davies makes a good point in his book on the origins of life, *The Fifth Miracle*. He says it's just a value judgment to place humans at the top of the evolutionary ladder using IQ as the criterion. He says that that is chauvinism, because we have selected the way in which evolution should be judged. Microbes win hands down for sheer numbers, turtles outlive us by hundreds of years—and compared to some species, we are rotten at seeing, hearing, smelling, flying, and swimming. Davies asks, "Is intelligence better in any absolute sense than, say, eyesight or hearing? Both of which are only moderately well developed in humans." I think it's most likely that all the species, humans included, are interdependent and vital in their own way. We are, all together, evolving through our different wave-fields. Life is just one big pulse.

You can see how humans evolve socially through wave-fields. At first, we evolve through the field of our family or caregivers, then in our teenage years and early 20s, we evolve in the wave-field of our associations with others of our own age. Then we mature and enter society as adults, and although we have a personality and an identity in that adult wave-field system, it is not greatly individualized at first. We follow the rhythms preset by others. Later, as we gain confidence and turn within to concentrate on the nature of who we are, we solidify and individualize. Sometimes the wave-field of life's tick-tock rhythm becomes an encumbrance, and we gradually gain enough courage to walk away to an even more individualized wave-field.

Lesser forms of evolution are simply in earlier, less complex wave-fields as are, say, individual cells in our bodies. To disconnect from nature is like saying, "I am important, but my body's cells aren't." We are the body of nature—and it is us

So when you're out in nature or when you have time to stop and contemplate, try to see or feel the bands of energy coming up from the earth. They look like bands of heat that rise from a tarmac road when it's hot, except that they are moving much faster. Notice as they pass through your body, and imagine how they might traverse the very heart of an animal's perception. If it's a little difficult to see the bands of energy at first, try *feeling* them instead. Pick a rock, preferably granite, and lay on it for a while; feel the way it gives off an electrical signal. If you stay an hour or more, its power will begin to make you feel quite spacey. You'll definitely know that the energy is there; it's not an illusion. Try this: Get a dowsing rod, and walk around the countryside. Watch the way it moves and responds to energy flows: ley lines, underground water, and so forth. We are in the middle of an enormous pulse of energy; it is all around us.

Embracing the nature-self is the act of grounding yourself geographically in a finite-particle body on Mother Earth, while developing your consciousness in an infinite hazy-wave dimension. The stress of life locks us into the world of mind and thinking, so we lose touch with the ebb and flow of life. Take a moment to notice and appreciate this current season, then move your feelings through all the other seasons that will follow during the year. So as the sun moves north toward the Tropic of Cancer, be aware and go with it. Notice how it changes your environment, and recall and remember why those changes take place. Then as it turns and comes south toward the Tropic of Capricorn, watch the opposite effect. How many people know where the sun is aligned at any given moment of the year? Not many. Yet it is the source of all life.

On a clear night, look up to notice where we are in relation to the other stars of our galaxy. Feel grounded, while thinking about the stars above and your position as a spark (star) of consciousness here on Earth. Look at the stars above, and take a moment to ponder that there are as many stars and galaxies under your feet as there are above you. I'll talk about the trick of placing yourself in an infinite context via the etheric and the stars a bit later.

The nature-self is a wave-field. The process of spiritual growth is a journey of various transitions from one field to another. To digress slightly for a moment, the concept of wave-fields explains why divorce is so prevalent today. Marriage is an institution of the old patriarchal system. It requires each to enter into a preset wave-field with all its inherent rules and regulations. That wave-field often regresses you to your childhood memories, when your mother and father were doing "marriage," and you were a child in their wave-field, not individualized as you are now.

When you fall in love, you lose yourself and your identity in the wave-field of romance. You become childlike, and each of you may give your partner a time-regressed name—Baby, Honey Child, Cutie Pie, My Little Dear, or whatever. Once the wave-field of romance peters out, you enter the day-to-day wave-field of married life. That may feel very solid and secure, so you don't mind the restriction and the duty of it. But as time goes by, and if you are now on the path looking at yourself, you might find the wave-field very stifling. You'll fight to get out. Often your partner is really lovely, and you can't understand why you are both picking fights for no reason at all. Without realizing it, you are suffering a spiritual-psychological asphyxiation. Neither of you can breathe. Each of you may be too insecure to allow the other the space needed to evolve. Eventually, you may have to go your separate ways.

There is no right or wrong, although separation is often fraught with acrimony because, having regressed to a childlike state via romance and marriage, the separation feels like abandonment. You'll feel orphaned and indignant—as well you might be if your parents threw you out at a young age and abandoned you. Your first reaction will be to insist that your partner owes you something, compensation for the abandonment. And they may demand the same from you. The wide-open space of a real, individual evolution is a scary proposition, just as the adult world feels scary to a young child. You desperately need a bit of security and a guarantee. Yet consciously or subconsciously, you walked out because you had to. There's no right and wrong, just wave-field after wave-field. Maybe that's why we call it waving good-bye. Tee-hee.

The wave-field of family, society, marriage, and individualization are fields in the human experience, and beside those are the wave-fields of nature. Those wave-fields have entities evolving in them. The writers of old spoke of the fairy kingdoms, the endines of the water, the sylphs of the air, and the salamanders of fire. Each are etheric nature evolutions not visible to the naked eye. (I've had a few experiences in the fairy kingdoms. In chapter 5, I tell the story of an occasion when I was out in the forest penetrating the fairy worlds, and I got knocked out of my body by some goblinlike entities that looked really strange.)

Now that the video camera has become so common in our lives, we are beginning to see things that we've never seen before. There's a group of researchers that specializes in filming what seem like etheric air spirits. Because a video can be slowed down and played frame by frame, we can now see things that may only be visible for 1/30th of a second. The group has hundreds of shots of air spirits that look like a small flying tube. They range from a few inches to several feet in length. They propel themselves through the air with fins that oscillate on both sides of their tubelike bodies. (The legend of the mermaid is our humanized version of a water spirit.) I don't think anyone has evidence of water spirits as yet, but I'm sure they are there. All of nature has etheric entities evolving in it. In fact, I was told once by a man in the know that there are many more nature entities evolving in the etheric on the Earth plane than there are humans. Our physical form with the etheric field that surrounds it is just one evolution, a part of many.

Then beyond our etheric and wave-field of nature spirits is the field of the universe as a whole, and beyond that, other universes, spirit worlds, and so on. As you develop the subtle shift required, you spread yourself and your memory through more and more fields, eventually reaching to the outer limits of this universe. Then you see that, while the universe is external to your physical body, it is, in fact, inside your inner-self. So as you watch the constellations cross the sky at night, they are, in effect, traveling through your heart, as well as above your head and below your feet.

You are poised in the center of a cosmic magnificence, connected non-locally to everything else. Make it a discipline to spread yourself a little each day. Say, "I am the wind, the fire, the earth, the water, the galaxies above and below. I am the etheric—aligned to nature, the animal spirits, the ancient wisdom, and the natural ways. I am open to all the information those fields contain." Make this a daily mantra. Within a short time, a shift takes place within you. You position yourself in a greater context. That's the first trick to expanding yourself. If you can spend time outdoors on your own, go to the mountains, sleep there, and embrace the ebb and flow of things. Quiet your mind, remain silent, turn within, and enter the etheric field, claiming back your natural humanity via the simplicity of your nature-self. It awaits.

The Power of Noticing Things

The next simple step in enhancing your nature-self and your sixth sense is to train yourself to become sharper by noticing things. I mention this a lot in my other books, so I'll keep it brief, but it's important. The mind is lazy. It has trained itself to ignore everything except those things that scare it or please it. By forcing the mind to notice things, you engage it, telling it you want to be aware of life, and to claim back that which has been lost. By stimulating the five senses, you bridge to the extrasensory perception of the subtle body. In addition, by stopping to notice, you place yourself more firmly inside this incarnation as a human. It's part of the process we talked about before. It's important that life doesn't just wash past you—so a day becomes a week, a month a year, and suddenly you're old and gray and dead! By stopping to notice, you are requiring the mind to come back from its world, its pleasures and needs, and enter another world—the real world of observation and comprehension. You are spreading your attention from, say, staring at a minute speck of dust on the windowsill, to looking up at the Great Nebula in Orion (M42) approximately 1,500 light-years away.

So, for the next 24 hours, every time your mind starts to talk to you, if that dialogue begins with the "I" word ("I think this, I want that"), stop it. Occupy it, instead, in the act of *noticing* something. Stopping the mind is a good discipline; it strengthens your force of will. You might remember from Carlos Castaneda's early books that his shaman teacher, don Juan, laid great emphasis on "stopping the mind" as the first step to the etheric world and the shaman's power.

If you are at home right now, stop to notice the room you are in. How many power points are there? How many lights? Are they all working? If you are reading in the bath, pause to count the tiles. "Yes," you'll say, "there are 132 white tiles round the bath, and three are cracked."

Now, think of a street you go down regularly. Write down everything you can remember about the street. Most likely you'll discover that you can't remember very much, and the pizza parlor you thought was on the corner is, in fact, two shops down. And although you've been up and down the street a hundred times, you won't remember half of it.

Then go to the street and fill in the missing bits. Write down everything you see. What do the traffic signs actually say? How long is the street? What parking regulations are enforced? What are the main features of the street—its shape, size, the shops, and so on? If there is graffiti on the corner wall, what does it say? Write a detailed map and description of your street, and remember it. Wait a few days, and have a friend test you. If you make any mistakes, go back to the street—as many times as it takes until you accurately remember everything. Let your mind know that you won't let it off the hook until it can remember each and every thing there is to know in your selected street.

It doesn't matter if this exercise takes you a month and you have to go back 12 times. What you are saying is, details are important, the effort is worthwhile. Make it a discipline to take stock of your situation every time you find yourself somewhere new. So, say that you're visiting an office today and you haven't been there before. As you walk in, pause, and cast your eyes around. What is your first and overriding impression? What's the feeling there? Happiness, anger, boredom, indifference? The office will be laced—painted, if you like—with people's emotions and their thinking. What can your inner knowing tell you about this office that you're just walking into?

What is there to *notice?* Start counting stuff. How many people are there? How many desks? What color are the blinds? How many phones? Are the filing cabinets gray or black or some other color? Try to pick up all that general information with just one or two casts of your eyes. Make a mental picture of the office in your mind's eye, and while you're waiting for your appointment, run through your mental snapshot, enhancing it and remembering it. Remember the picture that the room makes in your mind; don't try to remember the actual room. The picture can last for hours, days, years. Your physical presence in the room may be short.

Now try this: Take a pack of cards, and turn over three as fast as you can flip your hand. Let the cards make a mental picture in your mind. Pause, then turn over three more, and then three more—run through three sets of three, so you have nine cards in all. Now go back to your memory of the mental picture you had of the first set of three. What were the cards? And the second set of three? And what was in the third set of three? Don't bother to remember the actual cards—just close your eyes and ask your mind to give you the three mental pictures.

I used to teach blackjack courses to people who wanted to make a living out of the game. To become a pro at blackjack you have to be able to count the ratio of high cards (10s, Jacks, Queens, and Kings) to low cards. When you are playing, you are not able to count cards in real time, as the dealer moves them from your vision as fast as he or she can. So the way to become a great player is to remember the pictures that a group of cards make in your head. It's reassuring to remember that no croupier in the world can move faster than the speed of light, and that is the speed at which the picture comes to you as light reflects off the cards to your eye.

People asked me if I ever got intimidated in the casino by fast dealers. I'd tell 'em, "Fast dealers are good—hands come to you more quickly. The more hands that are dealt, the more money the professional player makes."

Remember, there's a subtle difference between reality as it is in the real world and the pictures of reality that reflected light creates in your mind. Reality changes, but the pictures stay. It's only a matter of telling your mind to hold on to the pictures. Eventually, you'll be able to remember cards you saw a month ago.

This card exercise might seem innocuous, but it's quite exciting, for it is the beginning of training yourself to develop a photographic memory. Part of the sixth sense comes to you in the form of visions and symbols, so developing the ability to remember pictures at speed is a handy tool.

Back to the cards exercise. If at first you find three cards too hard to remember, try turning over sets of just two cards, or even one card at a time. Once you have this part down pat, try more cards, expand your perception, and try flipping over sets of four or even six cards. Wait a few seconds, and see if you can accurately describe all six cards you saw and the positions you saw them in—say, from left to right. Don't be daunted; you are only remembering the image, the impression the light makes in your mind's eye. Eventually, you'll get so fast in your ability to notice that you'll be able to pick up cards or details of a room in a split second, hardly moving your eyes. Noticing is fun; it gives you a sense of achievement, and it instantly shows you things you never saw before.

Think of this: If you live 80 years and you sleep for a third of that, you are left with about 53 years in the waking state. Now if you only notice 25 percent of life, your 53 waking years come down to a real life span of just under 14 years. That's not much when compared to the full potential of a lifetime. Now, much of those 14 years while you are aware will be spent doing and noticing ordinary things, such as washing your body, mopping the floor, and hauling the kids to school. In the end, your life may come down to less than six to eight real years of quality, conscious, awake, valuable action—six to eight years to notice humanity in its real definition. That's rather sad, isn't it? Life passes most people by. They are asleep, or daydreaming. Copious thinking is a disease of the egocentric; it's their escape mechanism to avoid the insecurities of real life.

The only way to transcend life is by going through it fully, not by avoiding it or trying to duck around it. You raise your energy and go beyond things by experiencing them. Understanding what has happened, reconciling it all, and moving on through is the only way it works. By moving powerfully through life, you develop confidence.

Generally speaking, a person can't really become a noticer of life until he or she stops being obsessed with self. Our modern societies train people to become unreasonably self-indulgent and self-centered. Now it's good to look after yourself and honor yourself and to concentrate on your life, but there's a fine line between what is reasonable and the way some people operate. If the only thoughts going off in your head start with "I this" and "I that," then the ego has you in its grip. It will gradually shrink your world to where its whims and neuroses and its focus are all you ever see. It's much like a small child who will make a huge fuss and create a scene so that its mother will attend to it—putting aside whatever she's doing to care for the child.

People spend their lives mentally preening themselves, constantly thinking and talking about themselves, so they can't properly hear or perceive. When others talk, they don't listen, for they are listening to the incessant chatter droning on in their heads. It's very hard for them to perceive and notice what is outside of them. They walk up the street, meet a friend, have a meal, and several hours of life have gone by without them really seeing or noticing very much other than themselves.

An obsession with self collapses your universe down to a very small place. You are focused just on the outpourings of what is often a fearful and disconnected mind—one that's missing most of what is going on. Life becomes a blur; most can't describe what happened yesterday, never mind last week.

People resting solely inside their intellect and its ideas have a very one-sided view of the human experience. They have no frame of reference in which to comprehend the greater picture, for they have no solid framework outside of self and not much of a connection to the inner spiritual self. In the perpetual mutterings of the ego, you are in the wave-field of the mind, which limits you from spreading out eternally.

As you begin to open up, you'll want to discipline the mind away from itself and toward silence, energy, other people, and life. When the mind chatters, stop it. Say, "I don't need to think about that now. I will deal with these concerns later." Or, alternatively, as it speaks, say, "I don't accept that energy. I am serene and silent."

Then take a moment and notice something outside of you. Stare at the ant that's climbing up the garden gate. Look at a high building, and notice how the bricks on the third floor lock into the ones that make up the fourth floor. You are trying to "stop the world," developing the powerful side of yourself, the silent mind that is engaged in perceiving energy and the subtleties of life. The trick here is to get more information impacting your senses, rather than flowing past you at high speed.

Let's go to the next chapter and look at how the five senses form the pyramid base of the sixth sense—and how to use that to flip yourself from finite to infinite and back again.

ACUTENESS IN THE
REALM OF THE SENSES

Developing the Five Senses

The fastest and simplest way to open up to the etheric and the sixth sense is by delving more deeply into the realm of the five senses. The etheric field is moving more quickly than one is normally used to perceiving. By developing speed of perception and detail, you progress easily. Here are a few more ideas to mull over.

The first step is to crank up the awareness of your sense of sight. If you are not blind, you'll probably take this sense for granted. As humans, we don't have to make an effort to see, but we *do* have to make an effort to notice.

As a discipline, take a little notebook with you, and as you go through the day, make a note of things you see. It doesn't matter if what you see is unusual or not. Just write down events, or the descriptions of people and actions that have taken place in front of you:

> *"I was in the parking lot at the supermarket at 11.32 A.M. I observed a portly gentleman walk into a lamppost. He seemed dazed. He then became angry and he kicked the post. Grabbing his leg in pain, he hopped backward three or four paces into a shopping cart that was being pushed by a priest in a black cassock. The cart tipped over, and a can of beans rolled ceremoniously across*

the parking lot. A blue van marked 'Celestial Loveliness, Natural Cosmetic Products for the Young at Heart' squashed the beans. Interesting."

Filling in the notebook requires you to be attentive. It's a handy discipline if you ever want to become a writer. You learn to observe small details, and you become proficient at painting pictures with words. Writing a journal that describes events you've noticed takes the mind away from itself. It affirms that all information is valuable to you. It is important to gather even the most insignificant information: "I walked down the street and saw a glove nailed to a post, three feet off the ground. Weird." Later you will refine your instructions to the mind—so it cuts out the mundane and clicks in quickly when there is a special sign, or when something unusual is going on. But for now, write things down and remember everything, no matter how humdrum.

Training your mind to see in the shamanistic way empowers your subtlety. Your wave-field expands, offering you the chance to dream a bigger dream. If you can conceive a big dream for yourself, you enlarge your world and stretch yourself to greater possibilities. Dreaming the big dream is so much a part of the sixth sense, for it lures you toward the extraordinary, toward what is considered impossible. I think our world will be a dreary place in the future unless ordinary people begin to dream the impossible dream. The planet needs it. We have to do something different and quickly.

I don't think the big dream is necessarily egotistical. It can lie silently within you as a part of your spiritual concept of the Infinite Self and your higher ideals. It's important for us to attempt to reach for the stars; otherwise, our evolution grinds to a halt, drowned in the mundane insecurities of a mortal existence.

Try this: Wait for a starry night, and start by finding all the main constellations if you don't already know them. Perhaps you could start with your birth sign. Some of the signs of the zodiac are easier to see than others. Leo, Taurus, and Gemini are easy to spot; Aries, Pisces, and Cancer the crab, much harder. Of course, some of the signs may be below the horizon in certain locations, depending on the time of year. Get a star chart, and plot your way around the heavens. It's fun to know where your constellation is. There are 88 constellations recognized by astronomers. If you can't learn them all, it would be good if at least you knew the main ones. If you are keen, you can study the rest later.

Learning the sky is a spiritual exercise. It gives you a whole bunch of new friends, and it enlarges you. But most of all, knowing the sky gives you geography. You look beyond our small world-view to a cosmic panorama of light-years, enormous distances, and vast masses. By knowing the stars, you place yourself in your proper context, inside an evolution that is eternal. I can't stress how important this is, for the visionary is not a victim of his or her mind, but is in control of it. Visionaries are larger-than-life, eternal, beyond death.

Do this: Pause for a moment and remember that you are eternal— spread across a vast epoch—straddled across both the past and the future. In this grand mind-set, mentally cast a thought to the distant future, and think about people (your descendants, perhaps)—those who will be living here on the very ground you stand on right now. Think of them in, say, 500 years from now, in the year A.D. 2500.

Pause to reflect who these individuals might be, what their hopes and dreams might be, and how you might help them and strengthen them and wish them well. The future, you see, though not yet formed, exists in its virtual spiritual state *right now.*

So breathe in a long breath, and as you exhale, send love carried on your breath to your countrymen and women—those who are here right now, and those who might be alive on this very same day of the year, 500 years from now. As you breathe out, project the light into the future, place a positive energy forward in time, and feel yourself there as part of a future epoch. Via the eternity within, you will be there in a sense. And, of course, a small part of you will be there through the record of your current memories—those that you are currently placing in the global mind, which is a perpetual record of the evolution of humanity to which you belong.

Back to the night sky for a moment. Once you know the constellations, they grant you a security; you'll know better where you are. You'll also know, by looking at the positions of constellations, what month we are in, and you'll have an approximation of the time. I love getting out of bed at night and looking at the sky and knowing it's 3 A.M. or thereabouts. If you are one who seeks direction in life, knowing where you are right now is a positive step.

It has always seemed odd to me that so many seek direction, in the sense that they want a lucky break, or they need someone to help them, or they seek a path to follow. But if you asked them what direction they are facing right now, in the strictly physical sense, they can't tell north from south. They lack a relationship with this planet and its position in the universe—which doesn't say much for their hope of finding a direction in life. I can't help thinking that knowing where you are geographically, and your position in relation to the universe above, is a powerful statement of your maturity. Make a mental note from time to time during the day. Ask, "Where am I? How far from where? How close to what? Am I facing north or south? Do I have my head tucked under my arm like so many others, or do I know where I'm going?"

Sight is more than just looking at things; it is also knowing, positioning yourself in relation to things.

While gazing up at the night sky, pick a spot, which is black and seemingly starless. Stare at that dark spot and pull it to you in your feelings. Bit by bit, you'll see stars that were not there a few minutes ago. Get a pair of strong binoculars and you'll see thousands of stars, and galaxies made of up billions of stars. Many of them are like our sun, and astronomers now know that many have planets orbiting them, much like those in our solar system. Even if there aren't humanlike creatures up there, there is definitely an evolution going on; meaningful things are happening. The stars you see at night with the naked eye are all part of the Milky Way, our home. Beyond the Milky Way are the fuzzy hazes of 12 nearby galaxies, and beyond them a billion more. In a certain sense, it's a very big playground we find ourselves in. Very big—awesome, really.

The other direction in which you might need to crank your power of sight is inwards, through dreams, visions, and meditations. I am sure that all those are already an important part of your life. As you stand in a grander context, and you empower your perception of externals, your internal flow of information becomes richer and more meaningful. In chapter 5, I lay out some tips and tricks of the trade that have helped me understand visions and symbols.

Sensitivity and Hearing

Meanwhile, let me continue through the five senses and talk about sensitivity and hearing—which I am sure you will have guessed by now is more than just cocking your ear in the direction of noise.

Just as sight aligns to direction, hearing in its wider definition is comprehension. Now there is an etheric nature to hearing, which is both inner, from the clairvoyant faculty of the mind; and external, via the etheric self. I have lain in bed at night after a session at the music studio and have heard music playing outside my body, close to my left ear. It's always music I haven't heard before. It's not a replay of what I've been listening to during the day. The music seems external to the mind; it is in the etheric. How it gets there I haven't a clue, but it's a very different experience from the memory of a piece of music that goes through one's mind. To stimulate your etheric hearing, you have to start with your normal hearing.

Traveling over the years while lecturing, the one problem I noticed that was common to many was a lack of comprehension, which exacerbated their confusion in life. I have a lot of compassion for that uncertainty. Our human experience is so mind-boggling, heroic, sad, and so utterly strange, it's not surprising that people feel a bit unsure. Through comprehension, we attempt to develop a true spiritual meaning to life. I don't know that we will ever understand it all, but in the humble desire to comprehend, we are at least attempting to walk out of a cloudy life toward clarity and perception.

That's why the acuteness of your senses is important. At first it all seems so obvious that one would hardly bother to mention it. Yet in the case of hearing, say, there is an innate correlation between your ability to listen and comprehend and your ability to be open and to listen to the promptings of Spirit and to the voice of your heart—the subtle inner messages that lead you through the darkness to fresh air, and a spiritual and personal freedom.

As an affirmation that you will listen to your heart, in the sense of the promptings of Spirit, try this: Place your finger on your pulse several times a day, and as you hear your heart beating, pause to think about the spaces between the beats. Focus on them. The pauses are what death sounds like. The sound of the beat is what life sounds like to us humans. In taking a moment to listen to your heart, you are affirming that you will listen and act on its promptings. It's cool that we even have a heart. Try to love it.

Here's another. Try this: Sit on a park bench, close your eyes, relax, and stop your mind. Start by just listening to what is going on around you. Listen to conversations—hear life, its animation, its liveliness, and its grand emotion. It is all around you.

Now begin to stretch your hearing by reaching past what is normally audible. Visualize yourself with ultrasensitive, big elflike ears. Imagine them on a rotational mount so that you can turn your special big ears in every direction. Tell yourself that your hearing has become super-directional, that you can now mentally move your ears and search for sounds.

Focus on a faint sound in the distance. Then ask your auditory capacity to bring the sound closer to you. Mentally drag the sound toward you. It gets louder. It doesn't matter if you still can't hear it clearly; it's the act of concentrating on the sound that matters. In visualizing larger ears, you improve your hearing.

The other thing you can try is to cup one hand behind one ear, and cup the other hand in front of the opposite ear. That way you accentuate your hearing backward with one ear, and frontward with the other. Now you are even more multidirectional; you have created a wider catchment area around your ears. Suddenly you are bigger in your perception through the gift of hearing.

There are quite a few exercises you can devise to become more sensitive. Pick a piece of music you know well, and listen to it while sitting in a chair. Clear your mind and go through the piece, listening not just to its overall melody, but to each and every instrument. Then try to pick up on the feelings the musicians are putting across. If the track you are listening to has been recorded live, rather than coming from a sampler or a computer program, you'll find that behind the notes and chords is the real person playing through whatever emotion they felt at that very moment.

The music has its etheric color. Part comes from the frequency, and part from the human emotion. The color of music is an inner-sight phenomenon, but you don't have to see it to feel the color. The music talks to you in its emotional colors: anger—dark; music of an intellectual nature—yellow; sadness—orange; open and simple music—green. Music that aspires to climb would be blue going to indigo and then beyond that to violet. My old teacher talked a lot about the violet sound of music. It is pristine and often angelic in its nature. There is a lot of it in Mozart's compositions. I've tried for it with sopranos and altos on the albums that I've worked on. Here and there I've succeeded, or, I should say, I've talked about it to the singers and musicians, and *they* have succeeded.

I think metaphysics of harmonics and sound are coming into their own, although I don't think we yet understand why certain tones elicit certain emotions, or what real effect others have upon the physical body. For years, I have searched for a sound called the Sacred Hum. Supposedly, certain Taoist monks used the sound to open a transdimensional gateway into another world. At first, I was influenced and confused by the sound of the *om;* I always felt it was not quite the sound I was looking for. It was too deep, and sacred as the sound is, it never seemed quite right. Then I read a pamphlet by Chloë Wordsworth on Holographic Repatterning, which is a process that uses harmonics for healing. She pitches the *om* at 136.10 Hz on a scale, whereby A=220. Using tuning forks, I came to realize that the sacred hum must be in or around F-sharp. Years ago, a friend who specialized in kinesiology, which uses muscle testing to diagnose energy flows, told me he considered F-sharp very invigorating and strengthening for human muscles. Because of his advice, I put a piece of music in F-sharp under the main music that runs through my subliminal tapes. It seems to work quite well, so F-sharp is in the frame sacred-hum-wise.

I won't wax on any further about harmonics and music—it's a subject on which I reach my outer limits very quickly. If you are interested, there are lots of books that discuss the interrelationship between the musical notes, colors, and harmonics in general. I think David Tame's book, *The Secret Power of Music*, is one that is very well laid out.

Back to hearing: Next time you are in a face-to-face conversation with someone, focus your eyes on the tip of their nose. Concentrate on it, not moving your eyes, while you listen carefully to every word they say. Don't let your mind wander. Listen to the silence between their words, the sighs, and the poignant pauses. Listen to the inflection of their voice as it rises and falls. From time to time, move your concentration from the tip of their nose without moving your eyes, and watch their pupils and see how they open and shut slightly as they talk. There's comprehension to be had. As you concentrate on your listening ability, search for the subtle feeling behind what is being said.

When people are talking, most of the information they impart is in their feelings. The words they utter are only a code that describes a thought, which is an electrical outcropping of an emotion or subtle feeling. By listening to conversations in the way described, you honor the other person by concentrating on them, and you become aware of the subtlety behind what is being said. You'll begin to pick up loads of information, for by concentrating on the tip of their nose and clearing your mind, you are entering into their energy. It talks to you. You open to a natural clairvoyance.

Next, we ought to discuss the sense of touch. Gifted psychics can pick up a lot of information by touching objects—this is known as *psychometry*. Give a psychic an item of clothing from a person who has been murdered, and he or she can pick up on the energy of that person and the circumstances of their demise. How do psychics do that?

I believe we impact our physical reality with our spiritual, metaphysical identity—our subtle energy—and also with our emotions and feelings. There is a theory that says that sound striking a physical object leaves an impact or memory at an atomic or subatomic level. So, hypothetically, you could strip off a piece of the wall in your front room and there would be a record of everything you've ever said and every TV show you've ever watched. God forbid!

Still, aside from that, I feel that your subtle energy, emotions, and thinking probably act much like sound, impacting reality at a subtle, nonlocal level. In the end, it's all energy—subatomic, atomic, metaphysical, whatever. Yes, it changes, but I'm sure there is a perpetual memory that lives on—a record of the universe's evolution, if you like.

To expand your sensitivity to energy via the sense of touch requires you to become more aware of the texture and nature of life, to embrace its softness and sensuality. This is particularly important for men, who tend to abandon their sensitivity in their quest for wealth, status, activity, and competition. They often live in a world that is too hard and insensitive, and it hurts them in the end and makes them sad. They burn out with a garage full of stuff that gives them little real pleasure, while they could have experienced much via sensitivity and love. In doing so, they would have become bigger spiritually, they would have been less hard on themselves, and they would have experienced more goodness and pleasure.

Being connected to the real things in life is so much more valuable than the "biff-bang" world of the modern male. So much of the sensitivity of both males and females is lost in the madcap rush for security, status, and wealth. The idea that acquisitions will make you happy is a big letdown for most. Eventually, the coarse, plastic, electronic nature of modern living destroys our sensitivity, and with it goes much of our real perception of life.

So be in touch. Notice the feel of things around you. Touch a piece of satin or silk and feel its lushness. Feel the breeze on your cheeks as you walk in the park. Take off your shoes and walk on the earth, feel the dampness of the soil, and make a note of the way this marvelous planet feels under your bare feet.

Try this: Pick an evening when you know you will be home alone. Blindfold yourself. Now I'm presuming here that you are not already visually impaired. If you are, you can skip this one, as you will know it through and through.

If you are not blind, spend three hours with a blindfold on. Fix dinner, do household chores, walk around, and listen to the radio or TV if you like. Spend the evening in the realm of touch. You will be amazed. At first, you'll operate a bit spastically, and you might become frustrated and irritable. But your confidence will soon grow. You will be able to feel your way along and you'll know where things are, especially things that are alive, such as plants and your pets—they emanate heaps of energy. You just have to focus on it, picking up more and more.

So on this special evening, feel your way along, and reclaim the ability you had as a baby, when you touched things and licked them and fondled them to understand and learn about them. I wouldn't bother licking the cat if I were you, but you know what I mean. Claim back your sense of touch— it will help your sensitivity, and you'll develop gratitude for your sight. And that is part of understanding compassion and love, is it not?

There's a variation of this exercise we used to do in my men's seminars, which were called "Wilde Fire." I'd take the men to the edge of a wooded area, usually one that was rather hilly, and I'd blindfold them and make them walk through the forest, feeling their way along.

Each man was given two eggs to carry, which they were not supposed to break. The eggs signified a man's responsibilities in life: his job, children, family, and so on. Also, the eggs stopped the men blustering through the woods, macho-style.

For the first five or ten minutes, the men would whack their heads on things, often falling over. But bit by bit, they found that if they retired their thinking and engaged their feelings, they would know where the trees and the branches were. They could feel the etheric energy of the tree without having to see it. Soon they could walk through the woods at almost a normal pace. In this exercise, they had to follow a drumbeat, and often if the drummer (a staff member who was not blindfolded) wasn't on his toes, or if he dozed off, the blindfolded men would catch up to him lickety-split. The drummer would have to duck away quickly. I've seen blindfolded men get to almost a slow running speed, crouched over, holding their eggs, feeling out the positions of trees and branches, weaving their way through them at high speed. It was amazing to watch.

After you have done the "home alone" blindfolded exercise, go to the woods and try the egg routine there. Take a friend to help you stay safe so that you don't drop over a cliff or wander out onto a forest road where traffic might pass. Perhaps you could give it a go and talk about it, and then your friend might try it. It's heaps of fun. It teaches you things.

Then again, you can practice anytime, in the park or walking down the street. Take a moment to close your eyes and feel where you are. With your eyes shut, try to feel people passing you by—not just their presence or the displacement of air, but the overall feeling or energy they emit. You'll be astonished at how fast your perception grows.

Soon you'll be more aware of your surroundings. You'll recognize slight temperature shifts and air pressure changes, and you'll train yourself to enhance your ambient perception. Try to figure out when it will rain next. Use your feelings to detect the change in air pressure as a low front moves through your area, bringing moisture with it. You'll notice the shift hours and days in advance; the pressure change is very noticeable.

Reading people's emotions is not a lot different from noticing air pressure. Even people's most subtle mood swings will impact you and tell you things.

I'm sure you've had the experience of entering a room just after people have had a heated argument. You can *feel* the residue of their antagonism, and the emotional or verbal violence they have left behind. It's not an illusion—the energy is there. Have you ever visited an ancient battlefield and noticed a strange stillness there that is really spooky? You can feel the memory of the tragedy that took place. Sometimes the battle might have been many hundreds of years ago, but the residue of the event is laid down, covering the fields like a lead carpet. The stillness is in the shock of it all. It's the earth's spiritual objection—a silent protest that attempts to enclose the wound that was opened there.

There's a mountain village in Tuscany called Civitella. I go there for lunch sometimes. The Nazis shot all the men of the village against a wall in the main street. If you stand by the wall, it, too, has that same thick, silent feel about it. The residue of shock imprinted on the wall is eerie.

I have often felt that the Australian Aborigines are right about the Dreamtime, and that the memory of human and animal life criss-crosses the planet like the weave of a giant cloth, with each of us leaving a trace of ourselves as we move about, and each of our traces traversing the energy-grid left by others. If you go into a cathedral—a Catholic one, for example, look up behind the altar and you'll see a large, very faint etheric cloud just floating there. It's the hopes and prayers of the faithful, hovering there as an energy source, an offering to God. If you mentally pull that energy into your heart and curve it up toward the third-eye chakra in the center of your forehead, you'll energize yourself, and you'll find that your power of vision is temporarily enhanced. It's a bit like an energy soup kitchen; you get lunch for free.

There's a mass of energy out there—some of it spooky, some inspirational. Other energy pockets are bland. Sometimes you'll walk into a place and notice how the energy has become chaotic—that's when you turn and leave. As you develop your tactile sense, you naturally become more sensitive to very subtle energy, and in addition, you become more sensual. Life is more fun.

As a part of developing sensuality, you could work upon your sense of smell. You may want to invest in a range of essential oils and take the time to really smell each one so you can identify each flower or scent, maybe even mixtures of oils. Start to engage your sense of smell at the fruit counter in the supermarket, on the train going home from work, or in a restaurant at lunch. Try to really notice what smells permeate the air. Let your mind know that you want it to be aware.

It's the same with taste. Pause when you're eating, and really concentrate on the food. One of the perception-enhancing exercises I once used was to get people to concentrate on the intensity of each moment of life. I would give people one single raisin to eat, and I'd make them concentrate on it for a while. You may want to try this yourself.

Buy a pack of raisins, and put just one in the palm of your hand. Look at it for a few minutes; turn it over; and make a careful note of its shape, length, size, and color. Notice where the dimples are, and so forth.

After you've focused on it for a while, place it in your mouth. But rather than just swallowing it right away, move it around, taste it, feel it, and chew it ever so slowly. As you chew, imagine the sun shining in some place where the raisin grew, like California. See how the light filtered into the grape and remained there to become your personal sugary, sweet, very special raisin. Go through the eating of the raisin in slow motion.

What you discover at the end of this exercise—which, by the way, we used to call "Raisin' Your Consciousness"—is that the raisin becomes the most delicious, wonderful raisin you've ever tasted. Why? Because you've imbued your concentration upon the raisin, heightening your sense of it. Rather than eating the raisin in the sleep state of mechanical man, you've eaten it as an aware person, noticing the gift of sunshine that's trapped inside the raisin. The sun, of course, is yet another manifestation of the life force, the God Force. So life is more than just feeding your face. You are in this sacred blessing called *Life*, momentarily accepting its sacrament—in this case, a little piece of God Force that is raisin shaped.

Imagine how your relationships and love affairs would be if both you and your partner imbued them with the same intensity as the "Raisin' Your Consciousness" exercise just mentioned. Give your mate a bag of raisins tonight, and say, "Honey, I gotta new trick I wanna show you."

In passing, let me remind you of this: Concentration is actually a form of love. When you fall in love, you concentrate on one particular person and you make that individual special. As you concentrate on things—your actions, your life, a raisin, a lover, whatever—you are performing the act of love. By concentrating, you love; and by loving, you become more spiritual and more aware. You reconnect with your sixth sense—which, of course, is an act of concentration, so it is an outcropping of love and respect. In the act of stopping the chatter of the mind to concentrate on something, you are, in effect, loving it and yourself.

So as you move through the day, ask, What's happening here at a subtle level? What smells? What tastes? What can I hear and feel? What is the subtle overall message offered in this moment? Instantly, the universe responds. It tells you things. It's the shaman's world, the etheric nature-self, and all your subtlety honed to a pinpoint perception. It doesn't take years of practice, like golf or something—it's instantaneous, within a few seconds. If you want to see, it's there. If you want to feel more, you can. Just desire it and focus upon it, and the power flows.

Bit by bit, you'll become aware of the symbols and pictures that exist in your greater memory, inside yourself. Of course you'll want to heighten your subtle energy (the etheric), for that's the key to other-world perception. It comes once you have reclaimed your sentient self, and once you have entered into the subtlety of the five senses.

Come with me to the next chapter. I want to talk to you about closing the perceived gap between you and the rest of existence—the world that we normally imagine to be outside ourselves. Once you close the gap, your wavefield expands, and in that understanding is the doorway to everything else.

THE SHADOW, DREAMS, FAIRY KINGDOMS, AND THE GRAYS

Over time I came to see that there is a subtle trick to developing the sixth sense and a heightened awareness. To really grasp its subtle complexity, you have to gradually melt the perceived distance or gap between your mind and the outer reality of life—that which you perceive to be at a distance from you.

In the ego's domain, the perceptual distance that it needs to maintain between itself and the rest of the world is very important to its sense of self. It a part of the ego's scaffolding or security. It has to define itself as separate from others, different from other people, and special, perhaps. That's the function of the ego—to look after itself. The gap that it sees between itself and the outside world is an illusion. On an inner level, there is no gap; everyone and everything is joined. Yet the ego's illusionary gap is sustained every minute of your waking consciousness. It's vital to the ego-personality's raison d'être. "I am me and here and okay and good—and separate from everybody and everything else that is over there, at a distance from me, and probably less than okay or definitely bad."

We have to train ourselves to unravel that perceptional error, for the sixth sense requires you to be firmly in a nonlocal reality, connected to everything, which of course contradicts the "separate from everything" illusion. Once the gap has gone, all of life—both internal and external—becomes a symbol of self. Things aren't just happening out there inconsequentially. Eventually, everything has a meaning. The universe-at-large is talking to you.

Once the distance between you and everything else disappears, you metaphysically step forward. Now the enlarged you is expressing itself as a massive wave-field, which now covers what was previously the gap or distance (see Diagram #1) that the ego-personality insists is between you and the outside world. Once the gap disappears and you expand so everything is now inside you, you are much more in touch—your nonlocality becomes a given fact. Now you can expand your perception very quickly. It's as if your self-imposed prison wall has disappeared. Everything is now inside you.

DIAGRAM #1: Melting the gap between you and external reality.

Each of the techniques we discuss here builds on all the others, assisting your consciousness in completing the gap-closing process: analyzing your dreams, meditation, understanding and learning about symbols, personal discipline, quiet time, developing the five senses, exercising the etheric, developing the sixth sense, and so on. Suddenly you are in a two-way dialogue—first, with your subconscious; and second, with external reality—rather than what is often a one-way dialogue with a rather demanding ego-personality that is somewhat scared and needs attention.

If you have not yet read Carl Jung's book *Man and His Symbols*, do so—it will help you. If you're already familiar with the book, you might consider rereading it, as Jung really had it nailed down. The book will remind you of the subconscious archetypes and the shadow-self within, as well as the various components of our psychological makeup, the complexity of personality, and so forth. You don't have to be an expert in psychology, but you do have to have a working knowledge of it. Overall, Jung's book is interesting to read, it has loads of cool pictures in it, and it's simple to comprehend.

Melting the Gap

I can't stress enough how important it is to grasp the idea that there is no gap or distance between your mind's perception of itself and outer reality. Most miss this gap thing, so they never get anywhere. Realize that right now your conscious mind is probably standing halfway between all your memories and experiences (your personality), and what you perceive is the outer reality of life. Where you want to be is in the middle at the zero point, large enough so that everything is inside you.

Do this: From time to time, visualize an image of yourself out in front of you, at a distance, say, of 20 yards. It helps to animate the visualization— imagine that the *distant* you is waving back at the *real* you. Flip your concentration from your physical body to the distant image of you and back again. When your mind is in the distant figure, pause to look back (observe) the real physical you. Try to flip back and forth between the two versions of you as fast as possible. You may find that it's easy to look at the distant image of yourself, but when you have to reverse the process—putting your concentration in the distant image and looking back at your real self—it's a bit more difficult. Your concentration may slip to one side of the image and refuse to stay still long enough in the imaginary state for you to properly look back at the real you. If you find this tiring or frustrating, stop for a moment. None of these processes is supposed to trouble you.

Seeing your "out there" image looking back at you "in here" in the physical body helps you. It engages that part of your mind that knows about its nonlocal nature. Next time you're standing talking to a friend, facing them, imagine your etheric-self stepping forward out of your body. So, initially, the physical you would be looking at your etheric's back, and the etheric you would be between you and your friend. Now, mentally turn the etheric around to face you so it will have its back to your friend. Pause for a second, then step the etheric backwards into your friend's body. This stepping backwards of the etheric is performed deliberately with a certain amount of intent. It's not aggressive, but you are making a defined and deliberate move. Once inside, clear your inner dialogue and move your concentration over to your friend. Imagine that you are inside their head. It helps to stare at their temple. Feel what it's like to be them, inside their body talking back at you. It may feel very foreign at first, but it helps you perceive that you and that person are one. You may get a few subtle impressions from them as they talk. The trick is to try to keep your inner voice quiet while they talk, and perceive reality from a new place.

This reversing process is another version of the same distant mind-flip. I'm here and over there, and now I'm back here. It's the rudimentary beginnings of shape-shifting, in which the adept moves their consciousness in and out of normal reality and gives the impression to others that they are momentarily a bird, an animal, something completely different, or even in some totally different location. It's a shaman's trick.

You have to wonder if consciousness and light aren't two versions of the same thing. Reality comes to you passively via the effect of light reflected off things, so photons carry the impression of reality to you. But your consciousness makes the photons real, so you are in a symbiotic relationship with reality and light. The shape-shifter steps into that light-consciousness relationship, interjecting a thought-form between your consciousness and reflected light. So he or she, in effect, momentarily switches off normal reality, coming to you via that reflected light, and you see the shape-shifter's injected thought-form instead. Your normal perception of reality streaming toward your consciousness is involuntarily interrupted by another's mind.

I gave a funny example of this in one of my other books. It's worth retelling. I was on a bus with a pal going down Kings Road, Chelsea, in London. I wanted the bus driver to stop so we could get off. The bus was traveling at about 35 mph, approaching the pedestrian crossing just before Bywater Street. I mentally flashed a picture—a thought-form—to the driver, of an old woman walking across the road pushing a wicker basket on wheels. The driver saw her in his mind's eye and thinking her real, he put the double-decker bus into an emergency halt. Everyone went flying off their seats, and packages and stuff tumbled into the aisles. The driver got out of the bus and ran back toward the pedestrian crossing. The conductor at the back couldn't figure out what was going on, and the driver stood on the sidewalk, dumbfounded, scratching his head, unable to figure it out. My pal and I jumped off the bus and ran up the road. We were beside ourselves with laughter. My pal was suitably impressed as I told him what I was going to do before I did it. Shaman-wise, it was a lucky fluke. I was young in those days, and I didn't properly understand the principles, but somehow it worked.

Try this one: Let's say you're with two friends—we'll call them Sally and Mike. Sally is talking to you both. When she pauses in the conversation, try jumping in etherically and offering her a thought; it doesn't have to be a thought that has anything to do with what she's been saying. So she's been talking about her new car, and you jump in with the word *skiing*. Visualize skiing as you say the word. If you do it right, she'll mention skiing in the next sentence. If she doesn't, you could ask her, "Have you thought of driving to the snow slopes with your new car?" See if she says, "I was just thinking of that."

Lest you worry about mind control and infringement, remember that our thoughts jump from one thought to another all the time. And, anyway, it's not as if you're offering her a thought that contradicts her natural tendency. It's just you practicing your perceptional ability.

Do this: In the reversed etheric state, drop in on your other companion Mike, and offer him the word *love*. Watch for the slightest shift in expression, the hint of a smile. Remember, sometimes people's eyes smile even if their lips don't move. See if you can get him to respond in some way. I sit in airport waiting rooms doing this "love thing" to pass the time. It's amazing to watch people react in different ways. They sometimes turn around. Other times they smile or laugh. On occasions they stop in their tracks and do a full turn as if looking for someone. It's the same as the shaman's non-local world; it is you (the urban shaman) standing etherically in the gap.

Once the gap starts to disappear, there is less and less distance between you and everything else—which is good. But then again, there is less of a barrier between you and your inner subconscious mind. So one of the first things you will encounter is your repressed shadow. We all have one. How we usually handle our shadow-side is by displacement—separating the negative, and distancing it from ourselves while denying its existence within us. Remember, "I am over here and good; they are over there and probably rat bags." This works quite well for a while, for within the absence of any other reality, the ego can reign supreme. Yet when you over-energize your perception of the negative *outside* of you, you are, in effect, observing and substantiating part of the shadow *within* you. There is nothing really wrong with that—we all do it. The point is to understand it and eventually begin to change it.

The appearance of the shadow is described in the story of all spiritual journeys. It comes as a dark night of the soul, when you look at your life from a higher perspective and see whatever crud might have accumulated there—including bad karma with bus drivers!

A Strange Journey Through the Fairy Kingdoms

Several years ago, I was at a very private shamanistic gathering in the forest. I'd been hanging out with some of the local Druid types and a few of the more way-out citizens of those parts. We took part in an old ceremony whereby they call in the wisdom of the trees as a special teaching. It's a link they have forged over the years to the fairy kingdoms and the inner dimensions of nature's spiritual evolution. Later, we had a few gulps of a Druids' brew. It was an ancient recipe, mostly magic mushrooms, and maybe bits of other stuff—the Druids mentioned belladonna and mistletoe. Half a pint of that concoction and you're in the gap, pronto—straddled between two worlds!

I'd been walking in the forest with the others for about an hour, and one of the Druids was talking to me about the special medicine of the yew tree, which is sacred to those people. I listened intently. I can't say I remember much about yew medicine, but I recall being very impressed with the man's vast knowledge of natural pharmacology.

A while later, I came upon an old oak. Leaning up against it, I said, "Show me the ancient tree wisdom." Nothing happened at first. But shortly thereafter, I saw a tunnel open to my right. In front of the tunnel were some rather odd beings. At first I mistook them for very fat birds like turkeys, although they had no feathers. I thought they were pecking at the ground. They were bent over and had their backs to me. Their bodies were pear-shaped, dark gray in color, and on their backs were three parallel black lines either side of where their spine might be, in a V-shaped chevron. Their necks were long and scrawny.

One rose and turned toward me, and I saw a goblinlike being, then I noticed there were four or five more. They had the most unattractive long, skinny arms. I don't know if *goblin* is the right word, as one imagines a hairy fellow in breeches, wearing a Harris-tweed jacket and a pointed hat. These beings had no clothes. They were at the entrance of a tunnel, which had the texture and coloring of corpuscles. The beings seemed to be inviting me into their world. Having been up a few near-death tubes in my time, I instinctively began to move forward, but as I got closer, I noticed that the tunnel curved and went downwards at a sharp angle—not a good sign. Also, the red corpuscular nature of the tunnel bothered me. There was something negative about those beings outside the tunnel, so I turned and walked away. Seconds later, I went through one of the strangest experiences of my life. I had a spontaneous out-of-body experience (OBE). As it started, I felt my etheric wobble, and then I blacked out for a second or two. The next thing I knew, I was out of my body, hovering two or three yards above it. I have had OBEs before, but in those instances my body was in trance while I hovered over it. I'd never expected an out-of-body state while the body was wide-awake, walking through a forest.

I'm not sure if those spiritlike beings back at the tunnel knocked me out of my body in some way, or if the OBE experience was a part of the trans-dimensional nature of the Druids' journey. Maybe I flipped myself out, but if I did, I had no conscious volition in the matter. For a moment I thought I'd died, yet I could see my physical self walking through a thick group of pines. Next, I noticed I could flip my perception from my out-of-body state to my physical self and back again, like being perpetually in two places at once. I could see the golden lines in the forest that marked the memory of the people who had been in that place before me, and I could see the trees oscillate with an identity. It was obvious that they were linked to each other, as I was linked to them. I later worked out that the time dilation in that nature-spirit domain was approximately five-to-one. So two minutes of transdimensional fairy-world time is the equivalent of ten minutes in the real world.

When time dilates like that, you get bombarded by five times more information than you would perceive in the normal human world. First, I could see the real identity of my human companions—their true inner selves—not what I projected them to be, and not just what they projected out into the world via their bodies and personalities. I could see the real inner essence of each of them. In there I saw a lot of emotion, much of it hidden away. It had a comical edge to it at first. I'd watch from above as a man talked, and he might smile as he spoke, yet I could see his subconscious mind, his whole persona, and his spiritual energy all at once. It seemed like everyone was putting on a cheery grin to cover up the pain, disquiet, and fear in their lives. In the time-dilated version of them, no one could have lied—you'd know right away. You could see their hidden emotions as clear as day.

I gradually became troubled. I saw how much human life hurts people. It was not a normal intellectual understanding like, say, commiserating with the misfortunes of others. It was a very deep inner knowing that elicited a lot of natural compassion. I saw how life is so scary for people, and I perceived the sheer amount of pain they have to cover up day by day just to make it through. It's the resistance that hurts them the most. Fear forces them to stiffen, and in the stiffening, they take a lot of scary blows.

The other thing I saw was the loneliness these individuals suffered by being separated from each other and separate from life. The distance they had to establish between themselves and others in order to sustain the ego's image, and so deal with the pain of life, caused them even more pain. The illusion really hurt them, and through the illusion, they cut themselves off— not only from each other, but from the life force. You could see that each was an island unto him- or herself. Each suffered from a lack of life force, as if they were being denied oxygen. Now I was walking the woods with some very conscious, aware people who would have worked upon themselves a great deal. Yet the separation was still so marked and so sad that it really shocked me

Whatever judgments I've had in the past about people's lack of honesty, or about their weakness and lack of follow-through, I saw in a different light. It's not totally their fault. The external world of our lives is forcefully driven by the real person within, which is often so cut off and terrified that it can't help itself. It acts according to impulse, as if programmed by the condition. In the forest, my companions each seemed like prisoners shuffling along, chained to a terrible circumstance. My first impulse was to cry. I wanted to unlock them somehow. Then I realized that I had the same ball-and-chain on my ankle. Freakout!

I became really terrified. I was sure I was going to die right then and there. I was still out of my body, and my physical self had arrived at a very beautiful lake. It washed its face and hands and dunked its head in the water, as if attempting to wash away the terrible karma of being stuck in the human condition. Being trapped in the world of atoms and molecules and the Second Law of Thermodynamics, which requires everything to entropy and go to a heat death, is so utterly terrifying and eerie. To make matters worse, the inner-self can't defend itself against the personality and the intellect's reaction to all that. The inner you just accepts the program given. It's helpless.

I saw how the personality's fear was real and justified. I have always wanted people to be brave and strong and to face life head-on, spitting in the eye of circumstances. I went through a terrible realization by that lake when I saw that they couldn't. It seemed as if my whole life as a spiritual teacher had been a waste of time in one sense. Why try to boost the personality to transcend the fear and be brave, when the inner-self has been trussed up for years by terror and confusion? Bravery is fleeting; the inner impulse soon returns. If you have ever judged an alcoholic or a drug abuser or one that exhibits obsessive dysfunctional behavior, start to beg for forgiveness. In the light of the real self and the God Force, your judgments will look pathetic. You'll see how your judgment was forged out of your own illusion and separation, and how the rancor of it was sustained deep within you, fueled by the terror of your own collapse.

When you first have this realization, a great weight descends upon you. You may see that your whole life has been a terrible lie, a deception—one coated in righteousness and buried in denial—a position sustained for your own pleasure and sense of power. Because we are powerless to change our condition in the world of molecules and entropy, we victimize others with our power trips to gain a modicum of self-worth. It helps lessen the fear.

I saw that we each arrive at a crossroads marked in one direction Truth, and the other direction Power. Our tendency is to take the Power route. It's less scary. It elicits respect and observers and helps us in the illusion of our solidity. The path marked Truth is nonresistant, anonymous, humble; there's no glitz, money, or self-aggrandizement to help sustain the illusion. It's the path that reconnects you. The power trip only tends to accentuate the separation. If you don't realize it in time, that path kills you. You die a slow death by an asphyxiation of spirit, which in turn cuts off the flow of vitality to your human cells. Then, they begin their entropy sooner than they should.

Down at the lake, my etheric body gradually rejoined my physical body, although it was slightly askew, distanced from the physical self a foot or two, and off at a slight angle—like an overcoat that has slipped off one shoulder. I was still very much in the nonlocal state, in the etheric world of nature's vitality and the world of the real inner-self. I began once more watching my own emotions and those of my companions, which stood out like spinning orbs.

What happened next was the most significant part of my 24-year spiritual journey so far. I saw my whole life co-existing in a frozen but alive moment. In that frozen picture, I saw my childhood and my parents, and I saw how having to leave home at the age of ten had affected me by making me overcompensate for the pain of it. I also saw the good bits of my life, but most of all, my attention was riveted to the lousy bits—chunks, large chunks I should say, of the shadow vibe—in all its enormity. Every bit of bullshit hovered there in front of my eyes by that beautiful lake, flatly refusing to go away. I looked at my companions, many of whom I really loved and respected, and I saw something truly horrible: I saw how I had at times judged them for being dippy or incapable of getting themselves together. I saw how I had almost always been impatient with them because their weaknesses threatened me—not the grown-up me, but the ten-year-old child within.

I saw the grandiose nature of my life, and I saw it to be a manifestation of the child's pathetic attempt to defend and protect itself from an impossible situation. Imagine yourself 10,000 miles from home, with five pounds ($7.50) in your pocket, and adulthood staring you in the face—and you're just ten. Then I saw the sin of my intolerance—not an intolerance that stems from a racial or social hatred—but one that came more from establishing a tight frame of reference for people and emotionally discarding all those who were too stoned, inconsequential, or weak, or just incapable of making it up the achiever's ladder. I saw that my silly ladder was like the podium that athletes stand on when they win medals. Mine was a plywood box, a silly fake gold medal, tied to a cheap ribbon. My winners' enclosure: a psychiatric world for troubled children, demented egos lost in the illusion of competition and elitism, each held in the grip of entropy. To cut a long torment short, I saw how my action-packed world was no better or worse than any other lifestyle, just a different path.

I found myself walking with a friend from L.A. He began to talk to me about how he had seen the spirit of the lake rise up, and I looked out and didn't see it. The water looked alive, but its spirit, if that's the right way to define it, look diffused; it didn't have an identity of its own as far as I could see. My friend was a 21-year-old multimillionaire at the time. He'd gone into business at the ripe old age of 15 and made a slew of cash. The poor lad was pasted over with the same bullshit I was. Yet you could excuse his illusion as part of the exuberance and silliness of youth. My "stuff" was framed in the maturity of middle age. There was no escape.

Passing through the forest, Druids to the left of me, others farther back to the right, I came upon a dead goat—bones and a few bits of hair—no flesh. I looked deep into the eye socket of its skull. I was now slightly ahead of the others, so I had a chance to look at it for a while, uninterrupted. Peering into the empty eye socket, I saw the spirit of the goat, so simple and unassuming—beautiful and calm and so unresisting—deep in the arms of entropy and not batting a missing eyelid at its change of status. Do goats have eyelids?

I wondered what the goat had to say to me. It answered by offering me a profound stillness, which rattled me to the core. Remember, every emotion and event of my life was before my eyes and in my feelings, each shuffling forward in turn, seeking its place in my attention. There was five times the time dilation, and all the while, there was a nonlocal perception that was 50 times more acute than normal. So each minute felt like days, and several minutes like an age. Over a period of 12 hours, I saw every shadow-feeling that I had ever had. I saw how much of my attitude wasn't based on the spiritual beliefs that I had come to accept. I saw how my shadow and its impulse overrode so much of the positive nature of my attempts at goodness in this life. Jung said he was terrified when he met his shadow. I now know what he went through.

What was so embarrassing was that every emotion belonged to me. I couldn't distance or repress any of them. And even though there would be a contradictory positive feeling in me somewhere, the negative one was so forceful and real. And, worst of all, I saw that it was true. That's not to say that our shadow-self is all our fault, for much of it is formed in the innocence of childhood. But I saw how I could have gotten a grip on it decades earlier.

One of the people walking the woods was an American lady from New York. She was really pleasant, yet there was something about her that gave me the willies. I'd go out of my way to avoid her, and if she came close, I'd put out an involuntary silent growl. I was totally bewildered by my antagonism to her. There was no logic to it. Later I realized that the lady from New York had a great deal of repressed anger. She reminded me of a nanny that my twin sister and I had when we were three. The nanny was stern and loveless, violent and cruel. If my sister and I didn't toe the line, she would pick us up by our hair and count slowly from one to three. She was German, and the words "Ein, Zwei, Drei," if forcefully spoken in a loud voice, have always struck horror in me.

Once I saw that the lady from New York was just a reminder of the nanny, I felt better. I wondered why the American lady had so much repressed anger—and as soon as I asked myself the question, the answer came flying back: Life had been a rip-off for her. Men had ripped her off. She had been let down and betrayed, and she was pissed off about it. I made a point of trying to befriend her, and later I sat on a rock close to her and offered her some chocolate. I also had a little flask of whiskey. I extended that out in her direction as a part of my peace offering. She declined the candy bar and the whiskey, but I felt okay. I'd worked it out and had tried to fix it.

I finally reached home 12 hours later—so flooded and overwhelmed by the shadow that I could take it no more. If that was "tree wisdom," I think I would have preferred to start with something a bit smaller. Like a little bush: "bush wisdom." Or something even smaller still: "parsley wisdom." The whole bloody forest was too much for me. I was impacted and worn out and still frightened by the shadow. I remember a prayer I kept repeating out there in the woods: "God don't let me die before I fix this." My experiences in the past, up the near-death tube, were exhilarating. But because of having seen the light of the God Force at the other end of the tube, I now understood how you don't want to die with the shadow still in place, for it spells a terrible fate. I cannot imagine what it might be like to arrive in those spirit worlds after death and see it still there. What must be so extraordinary is that most people probably die never having seen their shadow. It would come as a terrible shock, made worse by the fact that once you're dead, there isn't much you can do to make amends and polish up your spiritual act.

Have you ever had a dream where you're in a public place with others, and suddenly you realize you don't have any clothes on? Or you have some really embarrassing combination of clothes, like a tuxedo jacket and pajama bottoms and sneakers at a formal dinner. That's the shadow talking out of the subconscious, trying to make itself known to you.

Embracing the Shadow and Fixing It

To close the gap and make yourself spiritually whole, you have to own your shadow and embrace it, realizing that the negative force is inside you as a part of the positive force. Once you own the negative as part of the real you, you have understood something that most miss. To own it, you have to look at it, and you have to be willing to fix it. There is a positive side to the shadow that often expresses itself as creativity. That's why so many creative geniuses have had such troubled lives. Both parts of their shadow are sharing the driving. First the creative impulse, then the destructive one, back and forth.

In the nonlocal world of the sixth sense, you have to get rid of the shadow in order to proceed. The earlier the better. It's an ogre on the path, blocking your way. I'll flip quickly through some of the common shadow impulses and traits that you may or may not relate to in your life.

Common Shadow Impulses and Traits

1. Feigning goodness, or being overly upset by what you perceive as bad in others.

2. Being overly uptight with people for what are often trivial matters.

3. Feeling unduly threatened or insecure.

4. Being emotionally or physically abusive. Using anger as a weapon.

5. Manipulating others through any misuse of power.

6. Passive aggression.

7. Being overly uptight with large issues that you can't personally fix, and refusing to get out there and actually do something about the issues that bother you.

8. Dishonesty, corruption, and shady business dealings.

9. Covert behavior and nastiness.

10. Selective memory. Using truth distortions to make the past look different from the way it was.

11. Putting others down through silent or overt judgment of them.

12. Using power trips and control; being unfair or unreasonable in your dealings with others.

13. Being vindictive and vengeful toward others. Bitterness.

14. Using "poor me" and a feigned helplessness to gain advantage and sympathy from others.

15. Unreasonably misappropriating other people's energy—that is, leaning upon them unreasonably for emotional or financial support.

16. Hatred, snobbery, and elitism.

17. Self-destructive behavior.

18. Being miserly.

19. Being overly grandiose or egotistical.

It's quite a long list. Once you see it and own the bits that are yours, you become free. It's part of how you heal yourself and the planet. Most would agree that our planet is in a bit of a mess; it seems like we've lost our way. There is far too much shadow being projected out; each person seems to be trying to take their insecurity out on others. And we are all collectively beating up on the planet. If you heal yourself, you truncate a line of darkness that would have been passed down to you, via your family line, for thousands of years. So if that dysfunction suddenly stops, you unravel thousands of years of bad karma, stretching back for generations. That is something to think about.

Because the dark impulse often swamps the positive, loving, creative side of your personality, there is a great benefit to getting a glimpse of it. Accommodate the dark, and the creative energy flows more easily. You are no longer separate and at war with yourself and the world; you are in touch with others and can empathize with their problems. And you are now in real touch with your inner-self and your creative originality. In addition, you reconnect with the light of the planet. The light of our planet is generous, open, and kind; it can lead you on to higher and higher energy and perception. All the love and creativity there has ever been is stacked in the light as part of its perpetual memory. That goodness is there to draw upon, while you, in turn, can contribute even more goodness to it.

Back to the gap-closing business. There are a couple of important items of expansion that we'd better not miss.

We think about infinity as being "out there" somewhere. We look up at the night sky and watch the stars and the odd UFO going past, or whatever, and we think, *Wow, there's infinity.* Of course, infinity is an internal as well as an external thing. So in order to incorporate all the information available on the physical plane, you have to become bigger than the physical plane. You have to begin to embrace that infinity—meaning you have to become larger than life in your feelings. That doesn't mean *more important* than others—more glamorous or more special—just bigger and grateful and humble and silently big.

We're talking about an expansion of a self that is already infinite and expanding. It's much like our physical universe, which is not expanding into anything, but it *is* expanding. The galaxies move away from each other, creating more space between them. Imagine them as raisins in a cake. As you bake the cake and the dough rises, the raisins in the cake move away from each other. You can also think of it as dots on the surface of a balloon. Blow up the balloon, and the dots move apart. That's how you can have an infinity that's getting bigger.

Your Infinite Self is expanding in the same way, as you turn within and seek to rejoin the life force more strongly. Clearing the shadow as you go, you allow your inner space to seek its maximum velocity. It's not held by the gravitational effect of issues handed down through generations, or those created by you in this lifetime. You move from the confines—gravitational orbit, if you like—of a finite perception, and the cramped quarters of an uncomfortable darkness. You free yourself from the idea of the ego at the center of everything, to the idea of an infinite identity that incorporates everything. There is a big difference: deluding yourself that you are at the center of everything, to expanding to where everything is inside you so you are connected to everything. I talk a lot about the Infinite Self in my book on the subject, but here I should talk about it in the general sense—that is, how the Infinite Self pertains to the symbols of your journey and overall perception.

The Infinite Self

At the beginning of your awareness, when you're tick-tocking (plodding along in your day-to-day reality) and learning ordinary stuff, nothing really means anything. You're not in a dialogue with the symbols of your inner-self, and neither do external symbols mean anything in particular. You tend to ignore them all. Furthermore, you are in the grip of the karma of our humanity. We often incarnate in the center of the vortex that is the global mind—in its tightest part, it's similar to water spinning down a plug hole. It's only later, when we become mature, that we can begin to travel up out of that psychological/emotional vortex to fresh air and freedom. Once we are out of it and we handle our insecurity, we can stretch to an infinite possibility.

As you move up and out of the tighter part of the global psychology into a spiritual open space, and as you close the perceived gap, you will see how the external universe is talking to you. You especially take notice of external symbols or events that are strange and unusual. So if you are just looking at a tree and the leaves are blowing around in the wind, that's nothing in particular. But if suddenly the leaves fall on the ground in a strange shape and a little creature jumps down from the tree and grabs three of the leaves and runs off, it means *something*.

The leaves and the little critter and the preciseness of the moment—and your presence in that moment as the observer of the event—make the event an external manifestation of you because you are there to watch it. The question is, what does it mean?

The meaning rests primarily in a degree of endless potentials, but don't let that daunt you. How many potential meanings there are is not important. What is important is what it means to you, for watching the leaves is personal. It's you talking to yourself. What it is saying is in your feelings. You have to delve into the symbol and then put it in the context of your life. First, let's talk about the delving.

The Importance of Dream Interpretation

Fritz Perls came up with a good method for the delving in his Gestalt therapy work. His method can explain both external symbols in the waking state, and the internal symbols of dreams and reverie. I'll fly through the interpretation system for dreams (hopefully without putting you to sleep) so you can then apply it to external symbols as well.

The standard dream-interpretation technique "a la Fritz" goes like this: You have to go back into the dream and analyze each symbol one at a time to see what it means to you. Usually you can't do that just after you wake up from a dream. The dream takes place at a low level of brain speed and comes from the subconscious, so you can't properly translate it via the waking brain, whose speed is somewhere between 14 and 22 cycles per second. And you can't necessarily engage the intellect, for it doesn't usually know what the subconscious means by a particular symbol.

To understand the dream, you have to first write it down so you don't forget it, then wait until you have a quiet moment so you can enter back into the dream from an altered state of consciousness. In a quiet state of mind, at a slower, more meditative brain speed, you access your subconscious mind more readily and more effectively.

The famous Perls interpretation was of a dream someone recounted: A man is walking along with a fishing rod over his shoulder, he walks under a bridge, and various things happen in the dream.

Fritz Perls's method requires you to act out the dream in your mind's eye, placing yourself first in the psyche of the main character—in this case, the man. So you say, "I am the man with the fishing rod. . . ." (and at this point, you insert your name, referring to yourself in the third person—let's say your name is Sally, so . . .) "I am the man with the fishing rod in Sally's dream. I represent . . ." You pause and allow the symbol (the man) to talk to you, telling you what it represents to you. Then you go back to that character and ask it how it feels, or you may ask, "Why are you going to the river?" Your subconscious answers, saying, "I am going to the river because the river is abundant, and I seek abundance in this life," or whatever.

You travel through the other symbols one at a time. So in this case, you would now take the part of the fishing rod. You have to imagine that the fishing rod can speak and you make it come alive. So you recall the fishing rod in your mind and it says, "I am the fishing rod in Sally's dream. I represent [let's say] direct action and the ability to bend." Suddenly, you remember that in the dream, the rod whacked the underside of the bridge. You realize it's telling you that maybe you are a bit too stiff in certain circumstances, that you need to bend or you'll whack your head on life.

You go through each and every symbol of the dream: the bridge, the river, and so on. Each component talks to you, and each symbol or action in the dream is a word in the sentence or paragraph that the subconscious is trying to impart to you. Analyzing your dreams is important, for it helps you understand the circumstances of your life. It also helps you understand your visions.

Now go back to the little critter that you saw grab the leaves underneath the tree. External symbols like this can represent either some part of your waking intellect (such as synchronistic events that often reflect thoughts in your mind), or the little animal's strange activity may reflect a part of your deep inner-self, the subconscious self. Both are possible.

If you can immediately relate to the symbol, you can attempt the interpretation of it from the intellect. So you ask yourself if the action of the little animal, and what it does with the leaves, is the same as any particular aspect of your life. Look carefully at the overall "picture" of the action, and see if it throws up some kind of congruence, for often the action speaks for itself. So perhaps the way in which the little animal was picking up the leaves and collecting them may link to thoughts you've been having about how you ought to go collect your debts, or how you ought to order your life and clean out your basement, or whatever it might be. Sometimes the critter is talking to you from an external action that you've taken or that you've been thinking about taking. If you don't get an immediate clue from your life's circumstances, then the symbol is reflecting some deep inner part of you, and you'll have to make a note of what the critter did with the leaves and think about it later. Write it down in your notebook, and later on, in a meditation, go into the subconscious and go through the event with the Fritz Perls method as if it were a dream. Enter into the various components, and ask them what they are telling you.

So you would say: "I'm the little critter . . ." and so forth, and then you ask the animal what it symbolizes to you. Then you say to yourself: "I am the strange pattern of the leaves . . ." and then the leaves talk to you, telling you something about yourself. You energize the comprehension process by engaging it. Much like the shadow, it is in the observation that the understanding comes.

As you have delved into the subconscious meaning of the symbol, it's helpful to put the symbol into the immediate context of your feelings at the time. So ask yourself, "What was I thinking and feeling at the exact moment when the leaves fell from the tree and the animal appeared?" Alternatively, you may ask yourself, "What has been my overall question or problem recently? What is the dominant issue on my mind?" By putting the symbol in the context of your current thought-stream, you may find a link, and you'll see that the symbol speaks to you out of current issues, rather than from your subconscious reality. There's a knack to interpretation, but you soon get good at it, and eventually you can unravel things for others by asking the same questions for them. It helps them to see that they are watching a movie out there, which reflects impulses and ideas that are internal.

Sometimes external symbols will be grouped together, several at a time. So you'll see a man fall off his bike, and later the same day, you watch as a tile comes off a roof and a taxi whacks a truck. All three are in the same cosmic sentence. They form a story line that's probably talking to you about a special seminar the universe-at-large runs called *balance and imbalance*. Perhaps you'll see how your life is too helter-skelter, too stressed out, and you'll remember how you bashed your hand against the elevator door this morning. And you'll think to yourself, *Slow down, bro', the universe is trying to tell me something. That's why I'm watching a taxi whacking a truck at the stop light.*

Watching life's symbols is important. Dream recall, and analyzing external symbols, are part of the same gap-closing process, one inner, the other outer. So write down, remember, and analyze incidents. Symbols and messages coming to you from outside yourself in daily life are more often than not reflected in your dreams and visions. And as you're now becoming a multidirectional being, there's no outside or inside. There's only infinity in all directions.

Sometimes, if you can't unravel a symbol right away, and if no hints come to you in your meditations, then you will have to leave it in your notebook for later. Some symbols you don't unravel until years later. They are predictions, signposts to the future, or visions that lead you in a direction from which the answer will eventually come.

In a vision, I saw a row of metal plates on the ground; in the center of each plate was a light bulb. A muscular man approached the plates with a hammer and knocked one of the light bulbs off its plate. It rolled in a very deliberate, curved way toward four other broken light bulbs that were nearby. They were placed on diagonals opposite each other, so they formed a square. The fifth bulb rolled into the square and settled in the center of it. The vision was something to do with the four forces of nature (the strong and weak nuclear force, electromagnetic energy, and gravity) and the mysterious and as-yet-undiscovered fifth force. The four broken bulbs made a square, and the fifth bulb that rolled into the middle marked the point where the diagonals of the square would cross. It has been several years since I saw that vision, and although I can see that it talked about how the power of humans in some way creates the fifth force or displaces it, there is still more to the vision that I haven't as yet unraveled.

UFOs and the Grays

One night about nine months ago, in a meditation, I saw a vision of two stars in the sky, quite close to each other, one lower and one higher. I couldn't figure out what the stars meant to me, so I just jotted it down in my computer to remember it. Later in the year, I was down in Australia, and I noticed that the stars Sirius and Canopus looked exactly like my vision, in the way they were placed in the sky. They caught my attention, and I watched them for a few nights in a row. There were some small lights in and around those stars from time to time, flying strange patterns. I thought them to be satellites, but they'd fly one way and stop, and then fly back the other way.

One night a friend and I saw three lights in and around Sirius and Canopus, flying in a V-formation. The three of them flew north, and another one was coming back the other way toward them. I started flashing that area of the sky with a million-candlepower lamp. I continued flashing every clear night for the next several weeks. Eventually, the moving lights I'd been watching between these two stars, to my absolute amazement, flashed back. I was with a group of friends, and they saw it as well. It was wonderful and eerie at the same time.

Now when I say "flashed back," I'm not talking about twinkle, twinkle little star. I'm talking about enormous flashes, like if you held your thumb up in the sky, the flashes would be as big as your thumbnail and enormously bright. The flashes I sent up followed the mathematical sequence of the Fibonacci numbers (1,1,2,3,5,8,13,21,34 . . .), named after the 13th-century Italian mathematician Leonardo Pisano, whose nickname was Fibonacci, so my flashes weren't random. Sometimes the little lights flashed back while moving in slow motion, and other times they flashed their lights while moving at extremes of velocity, traversing 30° of sky in seconds.

Anyway, all this flashing back and forth to those characters up there, in the Sirius and Canopus region, hasn't changed my life or anything like that—the rent's due, and the trash still has to be hauled—but it's a bit of fun, and it's taught me things. It has helped me reaffirm the galactic nature of our existence. There's a whole bunch of stuff going on out there that we don't know about. Some of it is benign, and some of it scary. But it's the spiritual warrior's nature to delve. If we don't seek, we will never know. Maybe the flashing lights will evolve into something; often symbols progress over the years, and things develop from them.

In passing, I'd like to say that I don't think UFOs are necessarily from other parts of the universe. From my experience, I feel that they are inter-dimensional in nature. The Grays certainly have an etheric identity, as they can come through walls. The famous French researcher Jacques Vallée (*Close Encounters of the Third Kind* was based on his life) suggested that the whole UFO phenomenon is a control mechanism. He felt that the UFO entities are an inner phenomenon—that is, beings from another dimension wanting to establish a power over us in order to lead us to certain conclusions. There are loads of abductees, channelers, and so forth who have stated as fact that the Grays and various UFO entities manipulated human DNA in the past to create modern man. I can't say if that is true or not. Maybe our DNA was manipulated by some higher beings, but I have a nagging doubt that it wasn't done by the Grays. Meanwhile, a lot of writers have bought the story, and the idea has entered modern UFO mythology. I've even seen it claimed that Jesus was sent here by the UFO entities to help us along.

I think it more likely that the UFOs are interdimensional, toward the demonic end of the spiritual ladder, and that they fly about to kid us that they have a special power and technology. It's their way of lording it over us. I also think that the abduction thing is true for the most part, and those who recount harrowing tales about being whisked off aren't lying, even though they may embellish their tales because the experience is so harrowing and confusing. I feel that the abductions and the medical procedures that are often associated with them are real to the participants.

Although I initially felt that the procedures were complete *BS* from a medical standpoint,. I imagined that they formed just another part of the control trip, kidding people that the Grays and others are performing great medical feats. But now that there have been thousands upon thousands of abductions, and as more and more details of the hybrid breeding program becomes widely reported, I can't say I know anymore.

The well-respected researcher David M. Jacobs, Ph.D., who is an associate professor at Temple University, wrote a book recently called *The Threat*, in which he details many abduction accounts and the hybrid breeding program. His book is scary, but it makes very compelling reading, and I came away more convinced.

The symbology of the UFO phenomenon is very important at this time, and it's not an illusion. The UFO entities are definitely here. I've seen two UFOs up close, and I've seen the Grays on a number of occasions, and I absolutely don't buy that they are Space Brothers helping us along. I think Vallée was right when he wrote in *Messengers of Deception* that the UFOs are deceptive and malevolent and that they don't have our best interests at heart—far from it. What I think is fascinating is that abductions, and the UFOs' attempted control trip over us, so closely reflect our modern societies.

I see the UFO phenomenon in the sky above as an aerial symbol that reflects conditions on the ground. It's the same ego-based power trip—the same manic control by a few power-hungry megalomaniacs, the same perpetual theft (abduction) of ordinary people's energy. It must be a part of our karma. The conspiracy theories that say our governments are in league with the UFOs may or may not be true, but you can see how people have made the connection because of the similarities between the two.

David Icke goes as far as to say that the secret government of the world is, in fact, run by reptilian UFO beings in human guise. When I first read Icke's books, I thought him sweet but a bit loopy. But as time has passed, I have become more and more convinced. I don't know if the proponents of the New World Order are reptilian or not, but there is something very demonic and fascist about some of our leaders and the power brokers who pull the strings in the background. It's the world shadow made manifest. I think that people such as David Icke are either very naive or very brave. So many of the whistle-blowers have been knocked off in recent times. There is an agenda that has to be protected, and assassination is a part of that protection. I hope they don't get to Icke. I love that bloke—his books are so wacky, yet there is truth in them. His book *The Biggest Secret* is his best so far.

The reason the UFO thing has never been satisfactorily resolved is that the UFO entities have an agenda that is secret—just as parts of our governments often have agendas they don't want us to know about. The other thing that is confusing is that the UFOs seem to have a solid reality, a semi-solid reality (the plasma state), and a nonsolid etheric reality. Perhaps the stories of UFO crashes are a myth, perpetuated to establish the extraterrestrial-galactic-visitor myth. It's interesting that we don't have even one decent on-the-ground UFO photo, given the hundreds of thousands of sightings. Perhaps flying saucers have no solid reality—only a plasma or semi-solid identity.

One thing is for sure: If the UFOs were extraterrestrials here to conquer us, they would have done it by now. They wouldn't wait for decades while our technology got more and more sophisticated; they would have made a move. So one can deduce several things from events so far: They don't want to conquer us, or, more likely, they *can't*. It's our minds or our bodies or our energy they want to control, not the real estate. Or, whatever it is that they want from us they must be getting, for they wouldn't keep reappearing if they constantly failed to get whatever it is they're after.

I've had a number of UFO sightings, some at a distance, and two very close up. On one occasion, a silvery disk, 30 feet wide, hovered for several minutes over my house, in broad daylight on a summer's evening at about 7 P.M. I wanted to run into the house and get my video camera, but somehow I knew that if I went indoors, it would leave. It had a rather sneaky, peek-a-boo energy to the way it hovered overhead. After a few minutes, I decided to go for the camera, and as soon as I had that thought, it began to move ever so slowly toward the southwest. In less than a minute, it was gone. I got the impression that it knew what my intentions were.

After I started flashing the sky, it wasn't that long before the Grays showed up in my life. (So if you are fascinated by the phenomenon, be ready for them to show up eventually.) They actually started to come through my bedroom wall. The first experience occurred one night when I was lying on the bed, wide awake, reading. I became aware of an orb of energy hovering near my knee. It was definitely etheric, not solid. I whacked it with my hand. As I did so, I noticed that in the center of the rotating ball—it was about the size of a tea saucer—was a prod about six inches long. As I whacked it, the prod retracted into the spinning orb to protect itself. It closed back inside with a slight mechanical click.

After that, the Grays showed up on a regular basis. Two once walked in the front door. I noticed them immediately, and I think that spooked them because they turned and left. On one occasion, a Gray was standing close to my bed, just watching me; I flipped my concentration through its eye, trying to etherically penetrate it. I was shocked to discover that there was nothing in there—blank, no emotion, no feelings, nothing, just empty space. Behind the Gray was a terrifyingly fierce, cruel, reptilian entity. Whether the reptilian was for real, or just putting on a shape-shifting show to scare me, I can't say, but in the heat of the moment, I bought it and fled in terror.

I've been out into the astral planes a lot over the years, and I've seen ghosts, dead spirits, and all manner of weird entities, but the Grays and the reptilians are the most spooky. The astral world is one of phantasmagoric ghouls, and so on, but the astral, when you get used to it, has a very unreal quality about it. The Grays are seriously real. Over the years, I've also encountered angelic spirits, unconditional love, and wonderful inspiration. And I can't help thinking that if the UFOs and the Grays are a good thing, they would *feel* good. There's no point in contradicting one's feelings. That is always a recipe for disaster.

In the extrasensory world of other dimensions, you have to protect yourself. The issue of the Grays is a tough one because they seem to be able to do as they wish. However, I feel I've learned a lot from deliberately going into their world. Even though I found it a very hair-raising experience. I feel especially sorry for abductees, as they don't usually have the benefit of experience to help them along. They must feel particularly vulnerable, confused, and scared.

Here is what I think I've found out. I use the word *think*, as in their now-you-see-it, now-you-don't world, it is very hard to be categorical. I'm almost sure that Vallée was also right when he suggested that the fairy kingdoms and the Grays'/UFOs' world are part of the same dimension or phenomenon. The Grays have an etheric identity—if they have a solid identity, I have never seen it. The silver UFOs, the orange balls, and various plasma-type phenomena that fly around are, I think, entities of themselves. In other words, they are not necessarily flying metallic craft, but "flying beings" like, say, a complex air-spirit that can shape-shift itself and change to look like a ball or a craft or a cigar-shaped mother ship.

The reason I'm quite certain about this is that the craft have been seen to divide and melt into each other in flight. They can also make right-angle turns at high speed. These actions have been caught on film, and no metal object can do that without tearing itself apart. So I came to think that the craft are alive. They are flying cells that can mutate and change, much as ordinary human cells can. The Grays are a component of that "alive and thinking" flying cell, as molecules are part of an ordinary cell.

The Grays seem to exhibit no personal traits, only collective ones. They work in unison with one another. They are each one part of a collective mind-set, a collective evolution—as bees in a hive. Whereas the Grays seem to exhibit a superior technology, they are not spiritually individualized, so I feel that their evolution is lower than ours is. Abductees report that the Grays are scared of humans, and that they only approach once they know they have immobilized the victim. I think most abductions are etheric in nature. I know abductees report returning to bed to find grass in their sheets, or their nightdress is now on the wrong way round. This would suggest a physical abduction, not necessarily an etheric out-of-body one. However, maybe the Grays want us to be confused. There is the famous case of a middle-aged Australian woman from Victoria who was abducted from her car in the presence of two UFO researchers who were not abducted. She never left the driver's seat. So that instance was etheric in nature.

There are some new, way-out scientific theories that suggest that there is no solid reality—that the solidity we experience is an illusion of this dimension. If that is true, perhaps there is only an etheric reality to everything in the universe. Maybe that etheric exists in a mirror world, and it only turns solid when it passes from the mirror world in which it exists and enters into our opposite universe. It might explain the shape-shifting nature of UFOs and the Grays. It may also explain why UFOs rarely land. Perhaps a connection with the ground is hazardous. It could alter a polarity and make it hard for the UFO to return to its lighter-than-air etheric state.

Whether abductions are always physical or sometimes etheric makes them no less terrifying. Some abductees report feeling their legs being etherically tugged down when they lie in bed. I have felt those same phenomena. If you feel like something is tugging on your legs, you can be sure there is something there, doing just that. You'll remember that the corpuscular tunnel of the goblinlike creatures was at a downward incline, and even though the UFOs seem above us, I think they belong to a downward world as well. There have been a lot of sighting of UFOs entering caves and plunging into lakes, especially in Puerto Rico, where locals are convinced that there is a UFO base in or under Laguna Cartagena.

The Grays have an agenda that seems demonic to me, but it may not be demonic to *them*—much like a scientist who has no personal animosity toward the mice he's conducting experiments on. Some writers have suggested that we are part of an experiment that the Grays perform for their own reasons, that cattle mutilations are food-gathering exercises, and that humans are just another species the Grays farm for their own reasons. I have seen no evidence to suggest that this is the case, although millions of people do disappear every year, never to be heard from again. So it might be possible.

However, my feeling is that if the UFOs are farming anything, it is energy they are collecting—human etheric energy. How they trap a human's etheric via abduction is beyond me, but there are a few aspects to the whole phenomenon that don't quite fit. Abductees report that the Grays are farming ova and sperm for a hybrid breeding program, and that eventually the hybrids will take over the earth, and humankind will be dispossessed. What I can't work out is how an etheric abduction can result in a real pregnancy and a solid fetus—a phenomenon that has been reported over and over again.

The interplay between the physical and etheric nature of the abductions is confusing, and the modus throws up some contradictions as well. I would think that if you want to capture someone's etheric, you could do it just as easily while they are sleeping as when they are awake, when they might resist you. Perhaps abductions have to be in the waking state. I came to see that the Grays might have to use the fear they generate to knock you out of your body. When I first saw the fairy beings, I wasn't scared of them, and I was definitely in my body, just walking along. Once I evaluated the tunnel and the red corpuscular nature of it, I became more fearful and wary of the spirit beings. Perhaps *my* fear was what knocked me out of my body.

We say things like, "I was so scared I nearly jumped out of my skin." Maybe that describes the beginning of the abduction process, the loosening of the natural etheric bond to the physical body by rattling the etheric with a fear-induced response. That might account for why abductions seem to take place while people are awake. Maybe the fear is needed to tug people out of their bodies. I noticed that whenever I experienced having my legs pulled down—for example, as I lay in bed—whatever was doing the pulling could only manage to get my etheric legs down a foot to 18 inches through the bed at most. So whatever it was ran out of energy or tugging power. That shows you one limit, anyway, which is quite encouraging.

I'm still not 100 percent certain if the Grays operate only in the etheric or if they can shift between the nonphysical and our physical reality. I have only had one incident that got me wondering. I was in Bath, England, resting in a hotel after a long day at a recording studio. I couldn't sleep; I was still a bit wired from the day's work. Then I felt the energy of the room change. (When the Grays show up, a room's ambiance gets thicker—it takes on a milky quality. I have never seen it as milky, it just feels that way.) A being was standing motionless between the bed and the door. The room was quite brightly lit, and since you lose sight of the etheric under bright lights, I couldn't see the being, but I could feel it. Anyway the room had definitely changed, which is a telltale sign. I was tired and bit irritable. So I screamed at it, "F—— off, you little piece of shit, or I'm going to get out of bed and punch yer effin' lights out!" Not very galactically embracing, I must say, but I wasn't in a very caring, sharing mood at the time.

The energy of the room instantly changed as the entity backed off, and all was clear. However, I woke up in the morning with two snakelike pinpricks on my arm. They were bleeding ever so slightly. The odd thing was that the blood on the pinpricks wouldn't coagulate. There were two tiny red dots on my arm for several days. So, "F—— off you little creep" perhaps only works to a certain extent.

UFO researcher John Mack says that the Grays are terrified of video cameras. He suggests that one anti-abduction trick is to run your camera all night. The problem with that is that most videos won't run that long, so I'd imagine you'd need a CCTV set up in your bedroom. The price of those is coming down, so it might be a good investment if you're being bugged by the Grays at night. The other thing they don't like is ultraviolet light. A UV bulb doesn't cost much—you could get one at the hardware store. The other thing I thought of trying was to rig a continuous copper wire under the bed, looped back and forth under the mattress, and then over and around the bed so that the copper wire made a cage. You would hook that up to a low-voltage battery so the wire had a small current running through it. That would alter the electromagnetic field around you, and it should put them off.

One thing I found, while examining the Grays for a while, is that they can skew your etheric off-kilter. I got the impression that the fairy folk in the forest did the same thing. On one occasion in London when the Grays were around, they somehow knocked my etheric legs off at right angles at the knees. It was a really spooky feeling. I got off the bed I was meditating on and fell over. Where I felt my legs to be wasn't where my real physical legs actually were.

I had the same experience once in a hotel in Copenhagen. My etheric slipped off at a 45° angle. I was in the shower, and I put out my arm to adjust the water flow and missed the knob by several inches. Again, I felt my arm to be somewhere where it was not. But the Copenhagen experience was different from London, as in Denmark I was suffering from exhaustion, and I don't think that experience was necessarily Gray related.

The Grays also seem to be able to tilt your chakras so they aren't spinning on their axes properly, and are suddenly off on an angle from their normal plane of rotation. So if you imagine a large platelike vortex spinning in front of your chest, normally the left- and right-hand side of the plate would be equidistant from your body. Suddenly I found that one side of my heart chakra was a full four or five inches off my body, while the other side was only an inch or so off. The rotation was tilted away from me on the left side, so the chakra was lopsided.

I found an etheric healer who straightened it all out for me, but it took several sessions. In the third session, while lying on the treatment table, I noticed that the Grays were off in the distance watching the procedure. The healer told me that one of the Grays walked into her room that night, and she told it to bug off—politely, of course, as the healer is very proper—and it went on its way. I have often wondered what energies attach to healers because of their work. I saw it firsthand on that occasion.

In the end, I got terribly pissed off with the whole Gray routine. So every day I sent them love in my meditations, and if they showed up in my room, I'd project love and mentally try to hug them.

I remember when I first went to America and I used to speak at Christian New Age churches such as Unity and Science of Mind, there would always be a couple of greeters at the door who would hug you as you came in. Being English, and somewhat shy and reserved in those early days, I found the greeters most threatening. I know they meant well, but I would have rather have rappelled off the church roof on a rope than be hugged by the stranger at the door—the one with the cheesy grin and the brown polyester jacket.

It must feel the same to the Grays, because any love or hugs and they push off double-quick. Of course, it might have been a coincidence in my case—maybe they were leaving anyway—but once I started the hugging and the "love-love" vibe, I never saw them again—well, not close up, anyway. But I've got my brown polyester jacket in the cupboard just in case.

A couple of months ago, a young man said on my Internet discussion page (**http://www.powersource.com/wilde/philosy/comments.htm**) that he'd been abducted, he'd used the same love-love routine, and it had worked for him. So maybe that's the only defense we have. Anyway, if the Grays are bugging you, you might as well try it. Can't cost you anything.

After I finished writing these pages about the UFO experience, I lay on my bed to meditate and rest. I saw a ghoulish character in my mind's eye, off in the distance. I pushed out toward him and hugged him. He was repulsed by it and turned and left. Several Grays then showed up, but they were very far away. I tried the same routine on them, but they were so far off I couldn't get to them. My meditation wasn't very deep, so maybe I was just skimming around close by, unable to really travel out to them. One eventually came closer, and I got him in the love-love hold, and he slipped from my grasp and went on his way.

The Grays, the Reptilians, the Watchers, the UFOs, plasma balls, and so on are all a part of our transdimensional evolution. Whatever the origins of man—via the apes or via a DNA manipulation by the Grays—matters not, for I know for certain that the God Force is within us, I've seen it. So we have to hang our hat on that and trust the process. My tactic is to tell God I love Him/Her five times a day and keep working on my shadow, while developing my sixth-sense perception at the same time. Who or what inherits the earth is not a part of my immediate agenda.

It's a weird and wonderful world, a part of our learning experience. What I find exciting about all this interdimensional phenomena is that it's a sign our energy is becoming more sophisticated; things are opening up. Whereas it might be a bit scary at first, that is the nature of the explorer's life. If we don't explore, we'll never discover anything new, and we'll be left with the same dippy stuff that was around a hundred years ago.

THE ETHERIC DOORWAY

L et's talk about the etheric and how it applies to the sixth sense. But rather than going into endless, tedious discussion—some of which is pretty complicated—I'll give you an exercise here and there that you can start right away; and the rest of the etheric information I'll drop in as we go along. I think it's easier to understand ideas when information is linked to practical examples, or in this case, to exercises you can perform. I hate jargon and nonsense and things that are tiresome. Best to keep it bright and breezy, ready-to-use, and clipping along at a steady rate.

Suffice it to say that the etheric is the subtle bio-electromagnetic emanation that exudes from the body. In certain subdued lighting, it is visible to the naked eye. You may not see it as yet, but you can easily learn to feel it. For years, scientists have said it's not there, but now they're coming around to the idea that it *might* be there, although they don't know what it really means, and they don't give it much credence as yet. I predict that in time it will become the single biggest breakthrough in medicine that there has ever been.

Once we understand the etheric properly, we'll command the energy that is at the root of our health and well-being. Acupuncture, which stimulates the flow of *chi*, or energy, along the meridians, is the rudimentary beginning of etheric healing. I'm fascinated by acupuncture. It is so advanced, and it was developed several thousand years ago when, in theory, medics didn't know about simple things, such as how blood circulates. I imagine that the sages who discovered acupuncture knew more than we realize. Maybe the secret of the etheric nature of acupuncture was lost somewhere in our ancient history. Certainly during a session, you can feel your etheric responding as the needles are placed at the various points. I am a great believer in the process, and I go to an acupuncturist on a regular basis.

A couple of years ago, I had a bit of high blood pressure—my lifestyle was just too intense. After the first session, my blood pressure dropped dramatically. By the end of the second session, it was at the high side of normal, and by the third session, it was well inside what is normal for my age. It's never gone back up again. I feel sorry for people with high blood pressure who are conned into taking pills all the time. I don't know if acupuncture will work for everyone, but it might be worth a try.

Your etheric is the *real* you, so treating it is more effective than just seeing a patient as a physical object. We are a pulse of energy. If you work on the energy, the physical body responds. The sages of old who knew the etheric technology would heal by lying beside the patient and rolling their etheric out of their own body. They would enter into the patient's body/etheric energy. Once in there, they would perform minor adjustments and move energy around for the patient's benefit. I have had a few discussions with some modern alternative healers, and we've often talked about how it was done. I know a couple of really proficient healers who are giving it a go. It's quite amazing what they can do.

Because the etheric is an evolutionary level beyond ours, we are all stumbling along. Through trial and error, we'll get there in the end—or our children will, or their children. But it will come. It's bound to; it is the next step.

Healing is not my expertise, but I've worked on the etheric now for just over 12 years in relation to consciousness, so I know how it moves. I have also uncovered some of the basic methodology as to how it links us to other dimensions. I am aware of the flow of the etheric around the body. I also figured out, in a rudimentary way, how to move the etheric and use it.

I'd enter a trance state and feel the energy within me, and then I'd come up with an idea of how to move it around and I'd try it out. Of course, some of the stuff I tried was way out. On one occasion, I tried turning myself inside out, and I got completely fried. Mostly, I'd try expanding my etheric and hovering it over my body so I could travel into other places in my etheric perception without actually leaving my body. It's not as hard as it sounds, but at times it got a little weird. Generally, I've enjoyed the challenge and the sense of adventure—and at times, I've scared myself stiff.

There are no books on the subject that list techniques in detail, so for the most part, I plugged away on my own for 12 years. Ninety-nine percent of the time, what I tried was fairly safe, but a few times I got into trouble through plain stupidity and a lack of expertise. But I worked my way out of it, so I'm here to tell the tale—which is jolly heartening.

If I discovered a maneuver that worked, I'd practice it on a daily basis, testing variations over and over until I knew that the technique was repeatable and foolproof and safe and—most important—that it worked. I'd try out some of the techniques with my long-suffering seminar participants (with their permission, of course), and that way I'd know if my techniques worked on other people. I was looking for a way to show people the reality of other dimensions, and the subtle body and the potential contained therein. The people I tried it on, more often than not, had had little or no previous training. I discovered that the etheric is open to anyone who has a bit of imagination and the ability to center their mind. I found that most of the techniques worked real well, which was lovely. However, some needed adjustment, and some flopped completely. I bagged the duds, kept the good stuff, and I honed in on improving the others. In this way, I unraveled bits of the knowledge, but the greater part of it still remains a mystery.

The etheric contains information about your characteristics, both emotional and mental, and it shows your stock of light—your metaphysical bank balance—as well as showing aspects of your physical condition and so forth. The chakras are, as you know, vortices of energy that spin through the subtle body. They are definitely there. The root chakra is at the base of the spine. The other lower chakras I don't bother with as they are very faint, and no one knows if they are really there or not, or what their real purpose is. I've heard a few theories, but they all seemed pretty loopy to me, and I'm dubious about anything I can't test myself. That may be a limitation, but it's also a strength. I test everything. If I can't make it work, I shelve it.

I've concentrated instead on the five chakras that are easy to feel, ones we know a lot about—the root, the heart, the throat, the third eye, and the crown—which is over the top of your head. As you get into the etheric, you'll start to feel them. But first you have to make it all real by observing it.

An Etheric Exercise

Here's an etheric exercise to start. It would be good if you could practice it each day if possible. Later on, I'll give you the more complex hovering and rotational techniques, but in the meantime, I'd like you to consider this basic method. I've made some simple changes to the old-established chakra-opening techniques. In fact, you'll see that I have flipped it all around the other way. That will speed your progress by heaps and heaps. You will remember that I said that when I was at the bottom of the near-death tube, I tried and tried to move up it with no success. Once I dropped that technique and pulled the other end toward me, rather than stretching up the tube to see things, it worked instantly. It's the nature of those mirror worlds. It's the same with the chakra-opening exercise. You'll see below that I have flipped it around the other way. I found that it works much better.

I changed the process because I felt that some of the teachers who taught in the late 1800s and early 1900s, who laid the basis for our modern knowledge, had made some simple mistakes. They got some of the techniques back to front. Their chakra-opening exercise is one example. Other techniques they taught were just flat-out wrong. In my early days, I saw those characters as the authorities on the subject, so it was hard for me to comprehend that they had made errors. It took me ages to realize that there were errors in the methodology that might need adjusting.

Even some of the modern writers have made mistakes. For example, Robert Monroe is considered the expert on out-of-body experiences (OBEs), and his book on the subject, *Journeys Out of the Body,* is fascinating. I have heard that his "focus ten" techniques work, but in this book— now a classic—he made a simple mistake regarding the angle of visualization at the start of the OBE. He put it off at a strange angle, and that's not correct, since in the OBE, one usually exits straight out of the crown. I said to Robert, some years before he died, that I thought the angle thing was wrong and that the technique didn't really work, and he admitted to me that he had made an error. Perhaps he changed it in later printings of the book. I'm not sure, as I haven't reread it in recent years. Anyway, Monroe did a fantastic job bringing those OBE worlds into a technological format. But the point is that if a technique doesn't work or if it is wrong—whether it comes from Stuart Wilde or someone else—you have to be able to bag it and/or modify it. Otherwise you'll get stuck.

Anyway, I've tested these etheric ideas over and over, on others as well as on myself. So I'm confident that they will work for you. You may want to read them through first so you're familiar with them. Perhaps you could write down the details on a card so you have them close at hand when you're ready to try the exercise.

Getting the Chakras Opened Properly

First, find a regular and comfortable spot for your meditations, and sit. You can lie down if you want, but you're more likely to fall asleep unless you're a real expert in meditation. Get a small concave mirror, one that bends inwards, like a shaving mirror. Place that close to your head. If you're lying down, it should be about 18 inches from your right-hand side. If you're sitting, place the mirror to your right on a nearby table, shelf, or window ledge. The mirror acts as a satellite dish. Remember, spirit worlds and other dimensions (the ones I have seen) are opposite us, facing us like in a mirror. There may be dimensions that are *not* opposite us. Author Stephen Hawking talks about Imaginary Time, a dimension at 90° to the physical plane. I can't say I've had any experiences of Imaginary Time, and I haven't seen any dimensions that are at 90°. That's not to say they don't exist, though.

The point about the concave mirror is that it bounces the energy/information coming in from other worlds in the right way for us humans. Maybe it also accentuates the energy. I feel it does, but I have no definitive proof of that—other than my subjective experience of it.

Okay. You've got your mirror, and you're ready to start. Close your eyes, breathe in and out, and relax. Begin by feeling the presence of the mirror near you; bounce your consciousness back and forth off of it a couple of times. It's like pinging a thought in the direction of the mirror, firing the thought with your will, and waiting a split second for it to come back. Now, before you get going, say to yourself, "I am shielded from any influence that is not of the Light. I invite assistance, cooperation, and guidance only from entities or energies whose wisdom and experience are greater than my own. Nothing negative or dangerous can approach me in this experience. So be it. I am love; I am light."

Now move your concentration to the base of your spine (the root), and visualize energy (light) going up and down the center of your body, from the root to the top of your head and back to the root. This is the *kundalini* freeway—imagine it running up through the center of your body. I know others say that the kundalini runs up the spine, and that's right. But here I want to introduce a slight change and ask you to envision a ray of light going from the root to the crown, up the center of your body. If you visualize it, you create it. See the light flowing up to the crown and back. Do this several times, then rest. This clears a path for energy to rise.

Next, go back to the root, and mentally collect a little bubble of the etheric energy there—say, about the size of a golf ball—and bring it up through the center of your being, all the way up to the top of your head. Visualize that light hitting the underside of your skull—"dong"—then allow the bubble to float slowly back down through the center of your body, back to the root. Do that three times. Move the bubble of light up faster each time. Try to get the last one to really whack the underside of your crown at top speed. You may even feel it the first time you try. If you can't feel it yet, just imagine it. If you have one or two sexual thoughts before you start, that will wake up the root chakra, and the golf ball becomes more real. The sexual thoughts aren't really necessary for the exercise; it's just a way of amplifying the root if you can't feel the bubble.

When you're ready, center your concentration back at the root, get another bubble of light, and move it up through the center of your being— do it slowly this time. Come up the inside of your body with the light, passing your navel, continuing up through your chest; then pause at the area of the heart. Imagine yourself inside the center of your body; visualize the heart chakra folding open in an outward direction. That is, mentally push out from inside your body, toward the outside world. See the chakra spinning, unfolding, and opening wider. Imagine it as a flower, and push its petals open. Once it's open, push out with your concentration through your heart and chest to the world beyond. Imagine you have a pair of eyes on the little golf ball of light. Imagine looking out through the chakra as if it were a hole in your chest, so you can now see into physical reality—the room around you, say, or the location you are meditating in.

This was the first adjustment I made. The old texts said to see yourself surrounded in light and open the chakra mentally from outside your body, as if you are unbuttoning a shirt. It doesn't work as well because you're trying to pull the chakra open, rather than opening it from within with the force of your will. Also, there is a special bonus in the process of trying to look out from the center of your body to the outside world. It's part of observation. In looking through the chakra from inside toward the outside, you naturally place your feelings and concentration in the etheric, as you are traveling through it and the chakra to the external world. The old method had you pulling the chakra open from outside your body, which leaves one's concentration in the intellect, on the outside of the chakra and the etheric. It took me ages to figure out that the old texts had gotten it slightly wrong.

It's a simple adjustment, but it's important.

Once you've looked through the heart chakra to the outside world, bring the bubble of light up a little farther to the base of the throat. The chakra is where your neck joins your torso. Open that chakra, and again visualize yourself from inside your body looking out. Then travel on with the bubble of light to the third eye, in the center of the forehead. Open that and push out from within. When you push out, attempt to reach for things at a distance. It's a mental process as you try to go beyond the location you are in at the time.

The heart chakra is big compared to the throat, and that is much larger than the third eye—usually, anyway. Next, move your concentration to the underside of the top of your skull, and push out and up with the light—imagine yourself punching a fist through the top of your head. Remember, at the heart, throat, and third eye, you push outward; at the crown, you are pushing upwards, vertically.

Now you have your chakras open. How open will depend somewhat on your level of resistance and how vulnerable you have allowed yourself to be. Breathe in and out slowly for a moment, then take a deeper breath and hold it for a few seconds. Holding your breath alters the CO_2 in your body. Inner perception is greatly enhanced by oxygen changes in the brain. While holding your breath, keep your mind blank, visualize yourself expanding instantly to the outer reaches of the universe and back again, then exhale. You are momentarily poised in time, saying, "I am everywhere. I am inner-knowing." Do the expansion breathing three times.

By the way, the expansion breathing doesn't necessarily have to be done in a structured meditation. You can do it anyplace—sitting on a bus, or waiting in your car at a light—whatever. It's good to expand yourself from time to time; it reminds you that you are everything and everywhere. You are a part of the light.

When you breathe in, hold your breath and visualize yourself expanding in every direction to the far reaches of the universe—at infinite velocity. Be particularly careful to visualize yourself as a multidirectional being. Make sure you think about what is above you and what is through the ground below you.

At the center of the earth's core is an enormous crystal of iron. It is very hot and about the size of the moon. As the iron blob revolves, it creates the earth's magnetic field—it's a power station radiating energy back up through the ground to us. In a minute, you're going to use it.

Scientists have recently discovered that the iron core is detached from the earth's crust—that it spins independently from the outer layers of the earth and slightly faster. So the iron crystal is, in effect, a planet within a planet.

Through the magnetic field of the core, you can add velocity to your perception. So, breathe in and imagine the iron crystal—and instantly expand yourself in every direction. Up through planet Earth to any part of the world on the surface, to any person or situation at ground level. Or you can ricochet up through the crust and beyond the planet to the outer reaches of the universe—which, of course, is below you and above and in every direction. When you do this, you'll notice how fast your thoughts are moving.

In this way, you are saying, "I am beyond time. I operate at infinite velocity. I am standing larger than life. There is a crystal mirror inside the earth, and there's a mirror by my head. My external life and my inner world of dreams, visions, and perceptions are now becoming two more mirrorlike effects that reflect reality back to me. All these mirrors are reflecting light, and as they reflect energy, they create an infinite burst of light—one that repeatedly bounces back and forth at high velocity, through three dimensions of our spatial reality and one of time."

And as the effect of these lights accelerates inside you, they combine with your mind and your feelings to form a further power source that projects itself beyond this dimension of spatial reality and time. It carries you into a new dimension. Just to recapitulate: There are four receivers—the iron core, the concave shaving mirror by your head, the receptivity of your feelings, and the storehouse of your subconscious mind. So there are four mirrors (forces) if you like, and you—that part of you that is your identity, the I am, poised in the center, where the diagonals cross, like the mysterious fifth force of my vision. Each force working together is now adjusted to focus a beam of energy. Imagine, for simplicity's sake, a square with one mirror at each corner: the iron mirror, the concave shaving mirror, a subconscious mind mirror, and a feelings mirror (see Diagram #2). We are going to focus those mirrors and hover in the center of that square. Using that, we'll scoot off into other worlds.

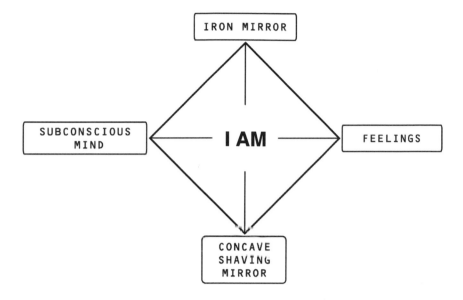

DIAGRAM #2

Because those worlds are mirrored in relation to us, they are facing us—our left is their right, and our right their left. That makes it a bit more complicated, for we have to make two adjustments in our "square" visualization. The first adjustment is needed because a square is a 2-D object—it only has length and breadth. We live in a 3-D reality, so we need one more "D" quickly. Otherwise we might regress into the mythical, simplistic world of Edwin Abbott's Flatlanders—that imaginary 2-D domain in which A Square (the hero of the story) takes a trip up into a higher dimension, known to us of course as the 3-D world. Our missing "D" in the diagram is, of course, height. The point in the center of the square, we'll call zero. It's the focal point of your energy. If that point moves up and down, along a vertical line that passes through the center of the square, you wind up with two pyramids base to base. One has the apex at the top, above the square, and the other pyramid's apex is below the square (see Diagram #3).

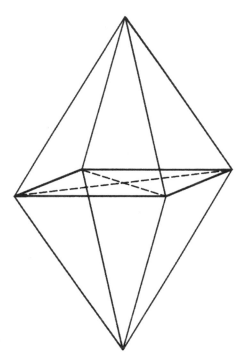

DIAGRAM #3: The square becomes two pyramids, base to base.

You can see how both pyramids are mirrors of each other. In fact, when you join the pyramids together, they become an eight-sided structure, an octahedron. They share the same square floor, and the zero point at its center is common to both pyramids. The two pyramids, base to base, are, I believe, a map of our immediate dimensions. It's quite complicated to explain, and there's a bit of mathematics to get around, so I've put the rest of the details in chapter 13, where you can ponder on it if you have a mind to.

I believe that when you enter a trance state and open the chakras, you are taking yourself toward the zero point in the diagram, at the center of the pyramid's floor. The zero point is the doorway to the opposite worlds. It accesses you to the other half of yourself, your mirror-self, you might say. As you pass through the zero point, you are, in effect, disappearing—that is why all mystical philosophies have taught that you have to control (disappear) the ego to reach nirvana and the celestial worlds. Of course, you are not necessarily disappearing from view, but you *are* disappearing from the wave-field of your normal identity.

When I had my spontaneous OBE experience in the forest, there was a moment as I came out of my body in which I blacked out. Others have described that same blank moment at the beginning of the OBE experience. I think it occurs at the instant that one crosses the zero point. In the trance state, one simulates death by slowing one's brain waves down as much as possible, to where they aren't ticking along at all. Zero-tick of the brain waves and you are "over Rover." In trance, we attempt to get down to where our brain waves oscillate at four cycles per second or less. This isn't weird, for we do the very same thing every night of our lives during sleep. Staying awake at that level of brain speed makes the difference between the visionary and the sleeper. The power of visions comes from the power to entrance yourself and stay awake. It's like sleeping and being awake at the same time. Monroe says it's the key to the out-of-body experience. In fact, trance is really a sophisticated, controlled lucid dream.

But before anything else happens, we should get a grip on this chakra thing so there's good energy flowing and you understand what you're doing. There are heaps of meditation techniques out there that you can use. However, what I found frustrating is that often no one really explained the methodology and what is actually happening. Understanding the rudiments was the key for me. Once I could explain it to myself, I started flashing along at speed. Up until then, it was all confusion and maybes.

Learning to use your mirrors in this unusual way will show you how to penetrate deep into yourself and other worlds of knowing. Discovering things about yourself is exciting.

Back to the process: You've now got the four main upper chakras open, and, hopefully, you are in a mild or deep trance state. Now you'll use the mirror system. First, bounce your mind off the little mirror to your right— see your thought-form pinging off and heading downwards toward the core of the earth, and then watch it ping back and return to your mind. The mental process forms a triangle. Then, turn your mind to a distant galaxy. It would be handy if you had picked one out at night and knew what it looked like and where it was at any particular moment. Get a star map and work it out. Pick one cluster or galaxy that you'll use. Learn where it is at a given time at your latitude.

For convenience's sake, let's say the galaxy is above. Fire a thought at it, let that thought ping off the galaxy and bounce back to you, ricocheting off the shaving mirror by your head and then the iron core in the center of the earth. Then have it touch your mind. Notice how the mental action of it feels slightly different from the one where you just went via the mirror to the center of the earth and back.

Now things are moving along nicely and you're ready. You have two satellites—the mirror and the earth's core; and two other mirrors—the subconscious mind and feelings. You've got four upper chakras open, you're relaxed, and you've spread yourself off into space. Now you can cast your perception in any direction you wish. The point is that you now have your antennae out, and you're seeing yourself in bigger terms—bouncing yourself around the universe and back again in the flash of a thought-form.

Establishing Yourself As Larger Than Life

Now here are a couple of visualizations I want to you to perform, either in the chakra meditation or whenever you have a moment. I've discussed them before in other places, but I'll mention them again quickly in case you haven't read my other books. They are just a handy way of establishing bigness, as your nonlocal sixth sense needs that to function properly.

The first visualization involves seeing the earth as very small. Stop whatever you're doing, and breathe in deeply. Hold your breath, and visualize planet Earth in the palm of your hand. You are as big as a giant, and there is a little, almost-round ball in your hand. You are larger than life because you are infinite. Now, for a moment, see any situation that bothers you; see it on the tiny planet resting in your hand. In this way, you see the insignificance of irritations in relation to the vastness of your real energy. The co-workers who've bugging you day in and day out are just tiny specks on the little ball in your hand; they're so small you can't even find them unless you look real hard. But you're holding your breath, so you ain't got time to mess with looking too long for an arseholic work mate. You are infinite, eternal, larger than life. Knickers to the work mate; we're doing "galactic" here.

Here's part two: If there's anybody who's really giving you trouble and you can't put them in an insignificant context because they've captured your attention and your emotions, then see them in the palm of your hand as a minute person, standing on the little planet. Send them love, and remember that most people act weird because they're just little children in pain. Sometimes it's hard to project love to people you don't care for, but do it anyway. Try not to throw up; it creates a bad impression God Force-wise.

Once you've sent that troublesome person a bit of love, bring your hand up to your mouth, take in a breath of air, visualize them, blow a short sharp breath of air into the image of that person in the palm of your hand, and blow them away. Allow them to seek an evolution elsewhere, out of your life; help them on their way. But don't do it with rancor and hatred—send them off with warm air and love. It's much nicer and more effective in the end.

Hating people holds them close to you. Often your anger and antagonism rob you of life force, and once they capture your attention, you lose sight of life and wind up doing "troublesome work mate" 19 hours a day. Eventually it can make you sick. It stymies your growth, locking you into a nasty situation that you'll possibly carry to the grave. Not a clever idea, believe me.

The second of the two visualizations involves seeing yourself straddling the planet. Now the planet is bigger this time, and you are above it—an enormous being, a colossus, thousands of miles high, astride the earth. One foot at the North Pole, the other at the South Pole, and the equator below you, passing between your feet. In this way, you affirm that you dominate your existence. You are the power, potentially omnipotent, universal, a part of all things.

Finally, one last item in this visualization category. The earth, I believe, has a spirit. It is aware of itself; it's not just an inanimate lump of rock; it has an evolution and it knows about its evolution just as you know about yours. The spirit of the earth is wise; it makes adjustments, and it knows things. Talk to the spirit of earth at times, and get into a sacred relationship with it. That helps you align to the nature-self and the mirror-world of spirit. You'll be amazed how the earth spirit will show you things about itself. The planet is expert at balancing itself, no matter how much crud is thrown at it. It can teach us things about balance and imbalance.

Back to the review of the chakra process. The whole thing should last at least 24 minutes. After the initial chakra-opening exercise, relax and breathe normally. Then see energy coming from the God Force through your heart—see it coming from every direction, from within as well as without. As that energy flows through your heart, engage your concentration upon it, and pull the energy up from the heart to the forehead and the third-eye chakra. In this way, you'll activate it.

If you are in a circle of friends who meditate together, try this: After you've all closed your eyes and opened your chakras, visualize the person sitting to your left. Breathe in, and as you breathe out, project your breath to them as light, and send them energy. Each person in the circle does that simultaneously three times to the person next to them. Then, you all move on to the next person, always going around to your left, in a clockwise direction. In breathing each other in and out, you build energy among yourselves. Once that energy is established, send three breaths to the center of the circle. A reservoir of energy develops there. You then mentally draw from that pool of energy up through the heart chakra, directing it upward to the third eye.

Once there is enough energy (light) at the third eye, pictures and impressions will appear. You can talk to each other afterwards about what you saw, or you can remain silent and keep it to yourselves. But whatever you do see, remember it, and jot it down in your notebook so you can ponder upon it at a later date. It's important to keep a record of impacting dreams and visions; it's an affirmation that the world of subtle reality is important to you. Gradually, a larger picture develops, and you'll see things about your life that you don't see now. Clarity comes in little packets of perception that make up the whole.

After the chakras are open and you've done the visualizations I discussed before, and when you've pulled energy up to the third eye, sit still and watch. Try not to let your mind drift. You may see nothing for a while—just darkness—but you have to push through the frustration of that and wait. It takes tenacity to get from here to there. From time to time, direct light to any areas of your body that need attention. Think of the mirror beside you, and bounce your mind back and forth off it and the earth's core and the distant galaxy you chose.

When the meditation period is over, take a moment to visualize the chakras closed. Do that carefully, one at a time. You don't have to close the crown as it never shuts—just the third eye, throat, and heart. If you worry about being too open, then don't go out into public places for about 20 or 30 minutes.

In opening up, one does become more vulnerable. So when doing this meditation exercise, you should avoid mind-altering drugs, alcohol, negative people, or locations imbued with negative energy. It helps to avoid burial grounds and cemeteries. I was meditating once at the Great Pyramid in Egypt. I'd been inside the King's Chamber for several hours at night when the place was closed to tourists. That was fine. But later that morning, I walked outside and meditated at the foot of the pyramid. I discovered that there were more earthbound spirits around that thing than there were tourists clambering over it. One makes silly mistakes through inexperience, but it doesn't take long to learn. I shoved off to breakfast double quick!

But don't get unduly hung up about negative influences or energies taking you over. It can't happen unless you allow it, or your energy is incredibly low, or you're into the dark side of things. As long as your energy is normal and you're not into weird stuff—heavy drug abuse, black magic, sado-masochism, and so on—you'll be fine.

By the way, if during a meditation you ever come upon a negative energy from the astral world, don't be scared; it can't really harm you. Pull up your strength, look it in the eye, and tell it to bug off. As you do so, expel a breath of air, directing it in your mind's eye toward the entity or energy you are dealing with. It's amazing how well this works. Negative energies rely on your fear and weakness for their validity. Any decent show of strength, and they melt away in horror.

Finally, I should mention that when practicing these etheric techniques, you need to keep away from electrical equipment, so you wouldn't want to be lying down next to your stereo system. Try to make sure that there's at least a few yards between you and any electrical gear. It causes interference. It also helps, when you're starting out, to get a theta metronome tape. It's a series of audible clicks that run at four to six cycles a second. They work as a biofeedback mechanism. Your brain listens to the clicks and lowers its oscillations effortlessly. Most stores that cater to "space cadets" and the alternative market sell the tapes.

Peripheral Sight—Becoming More Multidirectional

I want to give you some more ideas in relation to your being a multidirectional, infinite being—a person with a large vision, not a small one. Here are a few more mental exercises to try.

It's important to remind yourself that you are multidirectional. Normally, one faces forward—unless, of course, you turn your head; but your subtle energy can be directed via your will and imagination in any direction you wish. You should think in terms of turning it around and moving it in unusual directions. Moving your subtle energy around gets it to a higher velocity. It's sort of etheric aerobics. In most people, the etheric is quite sluggish—it moves only in response to emotion. It is very enlivening for the etheric when you start shoving it around. It responds quickly, oscillating faster. You'll find that you have more physical energy and that you need less sleep.

These directional exercises can be performed almost anywhere as you trot along through daily life. Here's one: Say you're at the supermarket, waiting in line at the checkout stand. Mentally visualize yourself turning around. Don't move your body, but etherically imagine walking back out of yourself. See if you can etherically touch the person behind you. You visualize your etheric body as blue-gray, a mist that is shaped the same as the physical you. Know that you can mentally direct it with your will, in whatever direction you please.

Now, let's say there is a person in front of you in the line at the checkout stand. Collect your thoughts, clear your mind, and mentally put out an etheric hand and tickle the back of their neck. See if you can get them to turn their head. If they don't move right away, imagine yourself licking the back of their neck. Make the visualization big, like you've got a very large tongue and you're giving the person a wet, sloppy cow-lick on the back of the neck. If they are not too distracted by their own thoughts, they'll feel it and turn around.

If, when a person passes you at a distance, on the other side of the street, say, concentrate on the space an inch or two over the top of their head, and imagine flicking that spot with your finger. If you are centered at the time, you may see them turn in your direction, since they can feel you touch their crown chakra even though they may not be aware of what's happening. If you can see their etheric anyway, and you just look at a person's crown chakra, you will have noticed more often than not that people pick up on your attention. They turn toward you anyway. The etheric is very sensitive. It's where all human feelings lie. So everyone feels it even though they may not be fully aware or be able to explain it to themselves.

Your awareness is not confined to the geographical position of your body. You can move your subtle body without moving your physical body. Of course, right now you might have to rely on imagination, but eventually you'll be able to see from inside the etheric body, and then you're not limited in vision to where your eyes are—you'll be able to move your eyes around, so to speak. Very handy for looking 'round the corners of life.

As humans, we define reality as a small band of perception that is slightly less than 180° wide—the line of direct sight that's in front of us. Everything else is blotted out or made less relevant. For the most part, we ignore our peripheral perception, yet we need it if we are to become multidirectional antennae picking up energy from every direction.

Your peripheral perception is more sensitive than your regular sight. You have to engage it if you want to see the etheric. So, from time to time, start concentrating on your peripheral vision and ask yourself, "What is to my far left, and what is to my far right?" Don't move your eyes—keep them focused straight ahead. Just move your concentration to one side, then to the other.

Get a pair of old sunglasses, and tape over the lenses so you can't see through them. Put the glasses on, and walk around your home for half an hour or so. With your forward vision impaired, you'll become more aware of your side vision. Try not to move your eyes too much; just let them stare at the tape. Do this from time to time as part of reactivating your peripheral vision.

Defining the Etheric Subtle Body

Let me talk to you a bit more about etheric energy. Over the years, things have gotten a little confused. *Etheric* is a word that comes from the Greek word *ether,* which means "to blaze." I like the word *etheric* because that was the term used in the olden days. But when the teachings were brought back from India, it all got very complicated. The teachings said that there were several different etheric bodies: the *subtle body,* the *astral body,* the *causal body,* and the *auric body,* among others.

The terms *subtle body* and *etheric body*, or just *the etheric,* are one and the same in my view. The term *astral body* was sometimes used in two ways. First, it was used to describe the energy field in the out-of-body state—in other words, the astral body was the vehicle one supposedly traveled in. But the term *astral travel* is also used to describe an inner meditative state, usually a flight of imagination and reverie, not necessarily a full OBE. So when used in that sense, the term *astral body* has come to describe the hypothetical energy vehicle (one's attention, really) that is used in flights of imagination and reverie. Mucho confusion!

The *causal body,* as far as I could make out, was the term used to describe the *feeling* part of the etheric. The *auric body* was considered different still, and that got all mixed up with teachings about the color of the aura. It was said that sight of the aura depended on an elevated spirituality. So a high adept would have the sight, and a lowly student would not.

Ninety-five percent of this idea is wrong. There is a fragment of truth, in the sense that an adept would have a controlled and disciplined energy so he or she would have more perception. But perception doesn't really flow as a reward for holiness, just from the nature of the etheric energy. Control your emotions and develop the acuteness of your peripheral vision and you'll see it easily. In my view, the spiritual elitism of the old writers was unfair. It disempowered people into feeling they couldn't develop their perception and see without going through an adept or master. That's a bit too control-trippy for the modern era. Everyone can feel the etheric, even if they can't see it. And with only a little training, you can learn to *see* it. So you can postpone your ticket to the Himalayas. This is cheaper.

You see the colors of the aura (etheric) with your third eye, your metaphysical inner perception—not with your physical eyes. The energy of the etheric in our physical reality is colorless. It is obviously made up in part of photons; otherwise, we couldn't see it. But when the energy is expressed around something that is alive, it is definitely not only in its subatomic or atomic state, as far as our vision is concerned—it is in its collective state. We can't see a molecule of water, but we can see the trillions of water molecules when they are grouped together in a glass of beer.

I can see why people split the etheric up into various components, like the auric body and the causal body, etc., but it's unnecessary in my view. The causal body is the sensitive, feeling part of the etheric, but I don't see that as a different subtle body, just a feature or property of the etheric. Out with the causal body!

The term *astral body,* when describing flights of the imagination, isn't actually a part of the etheric's action at all—astral travel is a mental state, one of reverie. The etheric hasn't changed or moved during astral travel (when the term is applied in this way). Then again, when the term is utilized to describe the vehicle used during an out-of-body experience, it only adds to the confusion. The part of the etheric that is *away* from your body in the OBE state is not different from, or separate from, the part of the wave-field of etheric energy that is normally *around* the body. It is connected in a non-local way. The link is the same as conjoined particles that are fired in opposite directions.

Also, I'm sure that even though part of your etheric is away from the body in the out-of-body state, the major part of the etheric's wave-field remains with the body. That is, one bit slithers off the other, and one bit remains. This is why you can get back to your body after the OBE is over. I can't say categorically that is so, since in the OBE state I have never seen my OBE vehicle. But I'm almost 100 percent sure it's correct. Anyway, a car in the garage or the same car out on the road doesn't make it a different car. So the vehicle in the OBE is the etheric. No need for the astral body differentiation. It's splitting hairs.

In passing, I'll mention the silver cord that writers have talked about. They've said that it attaches your out-of-body vehicle to your physical body. I don't think it exists. I've never seen it, and I've never met anyone who has. I think the silver cord was a subjective perception of one particular writer. It was his version of the umbilical cord. As I said, I think that what connects your OBE vehicle to the physical body is that your OBE vehicle and your body's etheric are part of the same wave-field.

The auric body is the regular etheric when one can see its inner colors. But, again, the colors are a property of the etheric or one's perception of the etheric—it is not an entirely different subtle body. Out with the auric body!

In the early days, I was so confused that I didn't know if I was Arthur or Martha, in my body or out to lunch, or what. It took me ages to figure out that all the various terms are part of one and the same thing. The terms *subtle body* and *etheric body* are interchangeable, and all the others terms describe properties of the etheric—or, in the case of the astral body, it is either reverie or the etheric OBE vehicle. So it's best that we connect the various terms and wind up with one term, the *etheric*. Much simpler in my view. Phew!

To recapitulate: The trick to transporting your perception into other worlds is the trick of entrancing yourself and not falling asleep. You have to hover at the zero point. I'm going to give you a bunch of etheric maneuvers in chapter 9 to help you achieve that. But first we'd better talk about the sixth sense in practical terms. The kind of sixth sense I like is a creative, tangible one—the sort you can haul 'round to the bank!

CLAIMING YOUR POWER

At this point in your journey, you have to step up and claim your power, if you have not already done so. By that I mean that you have to demand that each of your faculties of mind—your feelings and emotions, your metaphysical energy, your intuition, and your extrasensory perception—begin to engage their prowess and perception. For, as a part of developing the sixth sense, you have to insist that it be there for you. You have to exercise it by making it pull information from your surroundings.

Start with this: Prior to telephoning somebody, visualize their home. See if you can pick them up in your feelings, and see whether your feelings tell you if they're there or not. The trick is to see your friend as a composite of energy, not as a physical person. In other words, what is the overall feeling/identity of the person you're looking for? We remember people by the *feeling* that their character and overall energy give off, not by the shape of their face. Think back to someone you knew at school, or someone you haven't seen for years. You won't be able to remember their face in much detail, if you can remember it at all, but you can remember their character, and the feeling that came from that personality. So when looking for a friend in a distant location, look for the feeling that you're familiar with, and see if the feeling is at the location that you're about to telephone. Can you nail them in your feelings as being there or not?

Once you've decided, phone the person and check the result. See how often you're right. Don't worry if you get it wrong—by asking your extrasensory perception to perform many times each day, your batting average will soon improve.

The important thing is that you start asking questions of your inner power so that you establish a smooth nonlogical link to your higher perception and inner knowing. With it, you can look around corners, or into the future; you can perceive what is logically not perceivable. But you have to begin to convince yourself that you have the power, if you are not already convinced from previous experiences. It's mostly a matter of developing sophistication and expertise, rather than being hit-or-miss. Expect to be right 100 percent of the time!

Here's another one: When a person is talking to you, try to reach out and touch them with your feelings. It's no more than visualizing yourself with a long arm, and pulling back toward you a molecule of that person's heart—a molecule of their overall feeling for you to perceive, analyze, and understand. You reach out mentally, slowly, grab a bit of them, and snap back with it quickly. You are not there to pillage their energy in any way; you're just taking a small sample. Reach into their heart, where the heart chakra spins in the center of chest, and imagine yourself grabbing an etheric sample of them. In this way, you pull a molecule of their feelings back toward you. Now mentally ask, "How does this sample feel?" It will tell you much about the person's overall emotion, just as the symbols in your dreams will talk to you in their special language.

With respect to the person you're sampling, you may find that their underlying emotions are very different from the words they utter, or even their current demeanor. So in reaching out to pull a bit of them back toward you, you learn about how they actually feel, not how they *say* they feel.

When in conversation with others, ask yourself, "How does what they're saying sit with me? What is the subtlety of the communication here? Is it truthful or not? Scattered or solid, reasonable or flaky?" By asking questions, you instruct your perceptional capability to wake up and deliver.

It may seem a bit strange—testing out your powers before you've had much chance to develop them—but it is only through the testing of them that they develop. Extrasensory perception (ESP) takes mental effort; you have to corner your mind and make it work for you. It is lazy. You have to force it a bit. As long as your approach is not scattered or haphazard, and if you access the power in a disciplined and powerful way, all will be revealed. The exercises and concepts presented here and in the other chapters will help you a whole bunch. As you've probably noticed, they are designed to spread you out—in order to make you bigger and connect you to the power.

They all help, but it's only through practice and intention that you carry the concept of the sixth sense into your day-to-day reality.

The Psychometry of Daily Life

The important thing to remember is that everything, inner and outer, emits a feeling. And that feeling has an identity; it's a thumbprint of energy. A building, even though it is inanimate, has a feeling—because emotion and energy were put into the building when it was built. People have feelings about the building: They like it or they don't like it—they work there, it's functional, valuable, they earn money there, whatever. The building takes on a personality, a character, through the energy with which it is imbued.

Psychic energy is stored and made manifest in the feelings things give off. It's called *psychometry*. The psychic holds an item of clothing, say, and picks up a signal, the emanations given off. Why solid objects like a building are imbued with these emanations of past emotions is not known. Scientifically, no one is sure. The idea that something solid has a residue memory sounds odd, but all particles rest in fields of energy, and the idea that the field—rather than the solidity of a thing—holds information is not that strange. Sheldrake's morphic resonance is not widely accepted as yet, but scientists do accept that every atom has a wave-field around it. So-called intellectuals are also coming around to thinking that maybe an imprint is made by sound waves on solid objects like walls. It will probably be proven eventually that emotions are just mental sound waves. Or perhaps, energy waves of a person's etheric leave imprints on things. Certainly you can tell when you walk into an empty room whether it's a happy, empowering place to be, or if it is ugly and dangerous and negative.

Here's a good mental setup: Remember a building that you know has high energy—maybe a beautiful church, or a room in your home or someone else's that is particularly lovely; or an art gallery that's very beautiful. Set that up in your mind, and give it a rating of, say, ten points. Now contrast it by remembering a place you know that has a very low, unhappy, negative energy; basically, it's ugly. Set that up in your mind with a rating of just one. So now there is a spread in your perception from one to ten that you can use to evaluate places with.

Every time you go into a building or home or wherever, give the place you are in a rating compared to your preset scale of one to ten. If a place scores neutral, it will be in the four to six range. If it scores higher, it's a nice place to be. Pull energy from that location. It's a sucking in motion; you drag energy in via your heart and flip it up to the third eye. Pause and reflect for a moment—something might come to you from the energy of the room. If the location scores less than four, then you shouldn't be there. If you have to be there, then stay balanced and watch; be aware and make a special note of where the exits are. Remember: Never go into a building or a deal or a marriage or any situation in life without first looking for the exit. That's not the *sixth* sense—that's *common* sense.

Next, set up the same one-to-ten scale for people you meet. Make the highest-energy person you know the ten, and the lowest-energy person you know the one. There's your scale. When you meet people for the first time, exercise your perception right away. Grab a molecule of them from their heart, and remember: The first impression that comes back to you is always the right one. Later, your perception gets clouded by circumstances, or by knowledge of them that you may subsequently acquire. Or, it gets clouded by too much thinking. Touch them mentally in one of the several ways we have discussed, and have your mind give you the rating. Hightail it out of there if the rating doesn't come up to snuff.

Don't be too shy to leave when things are not right, if the energy of a place feels wrong, if a person feels odd, or if he or she rattles your sensitivity. That doesn't mean that you should judge places and people harshly—one shouldn't become too prissy. A place can be just right for others, but if it feels wrong, it is definitely wrong for *you*. So leave. It's the same when dealing with people. There is no God-given law that says you have to suffer low-energy people. Socially, we often feel the need to be polite and to accommodate people. One has to learn to set good boundaries in order to control one's life. So at times you may have to make an excuse and duck away.

Maybe in the heat of the moment, you've already said yes to a proposal, and later it feels wrong—perhaps the circumstances changed, and now you feel uncomfortable having to tell people you want to cancel. Start the conversation by describing your discomfort. Say, "Look Harry, I feel very uncomfortable saying this, but I can't come skiing next week. . . ." Excuses, excuses, blah, blah, whatever it takes. But start by admitting to your discomfort. That allows you a lot of leeway, as it shows you to be human—and people can empathize with that, no matter how much you're wriggling to get out of a commitment. Anyway, you have to follow your feelings if you want to build power and create stronger energy for yourself. Put these words on your fridge: "If it feels wrong, it *is* wrong. Period. Full stop."

Sometimes one's feelings can be a bit confusing—something can feel okay now, and an hour later it doesn't feel right. Situations are fluid and changing. People's feelings about situations change, or you have changed in the meantime. Perhaps an idea has been hanging about in your head all day, and now the idea is going stale. Over the last few hours, the universe-at-large has kindly shown you what a crummy idea it is, and what a nightmare it might turn out to be if you go to dinner at Harry's next Friday night. Maybe Harry's intentions, which where honorable when he asked you, have now changed, and things have gone dark in relation to the invitation or whatever.

Put Harry up in your mind's eye and see what your first impression is. See how much light or dark he emits. For example, on your scale of one to ten, where does he fit in? Has that changed since you last looked at him? It's easy—people can't hide their energy; there's no place to go in the all-encompassing light of the God Force anyway. You can also use the little bubble of light that comes up from the root chakra in the chakra-opening exercise, and fire it at people to get a more accurate evaluation. I'll give you that technique in exact detail in the next chapter; meanwhile, let's continue discussing the subtlety of the way things feel.

There is a psychometry to everything. The usual way it works is that the psychic handles a small object or piece of clothing. You'll probably rarely need psychometry of that sort unless you're one of those people who helps the police find bodies, murderers, and so forth. But if you *don't* do that work, I wouldn't sign up for it. The few I've met who do that kind of thing have all gotten very stressed out and sick; their lives have been threatened, and they take on a lot of bad-ass energy. Anyway, they say the pay is crummy; it's not worth it in my view.

But psychometry is worth trying out, as it helps with sensitivity. So go to an antique shop and pick up the various items there, and see what they tell you. The trick is to first mentally slot yourself in the historic time frame of the object. So if you are handling a piece of Victorian jewelry, try to project your mind into the Victorian era. In your feelings, join with how the Victorian emotions might have been expressed. What was important to people then? What were people's overall psychological characteristics? What were their issues?

In handling the object in question, the first impression that comes to you is usually the most accurate, for the longer you mull it over, the more your intellect gets into the act of trying to help out. Not very successfully, usually.

I imagine that psychometry would be handy if you were an art dealer or an antiquarian, as it would help you identify fakes. It would certainly warn you when things were not quite right. A crook might be able to perfectly fake a picture, even down to using the right paint, frame, and canvas. But you can't fake, say, the 500 years of emotion and feelings that have gone into a canvas. So if it feels "dead" as you handle it, an antique can't be as old as it is said to be.

You can use a variation of this same technique when thinking about a proposal. You just handle it in your mind. For example, say that someone offers you a deal where you'll be involved with him or her at a future date. Imagine holding the circumstance in the palms of your hands; turn it over, back and forth; handle it, feel it. Imagine it as a cube in your hands. Be sure to look at it from all sides, above and below. By doing so, you are asking your perception to show you all the angles to the deal. What level of energy does it give off? How much light? If the proposal feels bad in your mind's eye, you can be sure it will be a very dull event and that it won't have much energy for you. Also, this process is a handy way of figuring out how you feel about the proposal. Perhaps it seems fine, and perhaps you've made an intellectual decision to accept, but deep in your feelings the whole idea is tedious and boring, or downright grim. As you fondle it and look at it in your hands, it will feel that way—especially if you've taken the time to lower yourself into a meditative state beforehand.

That consciousness-lowering is important because you don't want to try this kind of mental psychometry from the brain speed of the active waking state, 14 to 21 cycles per second. You want to quiet the brain and be at a lower level.

If you don't have time to lower your brain speed properly via whatever meditation techniques you use, create a symbol in your mind that acts as a biofeedback mechanism for the brain that automatically lowers its speed. There are a couple of methods I use. The first is that I go back to a mental picture I associate with serenity. So I remember a mountain lake I know, and I imagine myself sitting there, levitating, hovering over the center of the lake, totally at peace, silent, surrounded by the water and the morning mist. As I engage that visualization, I can feel my brain speed clunking down a gear or two. Next time you meditate, set the same process up in your mind, and enforce it by thinking about the peaceful scene from time to time—

always use the same mental picture to reinforce the mechanism. Start every meditation thinking about the lake, and say, "This is serenity." Then the brain knows and remembers.

The other technique that comes from various sources, such as Silva Mind Control, is that of putting the tips of your thumb and first two fingers together every time you meditate. Soon the fingers touching together at the tips becomes a biofeedback trigger for the brain. It associates the action with a time when it was oscillating at a low speed, like in a trance meditation, say, so the three fingers together signals the brain to fire at a slower rate.

These two mechanisms—the three-finger technique and the peaceful lake—should be tucked into your inventory of handy perception techniques.

So, remember, as you walk along each day—20 or 30 times a day if possible, ask yourself, "How does this thing/person in front of me feel?" Push out your feelings into people, solid things, and situations. It's nothing more than grabbing a bit of energy as described, or you can just focus your attention on the thing or person in question, and suck a bit of energy back to your heart. You are a quantum-mechanical vacuum-cleaner sucking back to you bits of reality as you find it. Another way to perform this energy-collection process is to imagine a ray of light going out from you—imagine the ray has a hook on it. It goes out, grabs things, and brings back a little bit for examination. Simple stuff.

So go out into the street and start to pull from animate and inanimate objects. How does an animal feel? The birds—how do they feel? Pull from the inner character of the bird and ask, "How does it feel?" Do you feel the identity, the specialness of the bird? How do the buildings and the shopping mall feel? Grab samples of the people there. There's a nun on a skateboard hurtling through the park—how does she feel? There's a homeless person with a teddy bear sleeping next to copies of the financial pages of the *Herald Tribune*—how does that feel? Practice with lots of people and situations and things. Get used to the process.

In particular, do it every time you meet someone new, someone you know little or nothing about. You'll be amazed by how quickly you will be able to read inside people. Here's a technique that works: When listening to someone, imagine your etheric out of your body. See it standing behind them facing you. Get the etheric up real close to them, and wrap an etheric arm around their chest as if you were holding them tightly from behind. What impressions come to you? Then have your etheric step forward into that person in a powerful, definitive way, and as you step, clear your mind.

If they are spinning you a yarn to get you to do something, you'll feel the sneaky nature of it. The more covert and dark their intention, the easier it is to feel. Real danger feels like a hundred fire engines, sirens blazing, passing through your head. People can hide or suppress an intention, but they can't hide their energy. That is a jolly good thing—it keeps you safe.

The way to become proficient is to practice on hundreds and hundreds of people. Sit on a bench at the park, and do one person after the next. Try not to be influenced too much by the way people look. Sometimes, the way a person looks is an external manifestation of how they feel. However, very often it isn't. You want to go past the visual information they emit and just pull from their etheric energy. Don't look at the person in too much detail. Perhaps you might try keeping your gaze down so that you don't see the top half of their torso as they pass. Even looking down, you can still mentally reach out and pull a molecule of them back toward you. As you do, you'll get a sense of how they feel. You'll know things that others don't.

As you enter the world of sensuality, sensitivity, and feeling, the universe responds. It trains you and shows you things. I don't know why it does, but it does. The universe-at-large seems to have a vested interest in showing more of itself to us. So if you are looking for a friend, cast your mind out like a net and see where they are. Let's say your etheric sensitivity tells you they are at the bowling alley—make a mental note of it and check it out. Ask your friend, "Were you at the bowling alley yesterday at three o'clock, because I saw you there in my feelings?" If they say no, don't worry about it. It doesn't matter if you're wrong ten times out of ten—at the beginning, anyway. It takes time to go past that very human tendency of not wanting to feel like a complete idiot.

Making yourself vulnerable is part of the process of committing to the validity of subtle impressions—making them important even if many are wrong at the start. When you are not committed to your inner-self, it doesn't take you seriously. It can't be bothered to get things right because it knows you don't care, or that you don't take any notice of it anyway. It's used to you overriding its voice or feelings with the intellect. Your level of need and desire is important. If, for example, the rest of your life depended upon your very next extrasensory perception being right, then the inner you would make sure it got it right. It's strange how the system works. Going past the discomfort of being wrong is part of how you learn.

When you get a perception, try to act upon that impression—providing it's reasonable and hasn't told you to, say, jump off a cliff 'cause it thinks you can fly, or something weird like that. So if you feel that your friend is at the bowling alley and you want to see them, drive over and check it out. Taking action as a result of your inner perception is another way of affirming its validity. Sometimes, such actions will take you up a dead end, or your trip to the bowling alley will come to nothing, but that is part of the process, so don't worry about it.

When I trained to be a spiritualist medium in London at the College of Psychic Studies, one of the main things they taught was that communicating with the spirits really isn't that difficult. It's just a matter of opening the chakras and pulling energy up to the third eye. The spiritualist training mostly involved going past the inhibition of making a complete idiot of yourself. So we would sit in a circle, open the chakras, and bring energy into our circle; and then we would speak our truth—whatever we saw in the mind's eye, no matter how fleeting the impression. It didn't matter what we saw—the process was one of going past the inhibition of being wrong. The trick for you is the same: Ask, ask, ask—constantly—until you get to the point where you are more or less perpetually right. Talking to dead spirits is not most people's cup of tea, and it isn't mine either; it was just a part of my training. But everything helps you to learn, and perception can be turned in a million directions. Each will empower and enhance you.

To really embrace your subtle energy, you will have to start to meditate daily, if you don't already do so. It can be for just a few minutes each day, but it should be regular and at the same time. It's an important part of opening you up; it helps you control your mind. The human personality doesn't usually care for sitting still, for its domination of your life is set aside for a while.

Meditation helps you expand the etheric energy around you. It establishes a serenity from which the "feeling base" of your power grows. I've taught a lot of people in my time, and 80 percent of them were much too tight. Fear, self-consciousness, and inhibition closes people down. There's a stage in everyone's spiritual journey where they have to allow themselves to become vulnerable if they want to experience more energy, more power. To win everything, you have to loosen your grip so that you can travel on from here to somewhere different and better over there.

It's a matter of trusting and going with the flow, and knowing that you don't have to know all the answers all of the time. It's a fact of your spiritual journey and your ever-increasing energy that you won't know very far in advance what you're doing next. You're more spontaneous and have fewer personal rules in your life to restrict you. Your whole approach to life becomes less rigid.

You are open to offers, so to speak, and you're ready to hop the great freight train of life. You're goin' places!

IMAGINATION, OPPORTUNITIES, CREATIVITY, AND THE SIXTH SENSE

We've talked about standing tall, seeing yourself larger than life, and visualizing the planet Earth in your hand. The purpose of these visualizations, and of accessing the sixth sense, is to give you the extrasensory perception you need for your spiritual journey. As you get closer to metaphysically transcending the physical experience, you run out of books and teachers—and then you have to experiment on your own. Otherwise, things get a bit boring, and you'll be irritated by the limits of a confined mind-set.

Remember, you are *not* your emotions. You are an eternal being inside a physical body, operating through a mind that may—or may not—be experiencing what it considers to be a pleasurable or negative emotion. Once you detach a bit from the emotions of life, you develop a command of your destiny. The sixth sense and ESP flows once your subtle energy isn't swamped by excessive thinking and loads of emotions and reactions swishing around the etheric to spoil your perception.

You are coming to the point where you can command this incarnation. Many take that to mean that they must be rich and famous or very successful. Of course, worldly success is great, but it's not necessarily what your sacred journey is about. In the end, you'll want to command your life so that you can concentrate on love, and the experience of living. Commanding your destiny is just being in control of that part of the human experience you choose to be in control of. You can spend the rest of your life fishing by the river, and you can still be the initiate, the higher being in a spiritual evolution. We're kidded into thinking that money, glamour, and wealth are high energy, and everything else is of a lower energy.

Imbalance, dysfunction, being out of control, hatred, violence, gluttony, greed, and egotistical ideas—that's low energy. Balance, serenity, compassion, and spiritual ideals build high energy. There's no logical boundary to your perception, because you can pull anything to you in your mind's eye and place it in front of you and look at it. So you can see how it helps you to get in touch with your inner-self through consciousness-raising, discipline, visualizing the power within you, and seeing yourself as an eternal being.

Limitlessness is natural. Confinement involves effort. The entire universe is inside your heart, inside your charisma. Potentially, there is nothing you can't imagine and so create.

Einstein said, "Imagination is the theater of coming attractions." Imagination allows us to dream the impossible dream and to materialize it! People think that they have imaginations because they are used to daydreaming, but imagination and daydreaming are not really the same thing. Creative imagination is different from ego-pleasing. Most people's imagination is poorly developed. I don't think it is taught well in schools and, anyway, TV deadens the imagination. We don't have to imagine Niagara Falls or the plains of the Serengeti; we can watch it all in living color on TV.

Our couch-potato society thwarts our imaginative capacity. Most people are deadly dull, aren't they? Endless conformity, trivial chatter, the same stuff over and over, and all that machismo and violence and crud on TV, making the nation ill and the broadcasters rich—concepts to disempower people, making them frightened, apathetic, and easy to control. There are some very weird people on this planet whose motivation is money and power. They seek to control and encapsulate ordinary folk by getting them hooked on debt, drugs, and dysfunction—and also by desensitizing them— subtly controlling their minds by policing ideas and using disinformation to create a stereotypical conformity that suits the controllers and guys in power.

Will you succumb, or will you dream the Big Dream? Will you have the courage to be different and awaken your power to becoming an infinite being, keeping the sacrosanct, spiritual energy within you intact and well looked after? Will you move up in life and develop a greater vision for yourself, a good imagination? Most daydream a lot, yearning for a lottery win or for someone to come and "save" them. They wait passively, often pathetically, for an oversized dollop of good fortune to fall on their heads from the great Goo-Goo bird in the sky. Plop! I'm rich!

The Goo-Goo bird is cool, for it creates instant millionaires. The problem is that its bowel movements are few and far between. You're more likely to get hit by lightning. You can ruin your life wasting time and energy waiting for something that might never happen.

One day you will pass on, and the great Goo-Goo bird will be there leaning up against the Pearly Gates with a sheepish grin on its face, shrugging its shoulders, shuffling uncomfortably from one foot to the other, mumbling its apologies. And you could be looking back at a dull life. Maybe you'll see how you wasted your time, got nothing done; and got too suckered into daydreams of a cushy life and glamour and easy street— rather than acting to develop your creativity to secure such things.

Daydreams are pleasing to the ego; they bolster it up, for they don't usually require any discipline or action. The faculty of imagination, when used correctly, is different. Imagination allows you to see a future for yourself, but for it to make any sense, and to be real, there has to be a path from here—today's circumstances, where you find yourself right now—to whatever circumstances or vision you have for the future. Daydreaming is the brain in neutral, just ruminating, doing nothing. Imagination, however, is visualizing with pictures; it's not so passive, is it? Through imagination, you place yourself in the picture, and in the feeling, of a future circumstance or condition that you want.

In daydreaming, you disempower yourself, saying, more often than not, "I'm hoping for a break, but I don't really believe in myself. I can't really see myself in the vision properly, and by the way, my ego is real lazy so it won't allow me to take concerted action and do something." Daydreaming is easy; it involves no exertion.

Do this instead: If you are aiming for a distant goal and you want to direct your imagination to that, start by feeling yourself present at that future point in time. Enter into those circumstances—act them out. Allow your imagination to wander through the scene, so to speak, becoming a part of it. Enliven the picture and make it more real by imagining all your five senses present in those future circumstances. Grant the picture a sensuality that it would have if you were actually there, so give it its colors and sounds; and imagine the smell, texture, and taste of those future circumstances. Then come back from that future place. Focus your inner vision and intellect on seeing yourself progress through the steps it might take to get you from here, today; to over there, tomorrow.

Act out the steps in your mind's eye, and see yourself moving toward your goal through the intervening steps. You pull goals to you through concentration, while simultaneously moving toward them through concerted action. Remember, I've said many times before in my books that yearning for things pushes them away from you. In the emotion of yearning, you affirm that you don't have the thing you're yearning for. You set up an uncomfortable energy that others often have to climb over.

When you really need something and you're emotional about it, people tend to deny you, just because you need it. The emotions you express in yearning are often robbing energy from others, and they resent it deep down. They don't want you satisfying your emotional needs through such tactics; they feel their energy drop as you pull on them. They want you to tend to their needs, their ideas. It's an energy war set up by yearning. Don't yearn. It disempowers you. Act!

Imagination and Your Vision in Life

Back to imagination and the vision. Remember, see the goal granted by putting yourself in the picture; see yourself acting out your desires rather than striving emotionally to achieve them. Don't lean on the goal emotionally—stand straight. Externally move toward the goal. This is important because great opportunities usually carry a lot of metaphysical energy; they are heavily laden with goodies. So, great opportunities don't really travel very far. That might sound odd, so let me explain. Special breaks happen on the spot, rarely at a great emotional, physical, or commercial distance. In other words, you have to close in on your dream, emotionally and physically—shuffle up to it, so to speak—in order for it to happen. You have to be in the flow, in the loop, in the marketplace of life, acting out your greater vision—so your big break can find you.

This is because important people, who will open doors for you, don't usually scour the streets looking for others who might need a hand up. The important people are in the loop, moving in and around their successes, only hanging out with those who are in the same loop.

Moving close to your dream, practicing, perfecting your skills, gathering information, making contacts, and showing up in the loop gets you close to the target. Meanwhile, you concentrate on what you have to offer, polishing it up and honing in on the idea. People will only want you if there's something in it for them. They often only want you if somebody else wants you, and they don't usually commit unless they're sure they'll get what they want from you.

In other words, they have to know who you are, and they have to understand what you do. They have to see that you are endorsed and made right by others, 'cause once they see you in the loop, you're in, you're there. You have an identity, a special worth. You are valuable in the marketplace, and you're establishing a track record in whatever creative or commercial activity you've chosen.

So let's say you're a singer and you want a big record contract with a major label. You've stepped into the idea properly—you're singing in bars and clubs maybe, writing songs, hanging out in the studios. You've got a good demo, you know your stuff, and you understand what constitutes a commercial record. Now you've got a chance.

You're a cool dude (or dudette), and you've got a bit of music in you. So, theoretically, with a bit of power and the sixth sense helping you, getting a record contract should be a breeze—simple stuff. How are we going to get you there? First, you'll engage your imagination, and you'll see yourself with the contract, performing perhaps for vast crowds or whatever. You'll also see yourself moving through the various steps that will place you as close as possible to the goal—not only geographically, but also in your feelings. Meaning, do you belong to the idea of success, and does that idea or vision really belong to you? Do you really want what you're going for? Things that are too distant in your feelings are wishy-washy, vague, and ill defined, so they have little or no metaphysical pulling power.

If you want to make a hit record, give me the names of ten singers or bands that are in today's current Top 30. Then give me the titles of every record that made number #1 in the last 18 months. You've got music—sing me the tunes.

To make it, you have to know what's happening. You have to be in the business, and you have to be aware of what's hot and what's not, who's up and who's finished. If you can't tell me who's in the Top 30—who's made it recently—you're not giving yourself and your perception much chance. For you're out of the game, out of that part of the global mind that circles around pop music, for example. If you don't know your stuff, you're in the cold.

Maybe you're playing your music without realizing that it's miles behind the times. Or perhaps it's cool, but no one wants it. Sometimes it's a hard compromise. I know bands that are years ahead of their time, and others that are very original but too sophisticated for the popular market. Sometimes you have to make hard decisions. Do you go down-market and have a big success, or do you stay creatively where you want to be and suffer the fact that you might never make it financially? Because instruments make a noise, most musicians believe they can play. I think you have to be realistic, and perhaps a bit brutal with yourself. You have to be able to evaluate your music. Maybe your playing is a lot worse than you think it is, or maybe you can't generate the right emotions in your music.

Remember, you have to speak to an emotion in people for them to buy your stuff—be it music or any other product. All selling involves feeling out the emotional need in the market. Often, to have a big hit, you have to put aside what you want—get your ego out of the way, cooperate with others, accommodate them, and play music that others want. I've been lucky. I've made six albums so far of the kind I want to make—which is mostly transcendental, angelic music with a bit of rhythm. But I paid for those albums myself, and I luckily managed to sell a few hundred thousand of them, so that kept me afloat.

But if you can't afford to record and market your own compositions, you'll need others—and you'll need to know what they want. Back to the Top 30!

First you need to place yourself geographically close to your vision by getting in the loop. Then, you need to remain close to the vision in your feelings and believe in yourself. If you affirm that belief by acting out your dream—by doing sensible and useful things—then, and usually only then, will opportunities pop up. Once you're in the flow of your greater vision, there will be a strong energy around you. You will have shuffled up to those who are doing what you want to do—experts—and people who are part of the scene. Now and only now are you close enough to really engage the sixth sense to discover your strongest move—especially which particular person or organization will assist you in materializing your vision.

Also, when you're visioning and imagining, remember to start by mulling over what you will *give*, not what you will receive. I've gotten thousands of proposals over the years from people wanting help in materializing their ideas. I can't remember even half-a-dozen proposals that mentioned offering or giving anything. They all asked first, and often without even bothering to say *please*.

Your vision can't just come out of, "Gimme this, gimme that." Life is a trade-off. Either it's a win-win money trade-off between you and others, or

it's an energy trade-off and you'll have to give of your energy, your enthusiasm, your knowledge, or some effort up front. Maybe you'll have to compromise and shift a bit to get your vision off the ground.

I've seen people lose the opportunity of a lifetime because they were
scared of success—and the responsibility that success involves. Sometimes
they lost their big chance because they were just too disorganized. And
sometimes they lost everything because their ego got in the way—they
became too dogmatic and demanding and hard to deal with. They couldn't
feel it out and see that they had to give a bit to get going. The universal creative energy, which is open and fluid and seeks its own balance, soon gave
them the boot.

So what will you give? Energy, money, enthusiasm, innovation? What's
in it for others? As you meditate on your vision, try to hone in on anything
that's lacking. Do you need to polish your vision up a bit? Is knowledge
your problem? What's the plan? Does the plan make sense?

Some Handy Etheric Tricks

Okay, you're in the rock 'n' roll loop. In your mind's eye, let's review
the key people. Think about them intellectually and logically, but then think
about them inwardly with your sixth sense.

Here's how: Open your chakras using the method I gave you before,
and bring the little bubble of light up from the root to your heart. Make sure
you've totally relaxed yourself and that the chakras are open, especially the
heart. Now, put the people you wish to review up in your mind's eye one at
a time. Imagine them in front of you, as if reflected in a mirror. See them,
feel them, and watch them right there before you. Watch if any symbols or
feelings come up. Now pick someone in particular and put them up in front
of you, and hold them there with your concentration; don't let your mind
slip away to other things. Now fire the bubble of light that is hovering inside
you in the region of your heart—fire it at the person you wish to review. You
do this by willing the bubble to move in their direction; pushing it with your
mind; and expelling a soft, short breath at the very moment you fire the bubble with your will.

It doesn't have to be done with much force; in fact, the more softly you
do it, the better it is—you become more sensitive. Watch what the bubble
does. Sometimes it ricochets off the person you're looking at and bounces

back at you. Other times it goes to the heart chakra of the person you're watching and pings off in a strange way. The trajectory it takes as it bounces off that person will tell you things. Watch, notice, and remember. Then write it down in your notebook.

Everything you see at this level of consciousness, inside the sixth-sense faculty, is most precise and exact. It all means something. On occasions, the bubble strikes the heart chakra of the person you're looking at and goes straight up from their heart at enormous velocity, up toward their crown chakra at the top of their head. This is very positive—this person is a good person, and would be open to you—helpful and loving.

Sometimes the bubble hits the person and wobbles about like it's drunk, or it orbits around them incoherently, doing figure-8's around their head or body. It means they're confused and scattered, and their etheric diverts the bubble in a discombobulated way. They won't help you much. They may promise you the earth, but they won't deliver, and very likely they'll cost you time, money, and emotional effort.

Sometimes the bubble hits them and splats out like a soft tomato. It can mean several things: One is that the person in question is needy. They may have grabbed the energy of the bubble and absorbed it. Sometimes it means they are angry, so the bubble dies on the spot in the blackness of their anger—you may feel nothing coming back, or you may be vaguely aware of their anger. Sometimes, if they're not interested in you or your ideas or they don't care, the bubble dissipates and goes nowhere. If you get a splattered tomato, don't invest much energy in that direction, not now, anyway. Wait a bit, and try again in a week or two to see if the person's energy has changed. See if the bubble does something different next time.

There are a hundred possible trajectories and more. By firing the bubble into their etheric, you get a readout. Once you've done the process a few times and you're familiar with the method, it will all become obvious and you'll know what each trajectory means. It comes to you through practice.

The bubble process is a way of reading energy, a bit like sending a satellite to Mars. You've got a connection out there sending you back information. It's part of the "tapping" I talk about in my books, where you enter into people's energy, sometimes at a great distance, and you watch them and send them love while appraising their overall energy. Becoming familiar with their needs, you act accordingly.

Now you may wonder if it's possible to use these methods for malevolent intentions. The answer, of course, is "Yes, it is." Power is impartial; you can manipulate and hurt people, and you can scare them and use them. But if you do, one day something bigger than you comes along and it eats your lunch! Eventually you will live in the quanta of the dark, heavy particles you create around you, which block you from the life force. The light around you is enclosed and darkened, and you suffocate metaphysically in your own crud; you drift to a hellish state. That is soon reflected in your external circumstances—not a pretty sight! Something grim happens, and it takes you out. Like "Finito baby, hasta la vista." Energy is impartial; no one can stop you from doing as you wish.

Having watched the bubbles go to the various people, you'll want to review the situation, to appraise your opportunities better in the light of inner knowing. So, pull each person up in your mind's eye, especially the more interesting ones from whom you got a response of some kind. See those people one at a time. This time see them closer to you, feel yourself being more in touch with their feelings, their identity—pull them toward you.

You'll now momentarily grasp a little bit of them. Who are they—in their eternal, sacred sense? Don't get too hung up on their personality or how they have treated you recently and so forth. Just observe them unemotionally, with no personal criticism or judgment, pulling them up in your mind's eye one at a time.

Now, to get an even more accurate feel of their current emotion or attitude, you'll reverse into them for a second or two, at the level of the subtle body. Remember, there is no real distance at this level of operation; they are as close to you as you feel them to be. And as they come to you, you effectively engage the full force of your concentration upon them.

So you put them up in your mind's eye, and you've pulled them real close to you. Now mentally move your etheric out of your body so that it's outside you, as I mentioned before—standing outside your body, facing away to the distance. Then you turn your etheric around, so now your etheric is facing you, and you're looking at yourself! Then *will* your subtle self, the etheric self, once again, to step back gently but solidly into the character you're reviewing. As you enter, clear your mind and hold their heart in your etheric hands; be very still. Instantly, an impression or signal comes off that person you're visiting; you'll perceive their emotions or feelings—whatever is going on with them.

Sometimes you just feel it, and sometimes you actually see it in the mind's eye as a symbol or a sign they give off. And you'll comprehend that sign because it's usually obvious.

Just a couple of days ago, I was watching a fellow I know whom I'm doing a deal with right now. I'd just sent him a revised offer by fax and wanted to know what he thought about it. As I pulled him up in my mind's eye and stepped back inside him, I saw him wince and hold his nose as if he'd stepped on a dog turd. So I knew that the deal might not float, not in its current form, anyway.

Later I went back again, and I saw him throw his hands in the air. He's a nice enough bloke, but he's a bit of a dogmatic, demanding kind of guy— a real "gimme this, gimme that" type. He was reacting a bit like a spoiled child who's not getting everything he wants. I saw in his arm gestures that he'll come to the deal in the end, but he'll wrestle with his wounded ego for a bit. No doubt his fax to me will be on the machine later today or tomorrow. Interesting stuff, the etheric.

By using it, you'll pick up an indication of which is the strongest path for you, and you'll stay away from trouble and low-energy people. You'll engage your sixth sense to look inside things, people, situations, deals, organizations, etc., etc., to figure out what there is to know before you commit.

Most people are fairly weak but fairly honest, except when they're in a corner. Then there's a percentage of people who are downright scumbags. But they don't hide it, and they're okay in a strange way because they're so obviously dark that you know you should keep out of their way. But the worst sorts are the covert ones. They act righteously, but they are, in fact, closet scumbags, if the real truth be known. They are the people one turns the full force of one's perception on. You shine a light, so to speak, up their privates, and you see copious amounts of the stuff they're made of. And you do your best not to judge it too much; you just whiz off in the opposite direction even if it means you have to cut your losses and run.

Scummy people never seem to get any less scummy. In fact, the more you attend to them and give them your power by engaging them, the more they try to manipulate and use you. Remember the list of shadow traits. When you see an inkling of that expressed in the people you deal with, know that sooner or later they will turn and exhibit that side. It's so simple to comprehend. Never presume there will be an improvement—then, once in a blue moon you might be pleasantly surprised.

If you are a positive, loving person, and if you stay away from shady deals and so forth, you'll rarely become greatly entangled with scumbags, as they usually exist in a world of their own. But there are a lot of people out there, and some of the dark ones live right next door. You have to watch, and not take it personally, if the odd scumbag shows up in your life. Through the law of averages and the laws of physics, turds float. They drift around a lot, so one or two will inevitably float past your door. You just need to stay cool and distant, and establish good boundaries in your psychology. Let people know what you will tolerate and what you will not tolerate, and things should trot along quite nicely. Remember, it's not judgmental to observe a low-energy oscillation and keep silent. It's only judgment if you *vocalize* a personal judgment of it.

Now, a generalized judgment is different, so you might say, "I don't care for crack dealers. I think they cause damage to vulnerable people, and I would prefer it if they engaged in other types of commercial activity." That's different from saying, "I hate John Smith. He's a bastard and a low-life, crack-dealing scumbag, and he ought to be hung up by his testicolies." That's a judgment because it's personalized.

Onwards and upwards . . . as a part of the imagination exercises, do this: At night before you go to sleep, review the day backwards in time, from night back to dawn. Instead of just thinking about the day, go backwards through it in a mental silence, seeing the pictures of the day and noticing the feelings that were associated with those actions. This process helps you go from lots of thinking to more seeing and feeling. If something special happened today, like if you went to the races or the theater or whatever, go through those events picture by picture, feeling by feeling. Try to remember all the pictures you saw and the feelings you were a part of—"The roar of the grease paint, the smell of the crowd"—well, you know what I mean. By reviewing it all in your memory, using your visual and feeling faculties, you activate your imagination and practice your power of visioning.

Creative activities such as painting and drawing, writing descriptive stories, or even making up tales you tell to children make you engage the right brain and help with your imagination.

Then again, you can always enter a meditative state and shove your etheric around for a bit of visual practice. So let's say you're at the bus stop. Turn around within your subtle energy, as I've told you, and walk out of your body, facing backwards. Then see your subtle body leaning, say, to the right at a 45° angle; and then in the opposite direction, to the left at a 45° angle. Bring it back in front of you and lower it, slowly and deliberately, until your etheric nose is inches off the ground. Visit the ant kingdom for a bit; remind them of the danger of feet! They forget sometimes. Very dippy, ants are—one brain cell each, I'd imagine.

And take a little mirror with you as you go through the day, the kind that ladies carried around in their purses in the 1930s and '40s. See your image reflected there. Notice it carefully, and realize that that's what your etheric looks like when it's outside you—"beyond you" is a more correct way of describing it.

Now swivel the mirror quickly back and forth like you're signaling, and imagine your image quickly flying off the mirror's shiny surface to some distant spot, like the 7-Eleven across the road. Let your image help itself to your favorite snack, and imagine it coming back just in time for you to eat the snack prior to getting on the bus.

Dream odd dreams. Think up odd stuff. Let yourself invent strange stories you can amuse yourself with, stories that have good imagery. See the picture of the story in your mind's eye as you tell it to yourself. Read a bit of poetry from time to time, and feel out what the poet is saying. What pictures do the words evoke?

Just before you go to bed, run a warm bath and put lots of water in. Get a bottle of bubble bath, and pour a whole slew of it into the water. Get a manual egg whisk and whip it all up until there are suds up to the ceiling; then watch the bubbles float down the hallway. There's heaps of fun in that. Get in the bath and play and play and play. And clap your hands together real fast and watch as great columns of soap hit the ceiling, dangling there precariously, only to plop down on the cat's head a moment later. Get your mate to join you, show him or her the routine; there's a game in it, betting with your mate which dollop of soap will fall first.

Now you're warm and cozy and in bed, and you've gone through the day backwards in your mind's eye. Now you call on the "Powers That Be" to lead you to your strongest spot and to show you things this night that you don't already know. Ask the Powers to help you get from here in Soapsud Land, to over there in the Promised Land. You'll remind the Powers of your humble stance in life, and you'll mention the diligent things you've done today to help yourself and others. You'll review what you have to offer the world, and you remember that you were kind and gentle today, and that you thought about others as well as yourself. In passing, you'll mention that scrawny cow, Mrs. Higgins, who's been throwing trash over your fence, even though you've asked her a hundred times not to. You'll mention how you remembered to project love and caring and understanding to her, even though she drives you nuts, and deep down you'd like to wring the scrawny cow's neck.

And you'll fall asleep in the arms of angels, and they'll show you things, and in the morning you'll wake with those things on your mind—because you preprogrammed it that way. Before you went to bed, you remembered to tell yourself that anything important that came to you in the night would be on your mind in the morning as you wake up.

Upon arising, you'll jot these things down in your notebook and think about them. You'll take a moment to think about all the information you've received in the past, and you'll review whether you acted on it. Or did you ignore most of it? For the more you ignore the power, the more it dries up. And you might think it sensible to act on what you already know, as an affirmation that you are powerful and that you are ready for even more information.

And then you might think, *I'll have a little sit-down and a nice cup of tea,* or whatever; and then, *I'll take action next time. I'm ready now.*

HOVERING BETWEEN TWO WORLDS

Etheric Maneuvers and Other Subtle Stuff

Here's a series of hovering maneuvers. Again, you might want to write them out on a card and learn them. They can seem quite complicated until you get used to them, but eventually they become second nature.

Assuming you've got the chakras opened using the system described before, try this: Lie down with your head to the north and your feet pointing to the south. Open the chakras and really let go so you can get to a very relaxed state of low brain speed, deeply entranced. If you get to this state of relaxation, you should be able to descend to a theta rhythm (four to six cycles per second). The trick is not to fall asleep. You can tell if you're in trance, as you will find that you'll lose the sensation of your body somewhat—you can still *feel* your body, of course, but it is much less noticeable. If you have difficulty really getting down to a slow brain speed, get a theta-metronome, as I suggested earlier.

Now, once you're deeply relaxed, start by seeing yourself hovering above your body at about 18 inches. It's nothing more than willing yourself up. Don't worry about flipping out of your body—it won't happen. It takes a lot more to actually get out. So rest assured that you won't suddenly come out and disappear up the yin-yang, lost forever.

What you're trying to do is hover your etheric between our physical reality and the astral world, and then the spirit worlds beyond that. The astral world is one of discarnate entities, thought-forms, and phantasmagorical images. It doesn't have that much to teach us, but it's the first dimension you can access in the etheric-hovering state. If you do ever have a complete out-of-body experience, the first place you find yourself is in your normal surroundings, your bedroom, say. But the very next thing that happens is that you can feel the astral plane real close. Then you might become aware of holes or doorways, and they lead you out into other worlds. The etheric hovering discussed here is much easier and safer than a full OBE. It doesn't limit you one bit in my view; you can still see and hear and fcel things that you never knew existed.

The astral world is right here, permeating the lattice of our physical reality. As far as I can tell, it's this side (the Earth side) of the near-death tube, unlike the fairy kingdoms, which seem to be this side of the tube and beyond the tube as well. The point of the hovering process is not so much to access the astral, but learning to open up and let go. As humans, we have a very natural fear of the unknown.

Also, hovering the etheric over the body in a trance state, if done successfully, helps you loosen it, empowering its energy with velocity. One enlivens it by moving it around. The more energy in the etheric, the more lively your life and the more healthy you are.

So now you're hovering over your body, slightly above the physical but not totally out of it. Now try reversing yourself; it's an etheric pole-shift. By that I mean, turn your etheric head down to the south where your feet are, and allow your etheric feet to rotate to the north where your head is. It was after this maneuver that I once tried to turn myself inside out. Don't bother with that just yet—as I said before, it didn't work. Ya learn as ya go.

Next, rotate yourself etherically back the other way, with your head back to the north and your etheric feet to the south once more. Now, hovering over your body again, log-roll off to the right toward the west, say, five or ten yards, or as far as the etheric will let you go. Once out there, notice where you are, then log-roll yourself back to the center, over your body. Then head off in the opposite direction toward the east, twisting as you go. After a moment or so, come back to the center and rest.

Now take a bubble of light up from the root chakra, and push it through the top of your head. Try reaching up behind you to establish a new position for your head, an elongated one, perhaps a yard farther back than your head would normally be. Next, go to your feet, push through the soles, and stretch your legs out. Now you'll establish your etheric legs a yard longer than your physical legs.

Return your concentration to the elongated head point, and in your mind's eye, sweep along the floor or bed to your left, making a wide curved arc from your new head position to the new position of your etheric feet. Once you arrive at the elongated position of your etheric feet, make another wide arc from there up the right side, and you'll arrive back at the elongated head position. Next, make huge arcs over the top of your body, going from the new elongated position of your head to the elongated position of your feet, then do the same under your body through the bed or floor so the arc is underneath you.

Once you have delineated the arcs, they become your new imaginary expanded boundary. Now you want to fill them out with your etheric. Do this by breathing in slowly and seeing yourself blowing up like a balloon— so that you gradually fill the arcs with your etheric presence. Once filled, hold your breath and concentration on them as long as possible, then breathe out and allow yourself to come back to your normal size. Do that three times: filling the arcs, creating the expansion, and coming back to normal. Then rest.

Next, go back to the hovering position 18 inches above your body, and see if you can get your etheric to rock back and forth. Imagine that you're rocking a cradle gently, left to right and back again. The etheric may begin to rock back and forth of its own accord, but if it doesn't, try to see if you can give it a mental push by *willing* it to do so. The movement is a good thing. It shows that you're not too stiff, nor holding on too tightly.

Now you need to establish more distance. Remember that spreading yourself is the key. Imagine standing up forcefully, as if you're hinged at your feet. Send an image of yourself forward 10 or 20 yards. See the image as larger than the normal you, and place that character out there in the distance in front of you. In your mind's eye, give it a pen and a piece of paper, and instruct it to write lines over and over, such as, "I promise not to interfere in your life anymore." The large figure that you place forward represents the ego/intellect. Now you're keeping it busy, writing lines on a piece of paper.

Come back with your concentration, and while still hovering over your body; imagine a very small version of you, an inch or two tall, coming out of the crown chakra. It's your inner child. Send it, via a short breath or just with the force of your will, behind you off into the distance to play somewhere. Now you've spread yourself out. The intellect to the south, writing lines; the inner child behind you to the north, playing. Meanwhile, you're hovering over your body in the middle, expressed inside several enormous arcs from your expanded head to your stretched-out feet.

Now, in the expanded hovering state, you'll want to move the etheric around some more. At this point, your etheric body is facing the ceiling. Rotate it slowly so that it is now facing downwards—your etheric is face-to-face with your physical face, inches from your nose. Then twist it quickly back around the other way so it's facing the ceiling once more. Now try to have it sit up at the waist. Then lie it down again and see if you can stretch it by reaching with your imaginary etheric arms for the corners of the room. It doesn't really matter if you get there or not; it's in the trying to stretch that you exercise the force field.

One of the old texts suggested not drinking any liquid for several hours before trying these types of exercises, and taking a teaspoon of salt just prior to starting in order to induce thirst. They suggested that you leave a jug of water on the other side of the room. The idea is that your thirst will propel you etherically over to the water. If you suffer from heart problems or high blood pressure, I wouldn't recommend this one, but if you don't have these problems, it's an interesting exercise to try.

From time to time, take a new bubble from the root, and fire it up to your head and let it descend back to the root as before. This keeps the channels open. Then drop down and hover back inside the physical, and see if you can will your etheric legs to drop through the floor. This one is fairly easy, especially if you're really entranced. You will usually feel your etheric legs bending either from the hips or from the knees, and dropping a foot or so down through the bed or floor.

I used to rent an apartment on the second floor of a four-story house. When I did this exercise, I'd often wonder what would happen if a sensitive, psychic type ever lived downstairs. They might freak out when they saw two legs dropping through their ceiling. In fact, below me were a couple of young Japanese students. I didn't imagine them as psychic types. All was well.

Also, from time to time, clear the channels by shooting a bubble from root to crown, relax, and let go—then try this: Imagine that you have a set of elongated arms. Reach up with one arm, and enter your body through your heart chakra and take hold of your physical heart; feel it beating in your hand. If you do this properly, you will notice how precious you are, and what an incredible gift and learning experience your life has been so far. Next, remove your arm from inside your chest, and reach up to the top of your head. Go down through the crown chakra, extend that arm downwards deep within you, and see if you can get your inner spirit to take hold of your etheric hand. Tell it what you're going to do before you do it. Sometimes you'll feel your etheric hand being lightly clenched by your spirit identity. It's an awesome experience; if you can't feel it, just imagine it. Then, expel a fast, very vigorous breath, and scream in a loud voice, "Go!"

Your etheric and your spirit will fly off through the top of your head; you'll travel etherically to the borders of other worlds. It's not an out-of-body experience; it's more like an etheric stretching so that you're in another more distant area of your nonlocal etheric field. In my seminars, I'd set the participants up in a deep meditative state, and etherically they would get to the "spirit-grabbing" point, and when I intuitively felt they were ready, I'd fire a starter pistol. Through the shock of the sudden noise, their brain cells would fire a very deep theta spike, the brain waves instantly slowed, and because of the jolt, they would be ejected (maybe *catapulted* is a better word) to the edge of one or more nearby dimensions. About 25 to 30 percent of participants would etherically hear angelic voices in song—sometimes female; sometimes altos; on rare occasions, men's voices—singing sacred verses.

Of course, if you're on your own, a starter pistol might be a problem, although you could have it in one hand while in trance and fire it at the appropriate moment. But perhaps it might be best to stay with the fast-breath "Go" method if alone. Those pistols are real loud. If it goes off too close to your body, it can damage your ears. Your own "Go!" will do the job just fine.

I was presenting a seminar once in Canberra, the Australian capital. I decided to give the lecture from the back of the hall while the participants faced the front. So, in effect, I was talking to the backs of their heads. They had to remain motionless for 50 minutes, staring down at a coin in their hand. This was a variation of a method Pythagoras used; he hid behind a screen.

I had the starter pistol on the podium, which I'd moved to the back of the room, and at a critical moment in the session, the pistol slipped off, hit my foot, and went off. The flash burned my shoe and, being unprepared and so close to the noise, I couldn't hear properly for several minutes. In fact, I am a bit deaf in one ear because of another starter-pistol accident several years later. Anyway, what was real fun in Canberra was the fact that the Prime Minister of Australia, in those days, Bob Hawke, was in the next suite at the hotel attending some function. When the starter pistol went off, half-a-dozen security personnel—the dudes in the dark-shades-with-the-earpieces—were at my door pronto, asking questions. Picture it—six armed guards come through the door at the front of the seminar room, the participants motionless, eyes open, staring down at a coin, me talking to the backs of their heads. My shoe's black, the pistol's on the floor, the carpet looks like it's smoldering, and meanwhile I'm trying to dispatch a couple-of-hundred spiritual seekers to another world—what a scream! Life on the road is so bizarre sometimes! Maybe you shouldn't mess with the pistol. Scrub that.

There's heaps of stuff you can do once you've got the hovering sorted out. Try this: Raise your right physical arm at the elbow, and open your hand so the palm is facing east. Grab a bubble of light from the root, bring it out of your heart chakra, and move it out of your body so it is hovering just in front of the palm of your hand. Now tell it you're going to breathe out sharply and you want it to circumnavigate the earth and return to you. Expel a fast breath to shoot it off, wait a split second, and you'll feel it hit the back of your upraised hand once it returns. It's cute, this one.

As we are in bubble-firing mode, you might now want to try the method I described earlier, whereby you fire a bubble at someone to check them out. You are looking to see how the bubble responds when it hits them—does it splat out or what? Pick a few people and work on them one at a time.

After you've finished with some of these maneuvers, place yourself once more in the hovering mode just above your body; really clear your mind and let go. Watch and see if anything comes to you. It may not at first, as you may resist letting go because of fear, or perhaps you're still too stiff and controlling in the way you handle your life. Most people need practice to allow themselves this kind of etheric vulnerability, but it comes bit by bit as you let go of the intellectual handrail of life.

Using the trance state and the hovering mode was how I found the near-death tube. You don't have to pass out on a surgery table to get there; you just have to induce the same type of near-death scenario using trance instead of a medical trauma. So watch and see what happens, and remember to pull things to you rather than trying reach for them.

As I said, in the spirit worlds, you don't seem to *travel* to places, they come and get you. It's a part of the mirror phenomenon of those worlds; push is pull and vice versa. That's why pushing for goals in the real world is a big farce. You *pull* your goals to you—never push emotionally, because they retreat.

I'd better clarify a point here: The astral world of ghosts and phantasmagorical entities is not, in my view, a spirit world, even though it is a dimension of consciousness and it does have spirits in it. What makes it different is that it is this side of the near-death tube—the Earth side. I have never gotten the impression that the astral world is mirrored to us. I think the rotation that creates the mirror effect of the spirit worlds takes place once one is at the other end of the near-death tube, and those worlds beyond the tube are the ones I refer to as spirit worlds.

I suppose the nearby world of ghosts was called the astral world by early writers, since it is the first dimension you see in the out-of-body state. However, it is a confusing term, as *astral* means "of the stars," and that nearby dimension is definitely not out there in the heavens. It is right here in the room, inside our physical reality, between the molecules of our solid world. So a ghost from the astral plane can walk through solid walls. That's one of the reasons I think the Grays are astral in nature, as they operate between molecules in the same way ghosts do. That's also why I came to believe that the astral plane is this side of the near-death tube, compared to spirit worlds that are at the other end of the tube.

Some of the entities in the astral plane are a bit spooky, but if you master the etheric hovering, you'll never need to get out of your body—so they can't really trouble you. And you will still be able to see a long way into the other worlds without ever leaving your body. In many ways, the etheric hovering is analogous to an astronomer using a telescope to peer at objects far away in space. The astronomer never leaves home; the telescope brings the images to him or her.

In the etheric state, the perceptional crunch comes because we are used to reality and light coming to us at a certain speed. Yet visions and symbols from those inner worlds come right up the center of your inner sight at a very high speed—much faster than you're normally used to, and too fast for you to stop and concentrate on them. That's why the three-card trick I mentioned is important; it trains you to remember the knock of light that reality makes—not the object itself. The visions you see in the hovering state need much the same ability as the three-card exercise. They knock against the back of your mind so fast that you don't have time to look at them properly; you have to remember them from the residue of the intrinsic light of the vision that it leaves in your brain.

The point of these etheric exercises and techniques is to get you to a more enlivened state and teach you to perceive subtle energy that is moving fast. But they also have the function of getting you to see that inside each world there is another, and then another; and that there really are "many mansions in my father's house," as the Bible says.

These etheric exercises are designed to show you how to loosen up and stretch for the zero point in the center of the pyramid's floor—the doorway to the other worlds, which I mentioned earlier. If you need an extra boost, there is a short section at the end of the book in the appendix. It describes a technique using two mirrors at right angles that allows you to see yourself beyond the zero point.

But right now I think we should talk about the practical application of intuition and the sixth sense. All this woo-woo "other-world" stuff is fun, and hopefully informative, but there is a point on your journey when you will want to haul the proceeds of your sixth-sense faculty 'round to the bank. That's even more fun.

TAKING INNER
KNOWING TO THE BANK

You probably know if you've read my other books that I talk about aligning to whatever creative energy you wish: the greatest artists, musicians, talented athletes, and so on. It is just a matter of concentrating on them, learning about them, and entering into their energy field at a subtle level. It's not a personal intrusion; it is more a case of aligning to the creative splendor of their lives by studying them—watching them on TV, perhaps. By reading about these individuals and emulating them, you become familiar with them; then you can use the process whereby you "reverse into them via the etheric," as discussed before.

It is much like putting on an overcoat made of the legend's energy, imbued with their creativity and wonderfulness—or their ability on the playing field or whatever. In your mind's eye, you bring your hero/heroine close to you so he/she is standing in front of you, then just reverse back into them and try to feel out what it is about them that makes them special. To be creative, they would be tapping into their subconscious and inner knowing, so you walk into that subtle part of them, aligning to what it is they know that you as yet don't know. It's a nice meditative exercise—aligning to the creative talent of others as a way of affirming the creative splendor inside you.

To reach the height of your possibility, you have to push past the negative shadow and access the positive shadow, as discussed. It helps if you align to a truly positive view of your life. Most people think they are positive, but if you played a recording of their dialogue back to them, they would be shocked to see how much deep-rooted uncertainty and negativity is laced into their everyday attitudes—and the way they talk about themselves and life.

I mention it briefly, as it's all part of polishing up your act. Many a creative idea and moneymaking opportunity may be undermined by a subtle, contradictory energy emanating from you, like a trickle of water leaking from a pipe deep in the basement. Such an energy leak destroys your ability to empower an idea to its proper conclusion, and thwarts any kind of commercial return.

You should start by maintaining a clear and disciplined way of talking about yourself and your life. Never use words such as *pain, hard, difficult, terrible,* and so on. How many times do we use deflating and derogatory terms when speaking casually? "I'm dying for a drink. . . . It's a pain in the rear end. . . . It's hard getting a job. . . . Life's a rip-off. . . . What terrible weather we're having," and so on. Then there are all the subtle put-downs you inflict upon yourself. Not just your self-deprecating thoughts of, say, a lack of self-worth or self-confidence, but those instances when you vocalize inadequacy. So often you hear people say, "I am useless at this . . . hopeless at that . . . Nothing ever works . . . I'm accident-prone . . ." etc. If you have an internal disquietude, you can work on it over time, but you should realize that, by vocalizing it, you accentuate it and make it more real.

Start by developing a perpetually, ridiculously optimistic view of yourself and life even when things are at their worst. So when people ask, "What are your expectations?" never say, "I'm not sure . . . I don't know . . . I'll do the best I can . . . Let's hope and pray . . . It's in the lap of the gods." Be definite and powerful, and expect the best. More important, vocalize your positive expectations. When others express a negative expectation, saying, for example, "I don't see much chance of this working. . . ." or whatever, contradict that. Say, "Of course it will work. I'm sure we'll get a good result." Sound helps to create our reality: "In the beginning was the word. . . ."— what we say is eventually what we experience.

An Inner Pole Shift

The deeper understanding of this concept leads one to the faculty of auditory clairvoyance. That is the ability of your psychic power, or your nonlocal greater knowing, to talk to you via inner dialogue. The problem with the clairaudient faculty is that it is often mixed in with one's everyday mental mutterings. And these may be so cluttered with confusion and negative sentiments that you can't tell what's inner knowing and what's low-grade drivel.

What you are going to do, over a period of time, is to first quiet the mind via meditation and introspection, then eventually flip your inner dialogue over to the opposite polarity. It's a pole shift in your energy. Here's the concept in principle—you'll be able to work it out for yourself. One's normal inner dialogue is all pondering, wondering, and negative wave pulses; with a large dollop of confusion, guessing, and speculation. Negative dialogue and uncertainty, mixed with a low self-image and self-deprecating sentiments, cloud the auditory version of your inner knowing. You can't tell what is accurate information and what is just your mind sticking its nose in as usual.

It is very rare that a person has a naturally positive inner voice. Many people have developed—through training or just naturally—a totally positive external expression of self, meaning that they don't voice negative sentiments when talking to others. This is a good thing. It's the first part of the process, because a cheery outward dialogue, devoid of uncertainty and negative sentiments, helps you a great deal inwardly. The second part is flipping the inner voice from negative uncertainty to total positivity.

That takes a sustained effort. It's done by pushing constantly against the negative inner voice over a period of time, until you control your inner dialogue to such an extent that a positive energy within you takes on critical mass—that is, it makes up more than half of the total output from your memory/psychology. Eventually, when that happens, a polarity shift suddenly takes place inside you—your inner voice flips over, going from partially or totally negative, to being 100 percent positive all the time. No more inner doubts or self-deprecating sentiments.

Once the inner pole shift has occurred, you will have altered the electromagnetic polarity of your etheric. Then you'll find that the inner voice countermands your intellect's stance on things. It's real cute to watch. So your intellect may have doubts over an issue, but the inner voice knows, and it says, "It will be fine, go ahead." Or when it needs to instruct you on possible difficulty or uncertainty, it doesn't operate with negative dialogue or dire warnings. Instead, it expresses itself equitably, saying in a positive way something like, "See this person here, Ducky? The one you are talking to right now, here in this alley behind the grocery store? This person has an energy level that is less than one. Please notice and accept this timely information, and please vote with your feet. Like split, Ducky, like er . . . .right now would be best. Thanks.''

I can't say I know when the mental pole-shift might take place for you. Perhaps it already has. But if it hasn't, the idea is to get the process going so that you're reaching for it, developing critical mass, and heading for a new place—a dimension of love and positive ways. If you can make even part of the journey right now, it will make an enormous difference. For as the mental pole-shift approaches, there comes a new energy—a big one. And with that energy comes even more perception, and a heightened sixth sense of all kinds, especially the auditory kind.

For in the negative worry of life, you cloud the etheric, and you set up imploding waves in the field—waves that are tumbling in on you, curving back toward you. Negative emotion creates rolling waves of energy that ripple through the etheric—moving downwards, for the most part, toward the floor. Those waves carry energy away from the crown chakra and all-knowing, and away from the heart. That is why you lose your sensitivity, intuition, compassion, and your sense of love when suffering negative emotion. The rolling waves also burn up and waste energy, imploding and folding and tumbling as they do—that's why worry and negative emotion tire you out. The downward-rolling waves heading toward the ground are detrimental. They pull energy away from the seat of your perception and power: the third eye and the crown chakra. It's hard to get your head sorted out when you're an emotional mess—because the energy of your etheric is flowing chaotically, the wrong way, toward your feet. So at the very moment that you're upset and need to have all your guns blazing on an energy level, you're actually doing the opposite. You're carrying yourself down to a slower oscillation as the etheric flows downwards, toward the lower chakras and on to the ground at your feet.

If you are a female in an intimate relationship with a male, you might have noticed that your mate always seems to want "quick sex" when he's tired or has had a hectic, stressful day. Have you ever wondered why? It seems contradictory. You'd imagine that if your partner is very tired, it would be the least likely time for him to feel sexy and want to approach you.

In the emotion and the battles of the day, your partner rolls endless tidal waves of energy down to, through, and past the root chakra, so the chakra becomes activated and overloaded with energy. That's why many men are workaholics; it's partly a sexual, power thing, and, of course, overwork is one way people distract themselves from the effects of fear.

Once your partner stops work, comes home, and is not occupied by activity, he'll subliminally notice the kundalini energy at the root chakra. But he's too tired to relate to you properly, or to express much caring-and-sharing energy in your direction. And as often as not, he won't want to make sure you're stimulated or up for it—he just needs to rearrange his energy quickly. In the sex act, he dissipates a part of the day's rolling-etheric effect, and he will hopefully have your energy to assist him in firing his etheric back up to the crown.

The energy rises within the man partly because the woman will push it sexually and emotionally upwards, but it will mostly rise because a man cannot ejaculate easily without a mental picture in his head that stimulates him to orgasm. The early part of the sex act with his partner warms the power, moving it around. But it is in the ejaculation that some of the overload of energy at the root chakra is dissipated, and some is fired upwards, returning the etheric to a more balanced look. Then the male rests and recuperates, he relaxes or sleeps, and all the energy goes back to normal. It doesn't seem to work the other way for women. Usually when they're tired, they want to rest and nurture themselves, and sex is the last thing on their minds. I suppose it's part of the yin and yang of things.

Silent Talking

To recapitulate, in order to make the energy work for you, you have to get to the totally positive inner voice, and simultaneously use your sensitivity to make life easier for you. So, for example, if you are trying to convince someone about a deal, you can offer them your logic and explain the benefits of the idea, but the easiest way to win them over is to work internally first. It's a form of silent talking.

Bring them up in your mind's eye, and project the idea you want them to consider. Say you want your friend Harry to lend you his car so you can go fishing. You project the idea forward into his etheric identity, which you've brought up in your mind's eye, so it's now standing in front of you. So when you get around to actually asking him, he knows it's coming on an inner level, and the idea doesn't sound weird or new. When he's in front of you etherically, he may answer your request mentally from his nonlocal subconscious right then and there. He might say, "No, you can't have my car. I'm angry." So ask him mentally, "Why?" Listen for his reply. Maybe it is, "I am angry because you never returned my lawnmower." Now you know what tack to take. Return the mower quickly, take a six-pack of beer, and go overboard with your gratitude. Then leave it for a couple of hours so he's had time to settle—or better still, wait until the next day—then ask for his car.

When you're in a business meeting, you can offer silent ideas and thoughts to your associates and customers, offering them concepts you want them to appraise and accept. It's no different from actually talking to them, except that you're in silent world of the etheric, with your mind centered. Just look at the person. I usually stare at their left temple, just on the side of the eye. You gently push a thought into their mind, projecting it forward while you slightly lean toward them. You can, if you wish, fire the thought up via their root chakra to their crown. You do that by visualizing the thought in a bubble of energy and firing it by expelling a short, sharp breath. I deal with this particular technique, "turbo thought," I call it, at length in my book *The Quickening,* so I won't go over it again here.

Your special thought may say, for example, "This is an effective product. . . . This is safe. . . . This is beneficial," or whatever. It is understood that there is a perpetual communication going on between humans, silently at the subconscious and etheric level. The only difference is that, instead of that dialogue being random, you're *directing* it. If the people involved are dead-set against your ideas, you won't be able to shift them anyway. So offering the inner dialogue is a way of oiling the wheels, but it can't make a person do something that goes against their nature or their innermost beliefs.

Part of the sixth sense is knowing how to use your feelings. It's not a complex thing. It's nothing more than just projecting, from your heart, a feeling of safety and serenity. In a business meeting, you may be intellectually giving people a logical reason why they should buy your product, but perhaps deep down, your feelings are resonating disquietude and imbalance. Let's say you're not sure if the factory is going to deliver, or you don't feel worthy to receive the commission involved in such a big order. Or perhaps, deep down, you hate the customer. Those feelings are being transmitted, and the other people may be picking up on your subtle energy, intellectually or subliminally.

Just be aware of what subtle feelings you're projecting. Keep sending out warmth and safety. Remember, when people part with their money, they're giving up what they perceive is a part of their security—they have to feel safe to buy things. People only make purchases when the thing they are buying is more valuable to them than the security the cash in their pocket offers.

So as you move your energy upward, you have to police your feelings and thoughts to make sure they're not at odds with the situation. If you project fear and lack, others will become nervous, and the deal will fall through. So a positive dialogue is good, but positive thoughts and warm feelings are the real keys to success.

Trusting Your Feelings

I've never been much into the share markets—"shocks and scares," as I call them. But the bull-markets of recent times attracted me. So I gave it a go, knowing very little about the stock market. I started with $120,000, and within about six months I'd made $75,000. Now my account was worth almost $200,000. A friend that I trust told me about a technology stock that was a good bet, so I took a huge plunge, and I put three-quarters of my money in it: $150,000.

Everything was fine for a few months, then things suddenly went pear-shaped. A group of bad guys got into the company and ripped it off for $6 million. The fraud squad was called in. A boardroom war developed, the good guys lost the battle, and the stock became worthless overnight. My broker called to commiserate. I told him about the eternal Tao, and I said, "Up and down are like light and dark, just two versions of the same energy." He wondered why I wasn't throwing myself off the roof, doing a little "fast down" heading toward the pavement from a great height. My broker doesn't understand the finer points of metaphysics.

Now here's the good bit. I looked into my feelings, and I was positive and sure and definite that my mate, the one who got me into the technology stock, was a good guy and that he'd be right in the end. So I hung in there. Some weeks later, meditating on the subject, I had a vision. In it I saw a very beautiful, placid lake covered in a morning mist; it was so serene and lovely.

A split second later, there was a roar, something stirred from deep within the waters of the lake, and suddenly an enormous castle shot up out of the center of the lake, millions of gallons of water pouring off its roof, its battlements covered with weeds. The castle came up out of the water so fast that I was shocked at the speed of it all.

Prior to getting into stocks, I had the idea to make some quick money. I wanted to buy a castle in Europe and reestablish the energy of the legend of Camelot, with all its pageantry and esoteric mystery and the whole nine yards! I saw that the lake vision was saying, "Hang in there, Stewie. When it comes, it will come very quickly."

So I felt it all out and got a certain recommendation from the vision: that my mate was right and the technology mess was just a bit of bad luck that can happen sometimes. I decided to go with the flow and plug away. Some weeks later, my pal called to give me a recommendation on a weird, completely unknown Australian mining stock. I bought it because of the vision and because it felt right. It only traded at two Australian cents, so I wound up with three million shares.

Nothing happened for a while. My mate told me to hang in there, and I believed him because of the castle vision. Anyway, a while later he called again and said that the Aussie outfit had a sister company—he told me to buy that as well. So I borrowed on margin from my broker, who's a good guy, and I bought 200,000 shares in the sister company at 36 Australian cents.

Now I was totally tapped out. A stock operator with no cash, heaps of margin, loads of outrageous utterly out-to-lunch optimism, a vision, and great chunks of the Australian desert bought for virtually nothing. Not to mention a mate who was kind of a spirit guide to me. Yet it all felt okay to me—better than okay.

The parent company started ticking up. Not long after, the sister company went ballistic, jumping 20, 30 cents a day. Then the parent company ticked up some more, and in a very short space of time, I mean, two to three weeks, everything went megaballistic. My portfolio went up like the Concord on take-off. Almost vertical!

I went from struggling and a big loan to $553,000. I made half-a-million in 14 trading days! Smiling, man, smiling. I'm thinking, stock operator, cool, cool sideline, very cool.

"Tiddly om pom pom—the sixth sense is my chum!"

Now half-a-million won't get you a castle, but it will get you a draw-bridge, a moat, and a few turrets—and that's more than I had before I started.

The point is, if your dreams don't come to you right away, and if you mess it up a bit at first through lack of experience, don't worry. Up and down are just two sides of the same coin, and sometimes life tests you to see if you're all hot air. Or do you really believe in your visions? Are you a warrior or a worrier, (as author Martin Wetherill says in his books)? Are you a tiger or a mouse?

Remember this: As part of standing tall and developing your money-making ability and creative potential, you have to have the courage to embrace yourself and who you are. You are your own statement, your own calling card. It is you. And you have to *believe*, even if the calling card is a bit dog-eared right now. Even if your castle is still a long way off. Things can happen overnight when the energy is right.

Now here's another thing to clear out of the way. More often than not, we limit our creative potential because we feel we have to win other people's approval. We feel the need to justify ourselves, to fit in. We feel the need to be accepted. Yes, you might have to adjust to the vagaries of the marketplace, but you don't want to disempower yourself by being too shy or too timid, or letting others limit your dream. You are what you are. Look 'em in the eye and tell 'em, "This is who I am." Then be flexible, especially when there's money floating about!

I think the biggest culprits in the process of holding you back are, more often than not, family members. Because of their closeness to you, they can impact how you feel and can have a major influence on you. Often family members have an agenda of their own. They want to keep you where you are, or they don't want you showing them up as being inadequate. Or they don't want you heading out and leaving them back at the ranch looking up the back end of a thousand sheep! But in the end, your life is precious, and you can't necessarily keep everyone happy. You have to do your own thing.

Part of the art of developing the spiritual self, and inner knowing, is having the courage to know what it is that you do believe. You don't have to have the path laid out for you, tick-tock all the way for the next 50 years. You just have to know that you have the strength to go to the next step, and that you have the courage to follow through and hang in there. Of course, once you embark on the journey, more often than not there is no turning back.

As your consciousness grows, you become exhilarated by the flow of the God Force in your life. With every little burst of new energy comes new perceptions and original creativity, and there's no way you're going back to the old ways.

The problem is, people tend to follow along for a while, then they come up against a boundary—the boundary of their knowledge or the boundary of what they feel as a social being. Or, perhaps, they don't feel they're entitled to more. They may feel inadequate because they come from a very humble social background. Maybe they don't speak the language of success, so they feel inferior.

Don't let these hangups hold you back. Hop over them, and push against your comfort zones. It's easy enough to do. You just have to invent a series of actions or exercises you will perform, ones that force you to test your comfort zone.

A standard one is: If you're scared of public speaking, agree to give a lecture. If you're scared of heights, go rock climbing. Your comfort zone is an illusion. It's there because the ego is there, and the ego defines your position. But you're not a defined being—you're an infinite being—and your influence and perception are potentially infinite. You can pull information, money, and opportunities from all over the planet. You're not limited to just the family ways, or the tribal influence, or the group soul of the local tick-tock rhythm. How much of the force do you believe is possible? Lots and lots!

Most people one meets are fairly tight. They are usually either very meek, or they don't express themselves in a solid way. Or, they do believe in themselves, but they get hung up on silly points of the ego's argument. They don't see themselves as a fluid, caring, sharing, high-velocity being; they get bogged down in lack and the day-to-day politics of life.

A part of the function of the spiritual journey, the search for the Holy Grail within, is coming to a fine balance, a point of compassion in your heart. It's being able to reconcile your own needs, fears, and insecurities so that you can become bigger and have energy left over for the benefit of others. Part of bigness is generosity and caring. It's a form of tithing on an energy level: "I am silently big, so I have energy to give away"—that's the affirmation.

In our modern society, people are small and tight and insecure, and they have little time for others. How often have you been in a conversation with friends who are just yakking on about their life, their acquisitions, their job, their feelings, and their relationships? You can see they're self-obsessed.

So part of developing this sixth-sense spirituality within you is developing a magnanimous goodness within you that supports others with kindness and compassion. It is by being kind and supportive and loving that you reach the ultimate God Force within yourself. The God Force is the most kick-ass sixth-sense tool you have seen. A few dollops of that and you'll be the wizard on the mount. Pronto!

When you're with friends, as a part of your ever-developing perception and sensuality, rather than talking, become a listener. Ask questions that you want to hear the answers to. Don't just ask out of politeness. Someone might ask you, "How's the fishing going?" but they don't actually want to know. They just ask from a social standpoint. But when you're with people, make it a discipline to empathize with them; really care and relate to them at the subtle level of our humanity. When you ask them a question, look them in the eye, be there for them, and silently place your etheric hand on their heart chakra. There is a subtlety in it. You're not just looking at their physical form or relating from shared ego-based ideals. You're entering inside their humanity, inside their infinite etheric self, watching their eyes and lips move, watching the slightest shift of expression while they talk about their fishing trip. Now, the story of their fishing trip might be a long-winded bore, but it's part of your discipline to listen. The way you become more perceptive is to watch the world silently, without comment, forcing your concentration to lock on to an action or someone talking, without your mind interjecting. It's the act of stopping the mind once more.

It's part of your discipline to be loving and compassionate and to be there for others. It makes sense; you want more energy in your life so you'll have to offer more energy to others. In the act of service, you're standing strong and encouraging others; you naturally come inside a special sense of self—one that is wrapped in the spirituality in all things. It's an affirmation that says that you are the silent wizard. No one will ever know what it is that you know, but that is where the power lies, in the silence.

I make a point of hiding behind my "crazy guy" image; it's a persona that has allowed me endless silent progress. There is nothing contradictory or sneaky about that. You offer people an image they can understand, and you hide away the silent part of you that others may find weird or threatening. Offering people one view and living behind another allows you endless freedom. Sure, people will bad-mouth you and say you're a rat, but if you develop energy and perception they may say that anyway because your very presence pushes up against the fragility of their ego-based image of self. Deep within, they know you could tear them down and expose them, and because you can, you never will. You have to have compassion for their silliness, as it's not hugely different from your own. Anyway, he who draws the sword is lost. He who walks away is the winner, on an energy level anyway.

Remember, you are not short of energy, money, ideas, generosity, or anything else. You have an oversupply of everything at your fingertips, even if right now things are a little sparse. No matter the current reality, there's a mind-boggling amount of everything, and you are a part of it. You're in the line waiting to step up and collect, so you can enjoy it for yourself and offer it to others as well.

Now you can open the door and allow yourself to be more spiritually vulnerable. Most cut themselves off from the power because they're too deeply inside the ego, wrestling with their fears and pain. Often they're too mean and too small and too sick to become infinite.

It's very fashionable nowadays for everybody to be in some kind of childhood pain or past-life trauma. They've been abused and used, and as soon as you sit down next to them they have to tell you about it. Of course, it's good for them to be releasing their pain, but in our society there aren't enough listeners. It seems that there are more pained people than there are happy listeners.

Get rid of the pain, pronto. The emotions wreck your etheric, wobbling it, and that messes up your chances and your perception. It forces you to dive down a black hole within yourself, one that is often a bit self-indulgent. You can't see properly from down a hole.

The simplest and easiest way to go beyond your pain is by working on and concentrating on your strengths. I know that psychologists will tell you that you have to take your wounds, your inner-child traumas, and the various psychological fractures within you to a therapist, who will help you identify them. Then you have to relive them in your mind's eye and act them out, thereby releasing them. There's nothing wrong with that system, but it has one drawback. By dredging it all up and talking about it, the ego rises up because it's being noticed, and it focuses on the injustice of it all. The ol' ego hops up on its righteous soapbox, beating its chest, calling for attention and sympathizers: "Look at me, what a horrible life I've had. I need help and care and special treatment. I need attention, and people should commiserate with me and cut me a lot of slack . . ." blah, blah, yawn, yawn.

It's hard to finally get rid of your past experiences when you have to dredge them up twice weekly for the therapist. It takes years and lots of moolah, and it stops you from going forward at any decent speed. As you regress back to the dimension and time frames of childhood, or when things happened to you in the past, you stall, treading water, locked in a time-regressed warp of the memory for as long as it takes. Age regression that comes with inner-child work can make you very dysfunctional when it comes to outer, grown-up stuff like getting on with life and making a living.

Time passes, and all you're doing is *dis-ease*. You can grow old sitting in a puddle of pain. Love affairs, fascinating experiences, and great opportunities go elsewhere, saying, "He's in a smoky fug of his own; we'll come back later—much later—like the next incarnation, or maybe the one after that. Maybe he'll be ready for new opportunities then. Right now he's too busy with all his old stuff; better to leave him alone."

There's a middle road. Yes, hire a therapist, go into your childhood, rediscover and understand what happened, release the trauma, set yourself on the healing curve, and then drop it. If it goes on too long, you'll lose your momentum energywise. If you can't work it out with a good therapist in about six months of regular visits, then something is wrong, and maybe you're using the therapy as a crutch. Or, maybe they're using you as a meal ticket. It's our karma as humans to suffer setbacks; we seem to be innocent victims of life, yet we can't know in the infinity of things why certain events happened. Maybe there's a certain justice in it all that we just don't comprehend as yet.

Whatever the answer, you need to give yourself time to comprehend your childhood stuff and then go beyond it. As I said, at the age of ten I was sent away from home to a distant land at a time when there were no jets. I had to become a grown-up and fend for myself before I was ready to cope. It produced in me a sense of futility and abandonment—that was part of the downside. The other part of it was that it made me grandiose. I was the small child acting out grand fantasies to stop myself from being too scared. The upside of my abandonment karma was that it made me inventive and hardworking, as I had no security behind me to back me if I faltered. The grandiose side got me into trouble at first, as I was always way out of my depth. But in the end, I came to comprehend it, and I saw how it had helped me dream a big dream.

From weakness comes strength. Perhaps your karma has led you to where your life has a new meaning as you help others go through the healing curve because of the experiences you went through. Understand your karma and your pain, then file it. Come to serenity, detach, and work on your strengths. Bit by bit, the pain of your life goes away. We didn't come here for a perfect life. I wish we did, but we didn't. We came to learn. Each one of us was given something we had to go beyond. That is the nature of the journey—working on oneself to go past weakness to reach the Holy Grail within. You'll get there.

As you become more equitable within yourself, and more compassionate and open, you'll be in touch with the yin softness of life, and it's in your soft nature that you find the creative impulse—whether your interest is films, acting, painting, computer programming, sports, healing, or whatever. The inventiveness you can bring to those activities comes from the softness of the creative subconscious self and the centered disciplined mind. Through that serenity, one touches back into the God Force and the collective unconscious. Therein dwells the all-knowing. stepping back within, and knowing and believing that anything is possible.

As you begin to come from that magnanimous creative self, you're going to start to think in terms of the subtlety of who you are. It's not just an issue of how you will make ends meet or how you will vibrate an extrasensory power, but you want to start thinking in terms of how you will serve humanity.

As part of the sacred journey, each one of us has to take time out and serve. We can't just live in a world of self-aggrandizement, moneymaking, and issues of self. We have to serve to understand ourselves and to come to fruition in this human evolution. It's part of defining your purpose in life—claiming your power and having the courage to create limitless expectations and follow-through.

It's sad that many suffer from not having a purpose in life. But you can see how the problem comes about. Experiencing the activity of life, the ego-personality burns itself out; there is nothing more for it to do. Some settle for that and they carry on, accumulating bits and bobs. Nothing much makes them happy, and then they go on to another evolution. Others fling themselves on the spiritual path, which works for a while, but even that peters out, as there are only so many books and seminars and temples you can trot around before you find yourself beyond it all.

In the end, you have to become your own teacher, and you have to find something that has real meaning. It's part of understanding and expressing the God Force flowing through you. Discovering meaning is not a divine right; we each have to work to discover it. You win "meaning in life" as a special prize by creating energy. A lack of meaning is often a sign of a burnt-out mind that needs a new inspiration. Sometimes people fix the listlessness by going around the world on a boat or whatever, but that doesn't work long-term, for the listlessness travels with you.

You have to touch deep within and decide what you want in this lifetime. What are your goals? If you don't know what you want, I think it's important that you start praying to the God Force, Jesus, or whomever, and ask the power to show you.

Wandering around without knowing what you want is like a ship without a rudder. The universe-at-large can't respond properly and help you out. You don't need anything terribly grandiose. Maybe you just need serenity, freedom from money worries, a healthy body, and enough time off to enjoy the mountains. You have to decide, because in defining your life, you create and move the power within you. However, I think a purpose in life that doesn't include serving others isn't worth having. Through service, you develop meaning. You should decide how you will serve. If you've served, did you serve well? Did you serve the God Force and humanity, or was it a big ego trip?

Once you decide what you're going to do, then you stand inside a control mechanism that says, "Even though I don't know all the answers, and even though I can't see everything, I believe that this life of mine is in order, that it is divinely guided, divinely led! I can touch into the subtle energies, the Tao, the Christ Consciousness, the collective unconscious at any time by holding my breath and reaching into the sacred silence." Doing that, you flip to your eternal stance, reaching out at an infinite velocity. In that velocity is all the abundance you'll ever need. It leads you on, talking to you all the way. The test is to believe and follow the power—it *knows*. You just have to get used to really listening to the prompting of your heart and have the courage to follow through.

Gambling and the Sixth Sense

Life's a bit like a day at the races. The racing form says that #1, Acer Racer, will win hands down. But as you look at the horses, you know it won't; and in fact, #2, Johnny Rocket, is the best bet. How do you know? Intellectually you should back Acer Racer, but subliminally you've picked up that dear ol' Acer isn't looking too swift. And you subliminally heard the trainer, who was 20 yards away, tell the stable boy that Acer was feeling a bit the worse for wear, as it had banged its shin in the horse box; and subliminally you read the face of Acer's jockey. He looked bored as he walked up, and he seems to have other things on his mind, like the cute stable girl who's leading good ol' Johnny Rocket 'round the paddock.

And suddenly you have a strong intuition that Johnny Rocket is going to win. Yet intellectually, you don't know how you know, as your conscious mind is not normally in direct communication with your subconscious, where subliminal information is stored. So intuition is more often than not your subconscious showing you things in a quiet moment when your intellect has stopped waffling. This type of intuitive perception comes forward as you quiet your emotions, and it shows you where the money is, where the opportunities lie.

The universe-at-large talks to you—especially when there is a special need—at a synchronistic moment. You ask a question, and something happens by chance at that precise moment to answer your question. Or, someone unrelated to the situation or the question answers you, without them realizing that what they are saying is answering your question.

Let me give you an example. I was at Newton Abbot races one day. It's a small course in the west of England. I'd been throwing back a few beers, and I hadn't really been concentrating. It was now the last race, and I was about a thousand pounds down on the day. I suddenly realized that if I didn't get my act together, I'd walk away losing money, and that's against my religion. I'm very sanctimonious when it comes to taking money off the bookies.

Anyway, it's a slushy day, and it's a national hunt meeting—meaning the races are over the jumps. The track is wet and unpredictable. I'm in a private box, boozing with some racing buddies. I'm pondering the last race, and in walks England's number-one champion trainer. With him is England's most winning jockey. His name is Scudamore, and he'd been champion jock' over the jumps each and every year, as far back as anyone could remember.

I say to the trainer, whose name is Martin, "Who's going to win the last race?" and he replies, "Number 1." I can't remember the horse's name, but let's say it was Acer Racer once more. Sure enough, the champion jock' tells me that, barring accidents, Acer is a good thing. So I whiz off to the bookies with the view to plunging a thousand on Acer at about even money. Meaning, if it won, I'd get £1000 plus my stake back.

Now I'm standing in front of the fat bookie about to make my bet, and something in my feelings is worrying me. I'm not sure about Acer Racer. I always operate from the old axiom that says, "If you don't know, don't go." So I've paused, poised in a meditative moment, clutching the last of my cash, wondering.

I ask the universe-at-large, "Who's going to win this next race?" and as I ask, I look up and see the fat bookie, who's talking to a customer, pointing to #2 on his board of runners, good ol' Johnny Rocket! I take that as a sign, and I'm still there poised in my meditative state asking the universe, when a fellow comes past me and says to a friend, "I'm on Johnny Rocket; I don't fancy that Acer Racer; the horse worries me." I'm thinking, *You're right, dude, Acer Racer worries me, too.* So I step forward and plunge £500 on Johnny Rocket at four to one.

The race is now in progress, and Acer Racer and Johnny Rocket are coming up the home stretch neck and neck, miles ahead of the others, and it looks very, very tight. Three hundred yards out, I knew, categorically, definitely, that Acer wouldn't make it. Sure enough, a hundred yards from home, Johnny Rocket pulls ahead and wins by half-a-length.

That got me £2000 plus my stake back, less the £1000 I dumped when I was drinking beer and not concentrating. I came away with a grand for the day's effort. I'm back in the members' stand, and the trainer's there saying he's sorry he led me astray over Acer Racer, but he'd try harder next time. I thanked him kindly and told him how I had listened carefully to his advice, but that I'd changed my mind at the last moment and bet Johnny Rocket instead. He asked me how I knew, and I told him it was a lucky guess.

I didn't mention how the universe-at-large has a bloody good idea who's going to win, and in certain circumstances it talks to you if you settle down and listen. You just have to be in the right spot at the right moment, have no fear, read the signs, and plunge into your beliefs and back your fleeting impressions and so forth. I didn't tell the trainer all that stuff.

When you know things, you keep to yourself unless people really press you, or if they truly indicate they're interested in what you have to say. First, you don't want to come off as a hotshot; it's enough that the universe has blessed you with a payday. And second, you should never infringe on others by giving them esoteric information if they haven't asked for it.

Each has his or her own path through life, and it's wrong to dive in and try to change that, or to try to come off as a god and pronounce what their direction should be. You should disturb things as little as possible and let everyone head off in whatever direction they choose, even if you know they're choosing a long and winding path. Maybe they need to do "winding" in this lifetime. It's not for you or me to say, is it?

READING PEOPLE SO
YOU CAN HELP THEM

Archetypes and the Sixth Sense

O n with more of the psychic, intuitive discussion. It helps you to know more about people. Once you know and understand them, you can help them. In addition, by understanding people, life gets easier, and even more perception flows your way. To know people, you have to watch them and be interested in them, and you have to watch in silence with a still mind so you can get the subtle stuff as well as the more obvious stuff.

When it comes to people, there are only about a dozen life stories in the whole world, and each archetype has its own obvious characteristics. Of course, everyone has individual traits and an individual story, but the generalizations are true, as everyone is inside the one global mind, and that global mind is segmented into clear demarcations.

As a part of developing perception, you can start to slot people you see, in the street or wherever, into the categories I'm about to give you. It helps you understand the issues they have, as well as the nature of each one's emotion. In this way, you pick up psychic tidbits from their minds; it's loads of fun, and good practice to watch and notice.

In looking at people, you'll soon see what aspects you should avoid, and you'll know how to help them if they ask you. You'll develop a new compassion for all the unnecessary struggle people go through. You can see that most struggle is easily fixed, like it's not compulsory, man. Know whadda mean?

Here's the main cast of characters in no particular order. I haven't included every archetype, just the characters that are a bit dysfunctional. You'll spot them from among your family and friends. Once you have the categories under your belt, everything else drops into place. Bingo! People become obvious.

The Troubled Youth. Troubled youths are usually under 30, or they're over 30 and they never grew up. This aspect is called the Peter Pan Syndrome, where a mature person still acts like a child; or they still cling to their parents and never get out into real life.

The young version of the troubled youth needs acceptance and direction. They're anti-everything, because they can't accept themselves and their circumstances. They don't have a solid identity. Sometimes this happened because they were enmeshed with their parents, sometimes it occurs because of abuse in childhood, and sometimes they're just plain mixed up.

Troubled as they are, they play a kind a version of the game of "chicken," like jumping in front of trains. They're saying, "Hey, world, if you don't stop what you're doing and attend to me and notice me and help me, I'll cause trouble, and/or self-destruct. It will be *your* fault, and you'll be sorry."

As I said, in quantum physics, particles exist in a hazy-wave state with no absolute definition or solidity. When an observer concentrates on a particle, it changes, moving from its ill-defined wave state, potentially spread out anywhere, to suddenly becoming solid. Now it has validity and a definite location. Gone is the uncertainty. All this happens just because someone is observing the particle, noticing it. Weird, but scientifically true.

People are the same. If you want to perceive, understand, and perhaps heal the troubled youth, notice him. Take him from hazy-wave to particle. Make him solid. After all, he needs identity. And anyway, he's colored his hair lime-green, and stuck a thing through his nose and several "O" rings through his navel; he's telling you something. He wants you to notice him, so oblige him. Make a point of it. Don't judge him for being a twit; he'll run away. He can't take the pain of having no identity; criticism is useless—it won't work. Notice him. And try not to giggle at the chopstick he's stuck through his nose! Simple healing.

Once you notice him, he feels more secure. He's only out of control because he needs the solidity of the particle-state. Build him up. Endorse him. Assist him from hazy-wave to solid particle. Then he'll feel more self-worth; he'll eventually find direction and meaning, and he won't self-destruct. I think most kids go wrong because their parents are so busy trying to deal with their own issues and the frantic pace of life; the children are emotionally and intellectually ignored. They suffer a subtle form of abandonment. Why do you think so many young people straighten up once they find a romantic partner? Because if the partner is solid and not bouncing off the walls like they are, then the troubled youth has someone attentive to fawn over them. The youth heals.

Okay. Next character.

The Rabbit. Rabbits are scared. There are lots of them in the world. They can't handle life, much like the Peter Pan person. The rabbit is paralyzed by fear, and lives in a shell. Rabbits may be very bright, so they hide behind their intellectualism, and they fiddle around with their Internet gizmo, or whatever. But the rabbit doesn't like to come out of its hole and experience life. Deep within, the rabbit is often pissed off. Life is passing him or her by. The rabbit's psychology is full of injustice.

The rabbit needs encouragement and endorsement to feel secure enough to come out of its hole. So tell the rabbits the things they need to hear. Tell them it's safe, and offer to take them for a little walk and help them along. Etherically they are easy to spot, as their energy stops real close to their bodies. They aren't etherically "out there" expressing themselves, connected to life, so their energy peters out and looks weak. We all have a bit of rabbit inside us, so we can relate to the fear of others. The rabbit is overwhelmed and needs help to become more courageous. Use your courage to help them along.

The Wilting Wallflower is another variation of the rabbit. I talk about that one in my book *Life Was Never Meant to Be a Struggle.* Wallflowers use their weakness as a "come-on." They need people to rescue them; they're looking for the white knight. Don't buy it—unless you're into hauling a dead horse through life—for sooner or later, you'll resent it. Instead, try to get them to empower themselves out of their timidness. Help them out of their shyness, and teach them not to use weakness in a covert and sneaky way.

The Tyrant. Tyrants are angry, usually because they're scared. More often than not, they're tyrants because they were abused as kids. Sometimes they're angry because they feel they haven't gotten half the breaks in life they think they should have had. If their image is wrapped up in material things, or if it's trussed in a power trip, they will be threatened by anything that vaguely hints of a "reality check." The tyrant lashes out when cornered by the truth. Inflicting pain on others helps them feel less disempowered, less terrified by their monsters and dark memories.

They desperately need to be loved, yet they live in an emotional desert because no one likes them; most are scared of them. That reinforces the tyrant's warped idea that the world is against them, and that making life hard for others is a way of experiencing power. Sometimes, if the tyrant is really powerful, they pull lesser, would-be tyrants around them, and a gang or a fascist outfit is born.

The wounded child becomes the military or political tyrant, or the domineering father who lives vicariously through his children's performance in life to make up for his own failures. He won't think anything is ever good enough. Sometimes the tyrant is an emotionally tyrannical mother, or another female who's out of control and dominates and terrorizes through emotion and theatrics.

The tyrant, more often than not, is a nobody. Often he's a failure and a coward, and he needs others to march forward for him to fill the gap of his inadequacy. He places unreasonable demands on others, partly to dominate and control them, and partly in the vain attempt to bolster himself up to assist with his fears and insecurities. Meanwhile, he causes trouble, dominating, manipulating, and controlling those around him with negative emotion, violence, and threats. Tyrants are terrified of death.

If you don't have a Ph.D. in psychology and lots of time to spare, stay away from tyrants. If you have to deal with tyrants, remember this: Even though they're desperately unhappy, they become arrogant and dogmatic through the exercise of their tyranny. You will rarely get a tyrant to see reason. They live in their own rabid empire. Tyrants like and expect abuse. "Plank on head" is the only language they understand. Don't negotiate, don't accommodate, and don't try to please them. The more you try to do for them, the more it affirms their power of manipulation. It's sad to say, but you should never cut the suckers any slack. It's bound to backfire.

A tyrant is like the schoolyard bully who won't back off until he gets a punch on the nose. So the way to serve and help the tyrant is to be firm and not allow him to get away with it. He won't change until he experiences a big setback. The power that tyrants exert is too intoxicating, as it medicates their fear. So don't try to change them, and don't bother trying to keep them happy. It doesn't help. Just whack 'em in the head with the biggest psychological, contractual, emotional, or financial plank you've got. And when and if they get up, then whack 'em one more time for good measure. They expect it, and they'll respect you and cause less trouble. Over the years, I've tried love, kindness, and reason with this sort, but it rarely works unless some event has softened them up and made them open to change. If you can't just walk away, which of course is the best course of action, then engage them as little as possible and keep up with "plank on head" 'til they quit.

Tyrants may sometimes be hard to spot, since they often cloud their tyranny by feigning reasonableness. But you can spot them from their expression, as it's hard to hide the anger and violence they project. Usually the tyrant takes his darkness to the grave. But then again, sometimes the Great Goodness that loves us and gives as all a second chance comes along. Some special event is created for the tyrant, usually a painful one, and he suddenly sees the error of his ways and changes. Sometimes after he undergoes a spiritual or religious conversion, he uses his power to campaign for love and goodness, and that's a wonderful thing.

The Widow (or Widower). The widow is common all over the world. She (or he) may never have been married; instead, she is often married to an idea, and the idea sadly died. So that's why I call them the widows. They've suffered bereavement.

The widow has a vacant expression; she is uncomfortable and lacks direction, as often, the cherished idea that died was all she had. Sometimes it is a situation or a rhythm she's used to that died, or changed or disappeared in some way.

Widow types are typically 35 to 55 years old. Their dreams fell apart, they were unrealistic about them, they suffered from fear, or they never had the energy to pull them off. Sometimes widow types just had bad luck and got put off; they didn't dig deep enough, so now they're drifting.

The widow always needs an impossibly big break. Their currency is lowering all the time because they're concentrating on what they *haven't* got, instead of going for something new. In addition, their energy falls because they feel defeated or lost, so they drift. It's not that they don't have anything to offer; it's just that they're stuck, and their loss may have caused them to feel weak and insecure.

Solution: Tell the widows they're great and that there's a lot to live for. Entice them into action, no matter how small. Get them to set aside the old dream and to reconcile the loss. Encourage them to go out and meet new people, come up with some new ideas, fall in love, go crazy a bit, and dance all night. Get out of the old stuff and the dusty ideas, and swap them for something new—anything!

Widows are anchored in the past, so the trick is to get them to talk about the future. I used to tell the middle-aged types who came to my seminars and fit into this category to go crazy pampering themselves, buying stuff, traveling the world, and bonking goodlooking strangers! They'd be terribly shocked. Tee-hee! But their eyes would light up, and then I'd tell them that I didn't really expect them to be quite so radical, but that they should at least get their party frock out, and show up on Saturday night at the big bash, ready for action and looking good.

Tell the widows to hang out with young people, and to seek out creators and innovators. Tell them to pick up all the loose threads of any creative ideas that come their way and to follow them. The threads are like the universe's taxi that carries the widow type away from the graveside of their loss back to the real world. Tell them to read more; go to the mountains; seek out new interests; and to party, party, party. Life has a lot to offer. It's open and wide and big, and there's a lot of time ahead.

Widow types, whether male or female, are repressed and sad and labored; they only need permission from someone in authority, and they'll hop a freight train and be gone to a new and exciting life. So give them permission. Turn them into the Merry Widow—take 'em dancing, skinny-dipping in the lake, drinking a little too much, sleeping on the beach—whatever.

There's a variation on the widow—**The Rip Van Winkle** type. He or she has been asleep for 30 years or more, and wasn't having fun even in the old days. They've come to Earth this time to have a good nap. Let 'em be. At most, give them an extra pillow. You can't help them much until they agree to get out of bed.

The Priest is another category. This type will not necessarily be in any religious order, but he (or she—the priestess) thinks he is. Priests are very righteous and holy-moly. They often suffer from an inferiority complex, which they overcome by deciding that they've been chosen personally by

God to haul everyone to the Promised Land.

Now, you have to watch this lot, for quite often they'll have a magazine they want you to read, or there's something they want you to join, or they want you to buy some holy "something" that you don't want, or they'll try to get you on the green slime tofu diet. Or, even worse, they'll attempt to get you to read a thousand-page book of some obscure Indian from the Hindu Kush, who puts people to sleep for a living.

The Priests aren't any real trouble though; they just need to feel superior and chosen and special because they don't like themselves. They need acceptance. So accept them. Accommodate them. Tell 'em you love 'em, and tell them not to take it personally when you say that you don't want the green slime for 90 bucks a bottle. The priests are a bit weird, but one day they will love and accept themselves, and they'll throw away their robes and come back to the real world. Or they won't.

There are a few more characters shufflin' up in the line waiting to be discussed, so let's go on to them lickety-split.

The Terrorist. This character has usually been disadvantaged in life, and he or she won't fit in no matter what. Anytime he gets near success, he'll self-destruct and cause a scene. Or he'll join an organization, but in truth, he's not a supporter. What he really wants is to destroy the place. Anytime he gets close to the big time, where he'll have to fit in and join, that's a worry. He would feel judged and devalued if he joins, and anyway, it goes against his terrorist philosophy. He won't want to stick around in case he's evaluated and seen to be lacking, so he figures out a way of shooting himself in the foot. Or he'll run away, rather than bend a bit so he can make it in life.

The terrorist needs to know he's okay, and he needs to know it doesn't matter if he's not socially acceptable. He can make himself acceptable by just accepting himself. Once he sees how he hurts his own cause, he'll often change his ways. For deep within, he really wants success and money and well-being; he needs it to help him feel good. Deep within, the terrorist really wants to be accepted and to join and to have status. Status is very important to the terrorist type; he or she is desperate for it.

Once his desire for success is stronger than his conflict about being accepted, then he'll ease off. He'll be more reasonable and hang in there long enough to step up and collect. So tell him he's okay, and offer him some personal status, like feeling good about himself. And show him that it's more sensible to put aside one's ego and one's issues than to fight all the way. He has to put it aside—long enough to collect the prize, anyway!

The Professional Victim. The professional victim is really the wilting wallflower in another guise. They've been victimized, or they think they've been. Even if they haven't been victimized—no more than anyone else, anyway—they still like to make life into a tragic song and dance, a melodrama of epic proportions. Often they'll hire someone to help them sort out the story, which is embellished and wound up regularly like a clock.

Victims aren't strong; they need attention and drama. They've got a hang-dog energy. It's easy to see in the etheric; it turns in on itself, curved over like an ingrown toenail. Trouble comes and finds this character. Victims become accident-prone, because etherically, they're sucking energy from beyond themselves, pulling it into them from anything or anyone they can, anyone that might lend support to a hopeless case. That opens them up to a lot of grungy stuff.

Often, victims are lazy. Like so many, they want someone to hold them up, to provide for them, to save them. They don't want to do much, other than to tell their story and moan and groan and blame the world. Much like the rabbit, you have to get them to move on from their injustices, to open up and try new things. It isn't easy to persuade them, as the victim has a vested interest in their story. It's an asset. It gets them attention and makes them feel special, so the story is valuable to them. It's hard to get them to see that their story is just that—a story. It is a tale of a human experience seen from one person's eye. It's often an eye that's too tainted to ignore all the other directions, especially the exit.

Victim types can be a bit grim, as they are vacuum cleaners. You know 'em—you see them for a few minutes at the grocery store, and they've wiped you out energywise. They suck on you and pull from your energy. They need your life force because their etheric is turned inwards; it's not out there expressing itself, keeping them safe. It's limp and it feels unstable, so they feel needy. They usually won't let you go 'til they've got every drop of your vitality and you're on your knees, exhausted. And then they're a bit happier, and they trot off to find another mug to fill up from.

You have to protect yourself psychically from professional victims. Avoid close body contact, because etheric energy jumps. When they're talking to you, keep your distance—at least 18 inches. If you can manage 18 miles, all the better!

The way to deal with them is to keep offering them solutions; it doesn't matter if the solution you're offering makes sense to them or not. It's your defense. They will almost never act on anything you tell them, but keep offering the solution. Make up bizarre solutions if you have to. They won't want to hear them, but keep offering them. Don't buy the emotion, and don't ever, ever commiserate. Fatal. They'll jump into your heart chakra and set up camp. Before long, they'll be sleeping on your sofa, borrowing your money, and you'll have an emotional orphan on your hands, an etheric welfare recipient.

Sure, you can help a friend who's a bit low, but that's entirely different from becoming a paramedic for basket cases, isn't it? You've got to get these victims to see that the inward pulling motion of their etheric is dangerous. If they see that, they might change. In the end, one of two things will happen. They'll either take your advice and go fix their life (that doesn't happen often), or they'll get little joy from hearing you offer the sensible solution—since that means they will have to drop the story and get on with it—so they'll eventually wander off and find someone else to buy the emotion. They need sympathizers and listeners. They like people who agree that life is a bowl of sludge, hard and painful and thick and gummy— a bit like their psychology, really.

The victim is a common emotional energy loop that we all sometimes suffer. We get tired or something happens, and our energy drops. Suddenly, we feel threatened; we have moved from safety and life toward insecurity and danger. Some trivial circumstance becomes the focus of our concern. We build that into a great injustice, and we find that we have to lean on someone. Sometimes we have to induce an argument, or we pick a fight with someone to feel better. Now our adrenaline is pumping along, and we feel energized and safe. Married couples fight all the time over nothing. It's an energy war; it serves to give the relationship a shot in the arm. Arguing is often a substitute for sex.

Onwards and upwards. Here's another one, up front and center stage. He or she is **The Supreme Achiever,** the Savior. In a way, these characters are quite cool and fun to be with, since they usually have great stories to tell. They've done things in life, and they're usually natural-born leaders. So they carry the whole tribe on their shoulders, and they're responsible for everything. They'll go out in the rain in the middle of the night to close the shed door that's banging in the wind—very handy types, the supreme achievers!

Of course, they do all that stuff because they're sacrificial. They like to march headlong toward the guns and have everyone admire them for their courage. Often they like to be acknowledged for their service to humanity, and they're hoping for a prize. But even if you're prepared to grant them such an accolade, they will never stick around to collect the medal, as accepting praise and acknowledgment is contrary to the sacrificial lamb's energy, which forms a part of their religion. Instead, the supreme achiever likes to save everyone and then ride out of town, so everyone can say, "Wow, what a great guy. Who was that masked stranger?"

The supreme achievers are usually children of wimpy parents who expected a lot. The child has to overcompensate, win at everything, be very competitive, and show Daddy and Mummy and the rest of the world that he or she is okay. You want to be careful about this nonsense, as it can kill ya real early on. The supreme achievers are easy to spot. They have booming energies, but it's not usually contained and disciplined. Instead, it's usually billowing out in every direction, folding over the top of people, swamping them more often that not. People like to have this character around, but not for too long. Once he's done all the work and provided all the money and sacrificed himself, they tire of him real quick. They want him to push off and give them all a chance to feel their own energy. The supreme achiever takes your breath away, like an overly long kiss. You're sort of enjoying it, for a bit anyway, but after a while, you start thinking you're going to die, as you haven't had a whiff of oxygen for a hell of a long time!

Because of the supreme achiever's booming etheric energy, he or she will always feel ripped off. Why is that? Well, the achiever booms energy because he needs followers: people to accept him and admire his many and various achievements. So he sprays out energy, flashing across the sky like a shooting star, and everyone is lit up by his presence. Then he's wiped out, and he has no energy left, and everyone takes what they need and more. Then the next thing they need is to get rid of the achiever-savior type, quick.

So they'll say what a rat he is, or they'll make him wrong in some way, or they resent that they have had a bunch of free energy, and now he's moved off. Now they have to stand alone so they'll feel ripped off, and people will say he's dishonest, a rip-off merchant, a carpetbagger, and a rat to boot!

Of course the achiever-savior type brings it on himself, for he can't accept people's gratitude, and nothing is ever enough—no amount of money, fame, glamour, achievement, assets, or toys. Nothing works for long; he always has to go for more. And although he helps people out of the goodness of his kind heart, through his booming energy he also does it to satisfy his own agenda, as he doesn't think much of himself. And so, he didn't really get ripped off; he just didn't realize how he got paid. Namely, he got what he wanted, admirers and followers and fans. Deep down he wanted acceptance, and he got that, so he did get paid, in energy, anyway. Often he burns out early, but he had to be needed by others, and anyway, his overactive life kept him from facing his fears. And now he's a little less active—six foot down, and whatnot. And there you are. Everyone's story is a bit silly, isn't it? It gives us all something to work on.

"Tiddly om pom pom, here comes another one."

This one's **The Suffering Servant.** Once upon a time there was little girl who didn't feel loved. Perhaps she wasn't loved by her parents; maybe they were needy and leaned on her emotionally at too young an age. Anyway, because she didn't feel loved, she felt inadequate. She grew up to feel she owed the world a favor, so she started dishing *out* favors. Sad, really; it felt safe. She felt that by prostituting herself to life, she'd win acceptance and feel better. She didn't want to have to take responsibility, and she didn't want to stick out in a crowd or to amount to very much. Instead, she could latch on to strong people, tag along with them. She'd serve them and they would use her and she'd go to bed at night feeling sad but needed.

"I have served everyone today; in fact, I've done a pretty good rendition—well, impersonation, really, of a humble doormat. Doormat is safe. God loves doormats, and he's saving a special place for them in heaven. It says so somewhere, doesn't it?"

Truth be known, God doesn't treat doormats any different from anyone else. The God Force just reflects impartially back to you—what you are. If you are a doormat and you wind up at the pearly gates in the suffering-servant mode, then the first thing you'll see are the letters EMOCLEW, shining back at you.

And you'll wonder, scratching your head, "What in heaven's name is EMOCLEW? And why are the letters EMOCLEW covered, in part, by a dog turd?"

Suddenly, you realize you're looking at the mirror image of a Welcome mat. "Ah," you'll say, "E-M-O-C-L-E-W spells *welcome* backwards; the doormat reads backwards. Wow, cool. And look, look, the dog turd's 'round the other way. Fantastic!"

You don't want to be an EMOCLEW doormat—that's not LOOC, I mean cool. EMOCLEWS have etheric energies that say, "Use me. Plough over me, treat me like a fool, treat me mean and cruel. And by the way, when you've had your fill, pass me on to someone else who'll treat me badly, and that way I can make amends and feel wanted."

When healing the suffering servants, you have to get them to see that being of service to others is a wonderful thing, but you can't give yourself away totally within that service. You have to love and accept yourself, and you can't compromise yourself just to feel safe, to be accepted, and to give your life meaning. There's nothing meaningful about a doormat that everyone wipes their life on.

Then another common archetype is **The Egghead,** the Dr. Spock type. He thinks a lot, and when he finishes thinking about what he's just thought of, he starts right back at the beginning again and thinks it all through one more time. When he's finished with that, he wonders if he's missed anything, so he goes back and starts over.

Eggheads make their brain a god, and eventually they may become convinced that their mind *is* God, but in the end, they run out of things to think about. Sometimes, they lead hollow lives, thinking all the same stuff, churning through all the thoughts they've had a million times before. They lose a connection with the earth, with life, and so, in effect, they decapitate themselves. Their head separates from their heart. They lose sight of compassion, for themselves and others. That makes them miserable. They become critical and antagonistic. Often, they want others to agree with the idea that their mind is God, and they get very pissed off when people won't cooperate.

The problem with over-thinking is that you lose touch with a sensitivity for life, and that makes you neurotic. Your head and your heart separate, floating off in different directions. You lose touch with where life really exists. Eventually, your brain falls off its perch and hits ground zero. A bit like the French Revolution, really. The elite in France got way too far into their heads, and they were a bit too full of themselves, a bit too important and pompous. They lost a connection with their heart, and they didn't have compassion. And the people of France—the spirit of the French tribal soul—pondered what to do; and eventually it felt that the simplest solution was to cut its head off and allow the heart to grow and emotion to flow.

So they tried that one rainy Monday morning. Loads of heads and emotion flowed all over the place, and the spirit of France felt a bit better. As a result, the French heart did grow a bit, and the people became even more exotic, which is nice.

The only slight problem was that the head grew back again after a bit of time had passed. But at least now there's a power-sharing agreement between the head and the heart. That's why the French are emotional and passionate on the one hand, and intellectual and neurotic and endlessly argumentative on the other.

Lucky for me, I don't speak French very well. I can't go much past "two eggs and a coffee, please, and howyadoing? Thank you." But that's a good thing. I can pleasure myself in the passion and the arts and the food and the emotion, without having to buy the national discomfort or joining the argument. Merci beaucoup. So if you're an egghead, you'd better discipline your mind and make the 12-inch journey from your brain to your heart. And you might want to go out and join life— reclaim your humanity, play with children, and not be too serious. You could practice being lighthearted and funny, and you'd better put a time-lock on your computer and your bookshelf and all that dusty stuff. And you should run barefoot in the desert, love the little things of life, be kind, stay on the ground, and be human. Don't make your intellect a god; use it to help people, and try to love them and not judge them. Also, try to love the God Force as best you can, even if you don't believe in it.

We all suffer from over-thinking; for some it causes great turmoil, pain, indecision, and confusion. In my book *Silent Power,* I said that confusion comes from questions. You can't be confused if you don't ask questions. All confusion has to start with a question. Shall I? Shan't I? Will I? Won't I? You can't reach God through your mind; you have to touch the God Force in a thousand places: in nature, in people's eyes, in the loveliness of a sunset, and so forth. You can't brain-wrestle God into agreeing with you. The God Force is all heart; it ain't up for concepts and musty books and endless brain diarrhea.

Over-thinking destroys your perception because it blurs your feelings. It makes it impossible to visualize and vision and dream; and if you can't vision and dream, you're dead, bro', totally dead. So push the mind back, and when it worries and bitches, say, "I'll handle that later; we'll talk later." Then deliberately avoid mentioning the subject again. When it bitches, tell it life is fine, it flows, and there are better things up ahead. When it's neurotic, take it for a three-mile run, and throw it into a freezing mountain lake at five in the morning. Or, better still, engage it in helping others, doing things that are useful and that exist outside of itself, beyond churning. And when it wants things incessantly, tell it, "Tough, Ducky, tough, you can't have it right now—so relax, babe, relax."

When the mind drives you crazy and gets you into turmoil with other people and battles on for days on end, stop eating. Try that for three days, and if it's still grumbling and arguing, then don't eat for two or three *more* days. As long as it takes for it to shut up. The mind goes real quiet when you don't eat. It takes it personally, and it sits down in a corner and quits.

Thinking destroys perception, for perception is subtle, and when you think a lot, you rattle your etheric. You fill it with wave upon wave of clutter, and the field begins to wobble like Jell-O; it becomes agitated and gray and gummy like snot. Get your hanky out, blow your etheric nose, and stop thinking, for in the end, too much thinking kills you. You run out of power, and the mind worries you to death.

Feel the exuberance if life, join the sensuality of it, be in it, and dance and play. Perceive what there is to perceive, be lighthearted and carefree, and don't be pompous and serious. Allow life to flow so your Infinite Self can teach you things you can't find in books. Loosen up and party down, and go with the flow—the less resistance the better. Make sure you get out into the mountains or by the sea or in the desert as often as possible. That's where life is; that's where the heart is. That's where perception lies.

Another character is **The Emperor** (or Empress). The young version of the emperor and empress is, of course, the prince or princess. These folks were born very grand, or they became grand as a defense against the terror that they perceive insignificance offers. They desperately need the ego's illusion of distance to help them feel special and safe. I've never cared for them much, as they are often snobs. They exist in the charade of their own elitism, so they're often unreasonable, judgmental, racist, or downright rotten.

Luckily, you will rarely be called on to help them, since they are far too grand to descend to the world of ordinary folk and ask for help. And anyway, they are so deep in denial that they usually never see the illusion for what it is. Like the tyrant, there is little you can do until the empire collapses. So the trick is to butter them up, feed their illusion of specialness so they feel safe, and camp at the gates of the estate waiting until they're ready. The God Force is humble, and the emperor/empress is not. So they're cut off from the life force. To come off their thrones is far too scary, since it would mean that they'd have to face their shadow and their fears, and they'd have to descend to the real world and become human. However, these royal types are often very generous, since no one usually likes them. Therefore, they have to buy people. So while you're camped at the gates, order up everything you ever wanted. You might as well be comfortable while you're waiting!

There's one more character I should mention in passing, to fill out the deck of characters. It's **Mountain-Man Jack & His Ol' Lady Jill**. Now mountain-man Jack and his lady friend bought a couple of plaid shirts from L.L. Bean, then they got a pickup, and they went up the hill and stayed there. They are real earthy, and you can see them coming along a mile off; it's like they've got carrots in their aura.

I've always liked the earthy mountain type because he's easy to deal with. He's not full of self-image and thinking, and he knows simple stuff, like when the doodie-doodie rat mates and when it doesn't. His natural lifestyle makes him humble, generous of spirit, and close to God; and his ol' lady is nice—she makes pots, weaves things, grows veggies, and she's got heart. They're all-around simple people, and cool and easy to get on with. The only downside is that sometimes the mountain types are real loners, so they cut themselves off from people. Also, sometimes they get angry because they don't like people spoiling the environment, and because, living out in the middle of nowhere as they do, they often suffer a few financial problems.

You almost never see the mountain-man-Jack-type in therapy, since when he gets really pissed off, he goes on a walkabout. He processes his feelings through nature and hard work, like chopping wood and carrying water and stuff he has to do to survive, but his spirituality is in nature, not in his head. His feelings pass through nature and are processed and absorbed by it. He's in touch with his nature-self, as we all should be. He's got it right, and we urban types have got it wrong for the most part.

Go hang out with that dude and his lady friend, sit in the dirt by a little fire, have her tell you how the streams flow, and listen when he tells you about what coyotes sniff and what they don't like to sniff. Sit there and watch the stars, and think about the galaxies under your feet. Flit your energy to the end of the universe and back, drink a little tea, and she'll have a nice bowl of veggies gurgling away in one of her pots. You'll find that you'll remember things. You'll remember what God is, and you'll remember what life is really about. You'll perceive the sixth sense working through your nonlocal nature-self, and that will help you see the infinity within you.

You won't get hung up with dysfunction and trouble; you'll watch the doodie-doodie rat instead, and you'll say, "Cool, I like the way that rat smiles so much while it's mating. I never knew rats smiled."

Now, as you're watching all the archetypal characters go by at the mall, for example, identify who fits into what category, and see who might fit into more than one. Is the egghead in the rabbit category as well, or not? Some people are on the cusp, so to speak—like their moon is in struggle, and their planets are in silliness.

Anyway, by watching, you learn; so as people pass you, observe them carefully. Slot them in if possible, and feel out what their energy offers you—what's their issue? Then reach out mentally, tap the side of their head at the temple—like you're reaching with an extended etheric arm—and see what comes back to you. Maybe it's a word or an impression. Usually that impression will be an emotion—their overriding emotion. Sometimes you'll see a symbol flash in your mind's eye.

Alternatively, your mind will suddenly flit back to some period in your life, and the memory of a young boy you haven't seen for 20 years comes to mind. He's standing by the river the two of you used to play beside, and you wonder, *Why am I thinking about him?* It's the subconscious's way of showing you that the character in the mall in front of you is similar to—or has the same energy as, or the same feeling as—the one you associate with the little boy by the river many years ago. That's why you sometimes dream of school friends you haven't seen for years. It's the subconscious's language reminding you of feelings that were associated with people or events in the past—like the time you put ice cream down Susie Whatnot's dress, and she whacked you in the head with her backpack.

Sometimes the association is connected to a place rather than a person. Usually it's a location that you know from the past, which you associate with an emotionally impacting moment: a restaurant you had a fight in, a discotheque where you met a beautiful person, an office where you concluded a moneymaking deal, whatever.

In mentally tapping people, you make a connection—first to them, and then to the aspects inside you that are similar. We are all one; everyone is inside us. Using this technique, you get accustomed to picking up stuff from people's mind, their etheric, and their emotions. You expect it. It's easy and natural, and it's what you do every time you meet someone new. You scope them out in an inner way—like going back to the computer to ask for a printout of a file.

Remember, to learn, you have to be interested in people. Doing that serves to return you to your humanity. Their weaknesses remind you of *your* weaknesses. You remember to keep working on yourself. There's a humility in that.

CHAPTER 12

POLARITY, RELATIONSHIPS, AND THE LIGHTNESS OF BEING

Moving on from the last chapter, in which we discussed people's characteristics, we should now talk about polarity and inner knowing—and how that links to relationships and the masculine and feminine within you. So much extrasensory perception flows back and forth between the two yin-yang aspects of ourselves. In that elusive balance is the eternal Tao. We touch it, and in trying to hold on to it, we lose it—only to find it again later. It's bloody irritating, in my view. Perhaps it's called the eternal Tao because this yin-yang shuffle takes an eternity to master!

All sixth-sense perception is yin, because it is soft and delicate and stems from balance. Yet we have to exercise our perception amid the hectic pace of modern life, which often leads in the opposite direction, away from balance. The rules and structures of the status quo, which, of course, has yang qualities (after all, it was invented by men, for the most part), force us into unnecessary activity. We have to act a certain way to stay within the law. And we have to overwork to pay for a system that requires us to file and register and pay fees and ask permission, and follow a million silly rules—which, in effect, forces us to kow-tow to a manic control trip, dressed in a nanny's outfit: "Stand by your beds, button your shoes, and face the front, or else!" When you think of it, the function of the status quo is to milk ordinary people, forcing them to work. The status quo is a solidified manifestation of perpetual restriction that comes from the ego's psychological desire to control—which, of course, stems from the ego's fear of death.

All control trips at a deep inner level are death-avoidance mechanisms.

In his book *The Last Hours of Ancient Sunlight*, Thom Hartmann makes the point that we tend to consider tribal people disadvantaged, ignorant, and primitive, yet they are not isolated from each other as we are in the modern world. They operate an egalitarian system, and they have a unique identity, living naturally from renewable local resources. Also, each member has the support and comfort of the tribe around them. But most important, Hartmann says, tribal people generally work only two to three hours a day. The rest of the time is set aside for rest and play and ritual and social interaction with others in the tribe. This, to me, seems to be a yin existence.

Compare that to the yang nightmare and isolation of modern living— each of us going all-out to sustain ourselves and our families—under punitive rules designed to fleece us and disempower us. Bombarded as we are by one stress after another, each frantically competing with others to earn a living, we consume and pollute and destroy our environment. If half your money didn't go to taxes and imposts and hidden charges, you could live at your current standard by working half the week. The rest of the time you could play with your children, grow your own vegetables, recycle stuff, pedal to the pub for a beer, and live simply. So, in effect, we are enslaved to consume, pollute, and perform.

I have wrestled with this conflict for ages. How does one nurture softness and a lightness of being—developing one's spirituality and compassion—and still stay afloat financially? When I traveled the world presenting lectures and seminars, sometimes appearing 200 times a year, I suffered from exhaustion; my ego would feel threatened, and it would flare up. I began to lose a sense of what the hell life was all about. Yet it took me several years to break out of the programming that said, "Go. Go. Go." Eventually, I became sad. I heard myself up on stage talking about softness and compassion, awareness and sensitivity—embracing the yin way of life, and yet my path was the exact opposite. So, I decided to quit for few years to see if I could get my softness back. My income plummeted by 90 percent, which was a bit scary, but I landed back in the arms of the real me. Now I could think about God and the nature-self, sensitivity and compassion, and not feel that I was loaded to the gills with *BS*.

The Yin Path

As you take to the more sacred yin path, your perspective changes. You are less a part of a solid, yang, material world; and more in a soft, opaque world—a world of dimensions and shifting energies. It is a world where you can see through walls—not necessarily with your vision, but with your feelings—a surreal world where the past, present, and outlines of the future co-exist. This is a world where subtle energies intermingle, shifting and moving, opening some doors and closing others—a world where anything is possible, and the improbable becomes possible.

We incarnate into the idea that action is good and that stillness is boring. Yet, once you've had your fill of action and you've run out of ways to keep the ego happy, then you have to move to stillness. For in there is your teacher. It's the path away from the madness of the modern world to the serenity of the healed self. I had to give up a lot of material things to get away, but I had no option. My progress was stifled by the silliness of the modern idea that says materialism makes you happy and gives you security. In fact, it's quite the reverse, for activity burns energy, and that takes you away from security.

By walking away from most of it, I set myself free. Prior to quitting the job, I paid all my obligations, and then I became a perpetual traveler. So legally, I didn't owe any tax, as I wasn't a resident anywhere. I gave up the glitz and glamour that I hated anyway, and retreated into my own world. I was sandwiched between the 3-D yang world of the modern system, and the strange but beautifully opaque "other world" of dimensions and inner things—a secret domain where energy, not status or money, is the currency of choice.

Of course, arriving there as a novice, I had to traverse that uncomfortable place where I grieved for the world I had lost, unsure as yet of the existence in which I found myself. But in there I found, as I'm sure *you* will, the invisible passageways that permeate reality. Engaging the sixth sense, moving silently back and forth—somewhat spastically at first—I began to find my way. I traversed from a solid, heavy, oppressive state of being; to a lighter, more wispy, see-through energy state.

In that transformation, I had to process a great sadness. Ravenscroft says, in *The Cup of Destiny*, that on the way to the Grail, one has to process the entire karma of the world. I don't think he meant that one has to *fix* it, just that one has to reconcile it and transcend it. I can see what he means. I felt sad about the karma of ordinary people, trapped and bound into a silly idea invented by power-trippers. I felt for our collective ignorance. I cried for the pain we inflict upon each other. I felt bad that I hadn't fixed my shadow years ago. And I agonized that our children may inherit a world more dysfunctional and troubled than the one I was born into. Reconciling the yin and yang and the inevitability of it all took me three years. The hardest part was realizing that the solution for our people is so simple, and yet there is nothing very much I can do about it. So I prayed a lot.

Having been for many years an urban Taoist—one that hadn't ever spent any time isolated in a monastery or up a mountain—but one who had nonetheless embraced the concepts of the Tao and detachment, I was at least familiar with the teachings of the Taoist sages. But the detachment I managed was an intellectual one. Once I plunged into the sadness of our human karma, I had to fashion a new sophistication to my detachment, whereby I had to release the pathos of it all, and the burning desire to see the world become a better place. Letting go of that idea was the hardest lesson.

It is difficult to accept that the world is a manifestation of our collective mind-set. Although you may be on the spiritual path, heading in a different direction, the controllers of our world are firmly set in a system that suits them. Infringement, interference, manipulation, control, psychological mind games, emotional blackmail, contractual nastiness, financial control, and terror tactics over money and power, are, of course, the manifestations of an ego out of control. Yet our planet has to move through these dysfunctions in order to learn that there is another way. So sadness over these things, while natural, is just an evolutionary impatience. It might take humanity 5,000 years to gradually change—although I'd guess that in the current level of helter-skelter consumption and madness, things might fall apart sooner than that.

The lesson is to let it be and allow the eons to pass one after the other. One has to presume that God is not in a rush, so one has to back off and not be uptight. From an energy perspective, it's best to leave people alone and not infringe on their karma. Detachment is a terribly hard lesson to master. Yet if you infringe on others, you link your karma to those on whom you have infringed. You become glued to them. In addition, you become karmically responsible for them. You don't need it. And you certainly don't want to be responsible for unnecessarily changing people's lives. You have to let them go on their way, even if it causes you pain. It's the right way, the spiritual way.

Imagine that someone is going north, as that is where their highest destiny lies, and you, from your intellect or emotional agenda, persuade or influence them to go south. All of a sudden they've met the wrong bloke, headed off to the Yucatan, and their whole destiny changes for the worse. Maybe it will take them this entire lifetime to get back to where they were, psychologically, spiritually, and destinywise on the day they decided to go north—before you interfered and sent them south.

The spiritual lessons of this Earth plane are complex. We are here to learn to let go and trust our perception so that we feel safe without all the trappings of the material ego-world: burglar alarms, handguns, insurance policies, nasty lawyers, vindictive emotions, and so forth. But moving from fear to love and just trusting your inner power isn't simple in a world where manipulation, trickery, hatred, and violence are common. We have to become courageous where there is so much fear and insecurity. We have to detach when everyone is trying to suck us in as much as possible, and we have to believe in ourselves when the whole system is trying to mold us into a stifling conformity that pulls us down. We have to believe in abundance when people talk of lack. It's a funny ol' game.

But the central lesson is that we are here to learn to become more accepting and sophisticated and to go beyond our fears. To that end, the sixth sense helps, as it allow you a certain security. You feel you can weave your way through the morass of life and stay sane and safe. The other lesson is that one has to learn about oneself and how to successfully relate to others, as well as developing a relationship with all creation via the nature-self. And, of course, we are here to learn to use the creative force within us, which is such an important part of the human experience.

That's why relationships are so important. They are the school you attend, where what you are is reflected back toward you. They act as a mirror. That is why people suffer a lot of imbalance, emotion, and difficulty in relationships. They're looking at themselves and their shadow, and that makes them uncomfortable, fearful, and angry.

Interacting with other people and being in intimate relationships is how you evaluate yourself, and it's how you put your spiritual ideas into action. If you're sneaky and mean, lean on others unfairly (burning their energy), unfairly appropriate their possessions, or if you're perpetually fiddling the system, you'll see that come back to you in the way people treat you. If you wield emotional violence, that also comes flying back. People won't support you or cooperate. It's not for me to wag the finger, but having seen the shadow and the celestial, I'd remind you once more of the need to sort out the shadow, and to get real and true with yourself and others. Our planetary karma can only change if we each agree to change ourselves. But even if it never changes and this world becomes a living hell, you still need to grip your small part of it and head toward the light.

Deal fairly and equitably with everyone as best as you can, and set appropriate boundaries so others don't use you. But always try to offer a generosity of spirit. Turn a soft eye upon your brothers and sisters, and see them in the same context as you would see yourself—infinite, that is. Offer them compassion, hard as that might be at times. Understand that they are often weak, but they are learning, as we all are, to become infinite and angelic in our perspective of self. It may take a while, but in the end we're all on a winding path back to God—we never left our infinite state, and we're still in that infinite dimension of goodness even though our physical bodies are here on Earth.

It's hard to think like this, especially about others if they're giving you trouble, but try it. Your boss may be the biggest manipulator in the world, but he's still an infinite spiritual being. So offer the soft eye and the kind word to everyone, no matter how difficult they might be. It's a test. Somewhere beyond us are angels offering *us* the soft eye, even though we're a bit grungy spiritually compared to them.

Extending your subtle perception to your relationships makes them operate better, but it's no guarantee of success, for the pressures of life can soon swamp compassion and softness and turn a happy life into an ugly mess. The trick is in the balance of managing your energy well. For when you burn too much energy too quickly—via negative emotion, activity, or dysfunction—you soon plunge on a downward spiral, where the ego flares and you cut yourself off from the light.

Only *you* know how much of the yang "push-and-shove" you need. Each of us has to reconcile activity with the sadness of being isolated and cut off. Then again, if you retreat too far inside stillness, you may find a terrible loneliness there, as there won't be many in there with you. Back to that blasted yin-yang balance!

The Subtle, Unseen Part of Yin-Yang Balance

Because our entire existence rests in the tension between polarities, it's natural that it's hard to strike a balance. We see life's outgoing yang polarity, pushing on the soft yin inward-seeking negative polarity. Of course, when we talk of positive and negative, I don't mean good and bad—one could just as easily use a magnet as the analogy, saying yang is north and yin is south. Our life is sustained by the interaction of opposites. Our nervous system, which carries sensations to the brain, operates in a binary way: on-off. The whole universe works in this same way.

The masculinity within a woman creates a synapse of energy in her overall femininity, and the femininity in the male interacts with his masculinity to balance his power. In etheric terms, the yang polarity moves outwards, and the yin tends to pull inwards. I don't know how *you* feel, but a lot of the yin-yang stuff that I've read in spiritual books puts me to sleep. It's too wishy-washy. I've always had irritating questions up my sleeve, like where is the yang in the female, and what does it mean anyway? I presumed that there had to be a technological explanation that somehow locks the yin-yang interplay to the sixth sense and the etheric. Otherwise, yin-yang is all hogwash. Sure, you can understand the yin inside the male yang, but what does it actually mean? How does it work in practice, day by day?

I found a good explanation via a Taoist teacher who showed me the opaque bit in the yin-yang story. It might sound a little different from what you already know, but check it out and see what you think. The female has an inner spiritual identity. Think of it as part of the subtle body, a reservoir of light, her bank of perpetual memory. That inner spiritual identity is of a positive polarity; it's where the yang in her exists. Look at it: The feminine spirituality is nurturing—it expresses outward in the form of love, caring, mothering, compassion, kindness, love of the earth, and the little creatures. It is the outgoing supportive energy of femininity. Yet the physical body of the female is of the opposite polarity, yin. It pulls energy in to her. She sucks up emotions, she pulls the babe to her breast, she pulls to her the attention of others as she walks down the street, and she pulls the male to her body. So the feminine, in its physical expression, is an inward-pulling energy, and we would therefore consider it of the negative polarity. The tension or synapse between her yang spirituality and her yin body creates the electricity of the feminine incarnation.

On the male side of the equation, the body of a male, and often most of his thinking, has a positive yang polarity, a tendency to go out. The male ejaculates outwards, he moves outwards, trying to discover himself, while trying to develop his status in life. He feels he needs competition to prove himself and to establish observers. Or, he needs to be observed as being clever, exercising his intellect, solving problems. The yang in him requires him to attempt to conquer the world, sometimes sexually, sometimes through physical power. He needs the outgoing energy—initially, anyway—to discover who he is. A male in his simplest definition is what he *does*. The female is what she *feels*.

Opposite the outgoing, yang male energy of his thinking and his physical, sexual self is his spirituality—which is, in fact, yin. It's very inward—it pulls in. So men are very secretive about their inner selves, and they usually hide their feelings. For the most part, you'd imagine that they were all thinking and intellect, and that they don't have any feelings. It is not considered cool for men in Western societies to discuss their emotions. They are required to adopt the macho stance, ready to march toward the guns as soon as ordered. So the inner male is hidden away and secretive.

That inward trajectory is on the negative yin polarity, pulling in, while his external social self is on the yang, positive polarity, pushing out. A gap develops, one energy going outwards, separating from the spiritual energy within the male that is pulling inwards. A male's sixth sense perception, and his sensitivity, lies in balancing up the gap—in the same way as we all have to close the perceived gap between ourselves and outside reality. Most men push out, attempting to achieve, exhibiting feats of endurance and strength. They are, in effect, trying to establish observers, hoping that will make them more solid. In reality, too much activity makes them vulnerable and moody. They move so far away from their inner-self that they become disconnected, and so they experience difficulty in discovering themselves. Have you ever met a man who is very successful in the material world, a multimillionaire, perhaps, who is all "flash and cash"—and yet he comes off as a little boy? Perhaps you've wondered how he ever made it in the commercial world?

Of course, what probably happens is that when he's out and about making money, running his empire, he's in his grown-up, achieving, yang state, but that activity distances him more and more from his yin spirituality. In that yawning gap, he experiences a terrible confusion and insecurity. To compensate, a part of him age-regresses to his childhood, and there he seeks a surrogate mother for softness, comfort, and security.

Most men, feeling the huge gap inside of themselves, start to wonder, "Who am I?" In all that yang activity, they often lose sense of their real self. So the way a man discovers who he is, is by gradually pulling back from the yang and disciplining himself. The balanced male has to compromise, giving up the need for observers and status, and turning within—without becoming so dysfunctional in commercial terms that he becomes a burden on others, or turns to dishonesty to get by. All extrasensory perception is yin; it comes from softness and silence. A man who is out there, biff-bang, achieving, ejaculating, conquering, and so on, will tend to lose what little softness he has. So he'll win medals in one world, while decapitating himself and going blind in the etheric inner world.

He needs a bit of discipline to win back his spiritual self. It may be nutritional discipline, or a period of celibacy, or the discipline of putting his life in order. Perhaps he needs to settle his paperwork, pay his debts, take stock of where he finds himself, and get rid of any encumbrances superfluous to his day-to-day needs. Once a man has experienced the world and he has his fill, it's vital for him to put that aside and return within; otherwise, he will never rediscover his softness and compassion. Without it, he will never amount to much spiritually. The easiest way to make the turn is through meditation, prayer, and contemplation. We can all commune with God, sitting in a chair, thinking objectively about our lives, deciding what makes sense and what is just illusion. By looking at your strengths and weaknesses, you'll soon see what works and what doesn't. The spiritual path is an obvious one.

If you're a male, make it a discipline to express spirituality and softness at least once a day to somebody. It could be an act of caring, a soft remark, or a kind gesture. It might be picking up a child and holding it in your arms. Or putting your arms around an old person, and walking with them across the street, being interested in what they have to say, lingering a while to discover who they are and what they've learned in life. It's a spiritual discipline for the male to allow himself the vulnerability needed to reclaim the God Force within him.

For the female, life would be a breeze if she could her express her spirituality and her femininity in the relative simplicity of the tribal ways. But modern life requires her to be out there earning money to sustain herself—and her children, if she has any. So she is forcibly flipped to the yang world of productivity, competition, and striving. Of course, there's nothing wrong with earning a good living, as it grants you freedom. But wouldn't it be better if it didn't involve all the stress and strain that comes with holding down a job?

So a female also has to balance her natural desire to go outward (yang)—to experience the world, interact with others, earn money, exercise her power and the yang part of life—while guarding her natural spirituality. That's a softness she shouldn't relinquish, lest she fall into the vapid world of the spiritually lacking male. Unfortunately, the business world is male, for the most part, and to be a success requires a female to battle the discrimination that is so much part of the status quo. She has to don the armaments of a yang presence so that she isn't disadvantaged in a commercial game where men make the rules. But then again, we all have to push against some nonsense or other.

The trick for us all is not to become so deluded by the *maya* (delusion) of the outside world that we plop off the edge of life into a sea of trouble. A good bit of outgoing action helps us to earn money, experience life, have fun, and get things done. But too much of that and our energy cracks up. We suffer psychological or emotional breakdowns, and often our bodies react adversely to a loss of velocity and light.

The female's world holds together because, etherically, her spiritual polarity is expressing outwards. First, it creates a positive vibe that others react to positively; but second, it keeps her safe as it pushes incoming etheric energy back, giving her space. Third, if that spiritual, outward-moving energy is sustained in a loving, caring way, it will deflect negative vibes coming in from the outside world.

This subtle balance explains why, when a female is tired and yanged out, she may feel threatened and unable to cope. It's because what holds her together is the spiritual polarity within her—pushing out, acting as her protector. Once she overdoes her activity in the external world—and if she becomes angry and loses sight of her inner-self—the positive spirituality within loses its velocity and becomes erratic. Its ability to flow outward is impeded. Now she's tossed about on an emotional wave. with much less natural protection; things become scarier. The etheric ceases to enliven her; in fact, it begins to drain energy, buffeted about as it is, while the light of it is cut off from her cells. She becomes momentarily darker, disconnected from her true power and the God Force.

Meanwhile, her womanly self and the feminine body is sucking etheric energy in from all directions, without any outgoing spirituality to push it all back. Much of what she pulls to her is not helpful—or it is downright debilitating. So the incoming energy muddles her all the more, and metaphysically, the etheric wall around her starts to crack, and reality will feel like it's breaking up. Of course, it isn't necessarily breaking up. It's just that the etheric pulse around her, in which all human feeling lies, is fractured—and this may give the impression that she can't hold her life together.

Male or female, we all drain energy in this way: drifting to a more unstable state that carries with it the potential of problems and danger. Life may swamp us, and we can be faced with a tidal wave of darker, incoming energy, with little or no protection.

The spiritual female who understands the power and has agreed to step inside the opaque world of perception and the sixth sense will not be kidded by the maya of the physical world, glamorous and alluring as it is. She sees that she can walk down the etheric tunnels, which permeate life. She can step whenever she wishes, out of the physical-emotional mind-set of the normal world, into another world, another dimension.

Inside that strange and beautiful place, she can exercise her shaman's power, moving energy with no effort, commanding her destiny silently and powerfully. She will automatically pull to her all that she wants and needs. The incoming, undesirable energies of life that she is normally subjected to will pass her by. She is invisible to them, deflecting them via her natural etheric shield of power.

Inside the medicine woman's world, she has choices. She cannot be inundated by life's nonsense, because she is out of normal reality, inside a different evolution—living in the physical world, but moving through the silent gaps, the corridors of light. When she is in that crack between two worlds, she's behind an invisible wall, a solid etheric curtain, bathed in light and vitality. In there, she is perpetually safe. She can't be touched, because in the metaphysical sense, she does not exist here in the physical. She's way beyond the restrictive part of the global-mind, deep inside the balance of her yang spirituality and yin body. She's finally come home, back to the heartland, back to that special place where God rests and watches.

In there, she can crown herself queen of a silent world, exercising her power and expressing herself. And she will not worry about her external life in the solid world—for, with the power, she can effortlessly pull to herself all that she will ever need.

But look at our society, one that teaches our children to go out and compete, strive, push, pull, buy this, acquire that, and mortgage your life for a few bricks in the suburbs. We don't teach power and balance; we teach instead that chasing a material dream is where it's at. Girls are expected to be yang and sporty and drink with the lads, biff-bang and compete—not only on the playing field, but also sexually, in careers, financially, and so on. That's where happiness is, we are told. But all that makes for a hollow shell of a person. And that shell has to be filled with something: drugs, alcohol, mood swings, and dependencies of one kind or another.

So we are each trying to balance the demands of life with the tension of polarities. And our relationships, when they are balanced, help us a lot, because energy is shared, and each one can support the other. In a male/female relationship, the female can assist the man's spirituality to develop, and he in turn can show her the strength of the yang by offering emotional and physical strength at those times when the female's energy drops. In addition, she can become more confident in the yang world by bouncing energy off the male in her life. If she is strong, she'll help him by pushing his etheric back up to the crown, and she'll carry him (if he will go, that is) back to softness and compassion.

If a female becomes too yang, she will boom that yang etheric out as the male does, and often she will pull to her a very wimpy type of guy. Wimpy guys are attracted to overly yang females. How many of those women do you know? I've met many women who are very powerful in the yang sense, and they have a wimpy character that they tow along as the boyfriend. The wimpy guy will be sexually attracted to the powerful yang-style woman because she won't require much of him. It isn't like he's going to have to stand there and be a John Wayne-protector type. He is attracted by her masculinity, as it allows him an effortless free ride.

If a woman is more feminine, and she is confident in her spirituality, that combination expressed as an outward spirituality is very lovely, and it will attract a stronger sort of partner. Only a strong guy would be attracted to that soft, feminine self that a woman may want to show. There is also a need for balance on the male side, because if a male is too yang, he'll bore you to death talking about himself. He comes off as an egocentric jock, constantly ready to ejaculate his masculinity over others. Of course, if the male is strong but also sensitive, and if he can relate to his inner femininity, then he will not be afraid of emotion. He'll be able to express his spirituality and communicate his feelings properly.

A woman needs a sensitive male she can talk to—one who isn't going to necessarily fix all her stuff for her, but who will be there to listen and understand when she needs to discuss emotional aspects of her journey— ones that deal with the subtlety of feeling. Strong, sensitive males are few and far between. Yet again, it isn't easy to find a woman who hasn't been polluted by the maya of glamour and the material world, a female who has really developed her medicine woman, shamanistic self. So, if you are on the spiritual path, it's very important to hitch up with someone of like mind;

otherwise, you'll soon find yourselves heading in different directions.

I have always felt that one has to marry oneself first. Once you have made the commitment to yourself and the inner journey, you are more solid. Then if the partner of your dreams shows up, all well and good, and if they don't, you still have a good relationship anyway, with the God Force and your inner-self. In the solidity of that, you offer a better proposition to a would-be partner, so marrying yourself is good idea. You might want to have a little ceremony in the bathroom mirror, with a ring and all.

"Do you take . . . [yourself] to be your lawful wedded partner?"
"Yes, I do."

In effect, it is the marriage of the yin part of you to your yang counter-part. It's your pledge to be faithful to your spiritual ideals and the light within you.

At the very core of your being, you are a spirit. If your relationships or the stresses of life become too much, you become darker and heavier and lose sight of the lightness of being. The trick is to stay in the gap and embrace softness; if not, your relationships, and/or the material yang world will eat you in the meantime.

I am not very qualified to tell people how to run their relationships. Mine have all been exotic roller coasters, upon which I became so giddy I had to get off. Then again, some of those books that talk about the interplay of male and female—"I'm a Martian, and you're from Venus"—that kind of vibe, seem a bit mass-market to me. It's like reading a manual on how to become a race car driver. It's all very nice as a concept, but once you're hurtling toward the first corner at 180 miles an hour, the manual is bloody useless. It doesn't relate to the real experience, like, "Brake! For Christ's sake, brake!"

The other thing I've noticed is that as we embrace the spiritual path and open to the light within, we become less and less stereotypically male or female. In the spiritual marriage of yin and yang, one becomes more diffused and androgynous. How that is supposed to fit into the old-style patriarchal marriage contract was never explained to me. The only way it seems to work is, if you are both secure enough to offer your partner lots and lots of space, each of you has room to move and grow. Then again, being married to someone who's perpetually up the Hindu Kush visiting his guru might be a boring experience. Suddenly, tick-tock and the pizza deliveryman might seem to be a good proposition.

Fear kills relationships. The ego's self-centered and insecure perspectives, and its overall survival trip, gets in the way of love, so things can go wrong. Love is giving people space, letting them be, having compassion for them, feeling secure without having to imprison them emotionally. But when the ego kicks in, you'll get scared and insecure. You'll tend to want to control; that will stifle your partner and they may react.

You might have been initially attracted to an individual because they were different. Maybe they seemed unusual, interesting, powerful, and strong. Then, as you get into a romantic relationship with them, each of you enters into the web of the other's energy, and you both try to create more power and energy. That usually works initially, and things move faster metaphysically. You create a quickening.

All of that is fine when you're both coming out of love and cooperation—when you're both still on your best behavior. But if one or both of you freak out at the speed of things, or react to the responsibility of having another person in your lives, the ego may kick in with a power trip, and things will turn the other way.

Suddenly, one person is fearful and wimping out, and perhaps they're now trying to hold the other one back. The stronger one reacts to having energy pulled from them; they want their partner to stay with the pace and don't like the implications of what is happening. An energy war develops. "It's your turn to do the washing up. I'm tired. I work and pay for this and that, and all you do is sit on yer back-end watching TV. It's your turn to . . ." So the whole relationship descends into a quagmire, one partner trying to enforce the law by standing over the other, and the weaker one trying to hold things back by controlling, manipulating, cajoling, screaming, and shouting to get things to go at their desired pace. Then the situation might change: The gung-ho one now has the flu, he or she wants to pull back, and the slower one is happy. They take control and drive the bus, so to speak, and then the gung-ho one sooner or later reacts, and the war's on again. It's a teeter-totter, back and forth.

The other thing that happens is that both partners owe a certain amount of their newfound extra power to the other person, but the ego doesn't like to admit that. So psychological turf wars ensue, where one claims that all the power is his or hers, and the other one knows that it isn't so. It's a political thing, which develops when a relationship goes into a tight ego-mode, rather than an open love-mode. A shift takes place. That shift should be sorted out quickly through love, compassion, and good communication—quality talking—where you and your partner express your concerns and discuss whatever aggravations have built up. Each of you should be listening to the other without blame so you both can see clearly what's needed and how to get things back on track.

So, you bring perception and the sixth sense to relationships by watching the flow of energy—reacting with positive action when needed, or pulling back when your mate needs space. It's all energy in motion. By watching it ebb and flow, you'll eliminate any trouble before it starts—and before resentments set in. Each of you has to become the custodian of the energy of the relationship, and each has to make adjustments for it to rest in harmony.

The trick here is to remember that the person you are with is not just a male, a stockbroker, or a construction worker—he's an infinite spirit temporally *doing* male. And she isn't a technocrat, a mother, or a part-time teacher, she's the same—infinite—inside her feminine identity. It sounds obvious, but how many times have you thought of anyone as an infinite being? It's so easy to see people stereotypically as a male, an African, the phone engineer, the schoolteacher or whatever, rather than thinking of them as *energy.*

Mind Reading: Uncovering the Hidden Messages

The way to develop a deep sensitivity to the energy of a relationship is to first ask yourself the standard questions in relation to people's actions—that is, what do their actions mean? And then you need to delve more deeply into what the subtle message or energy is that underlies their actions. Actions are the external manifestation of thoughts and ideas, and the impulse for those thoughts is always somewhere deep in the subconscious. So action is the external manifestation of an impulse driven by a desire or need. When people act in a certain way, there is an explanation. It may not be obvious at first, but in your subtle perception, it's easy to see. I think women are much better at policing energy changes than men are. Most males plod along, oblivious of what their partner thinks and feels. Yet it's much like unraveling a dream, as we talked about before. Its symbols and messages seem crazy at first—until you adopt the correct technology for looking at it. Then you see the dream in its proper light, and it all seems obvious.

Okay, how will you discover what inner messages people are giving off?

At any given moment, each person has a number of impulses they are operating under. It's as if there's a multifaceted beacon driving the person from deep within. When people talk, there is a hidden message inside the speech. Even when they're not talking, there is often a subtle message in their silence. There is always more. People can only enunciate a small percentage of their overall reality. That's because there aren't enough words to describe all that they feel or want to say. They may be covert, but more often than not, it's just because they're simply not aware of their subliminal, subconscious impulses. So they don't know what's moving them. It may be some very distant feeling in their subconscious, of which they are totally unaware.

You can quite easily discover the hidden message. Here's a simple way to get you started: Clear your mind, establish the silent gap we talked about, and as a person talks to you, pull them into the field of your concentration. First, imagine your etheric arm outstretched. Place it behind their neck, and pull them ever so gently toward you, placing them closer to you on an energy level. When you do this, you might see them bob toward you slightly.

There's another way of holding them. It's a bit more complicated, but easy enough to do: Imagine a beam of light, or a thin steel rod like coat-hanger wire, going from your left eye diagonally across to the other person, and imagine it going behind the other person's left eye. Imagine you are holding them with the rod or the beam of light. It's a way of sustaining them momentarily with your concentration, by establishing a close etheric connection with them for an instant. There is nothing negative or untoward in holding a person in this way, as concentration is a form of love. When you love someone, you focus on them in a positive way. You are there for them, rather than inside your own head, with its thoughts and feelings. That's love, isn't it?

So once you have them in your concentration—mentally pulling them closer to you via the eye-to-eye connection, for example—center yourself, clear your mind, and ask that your inner sixth sense finish any uncompleted sentences they may utter. That will give you guidance as to what they are really thinking. In effect, you are tapping into their subconscious, linking to that part of their reality that is unspoken. So your friend might say, "I would like to go with you to the movies next Thursday but I'm not sure. . . ." And you clear your mind and ask it to fill in the missing bit—the answer comes back as words in your head. The first words are always the correct ones.

As long as you're in the blank mind mode—a mental silence—the rest of the sentence comes to you. Your power knows. We are all inside the same collective super-mind. So it tells you because you've asked it. In this case, let's say, the rest of the story goes: "I'm reluctant to go to the movies with you because I want to bring my boyfriend, and I've noticed subliminally that you look at my boyfriend in a way that seems odd to me. I fear you might be after him. I don't feel so good about myself, and I think you are prettier, better, and more sexy than I am. I worry that you'll both hit it off and I'll lose him."

The rest of the hidden story that goes off in your head is not usually as convoluted as the example I've given, but I've laid it out here so you can see it. Now, listening to your friend's inner answer, you make adjustments to ease her insecurity. So you talk about the great boyfriend you've got, and how you're really committed to him, and you'd never dream of sneaking off with anyone else's guy—and anyway, people shouldn't infringe upon each other. And then you go on to say how neat it is that your friend and her boyfriend are together, and how endearing it is, and what a perfect couple they make. You say all the things required to reassure your friend that you're not after her guy. Then you ask her again, "Are you sure you don't want to go the movies? I'll bring my boyfriend, you bring yours, and we'll go on a double date." And your friend loves you deep down, and now she's not placing fear in front of her friendship and love for you. So now it's safe for her to say, "Yes, I'll come to the movies."

Life is simple when you know what others really think and feel. Sometimes when you're in the mentally blank concentration mode, asking questions, you're not necessarily hearing an unfinished sentence; sometimes you're mentally receiving an added, silent thought that explains what's been said. So in this example, your friend might say, "I don't know if I really want to go to the movies. The weather is bad." Then you may want to ask her for the rest of her thinking. It comes back as a telepathic transfer that says, "I really want to go, but I want you to drive across town out of your way and pick me up, and by the way, I want you to pay for me, as I'm not very flush at the moment." Then you can decide on the basis of the silent information whether you want to be the chauffeur and financier of the trip to the movies or not. You cut across the unspoken stuff to the real issue.

It's the same in business. The agenda is often unspoken. It is often one of ego, power, status, and not losing face, or it's about positioning and control and so forth. It's not necessarily a money issue at all. Sometimes you can offer people status or an ego boost instead of money. You keep the money and take the humble spot and let them have the status. Sitting at the office meeting, ask yourself, *What do these people want?* Everybody wants something. I don't think that is bad, necessarily; everyone has needs. It's rare that you meet people who don't want anything—very rare. If you ask your sixth sense constantly, it tells you what people want. Often their wants are framed inside an emotion, so it's easy to work out.

Remember, most have little or no real free will because they don't own their power as yet. They only have the potential of free will, not the real thing. Mostly they act from a Pavlovian response to life, moving away from pain, fear, discomfort and effort, toward anything that makes for a cushy life and an ego boost—such as importance, glamour, or status. This is not a bad thing or a good thing; it's just the way it is. Because of people's needs, they project outwards, etherically stretching for things—it is a subtle out-going etheric wave, but it's there—so it becomes simple to figure out what they really want. Just ask inwardly, as I've said.

Sometimes your subtle senses show you the *feeling* involved, rather than the exact opinion, thought, or intellectual aspects of their agenda. In other words, maybe on this occasion your friend has no precise reason why she won't go to the movies, it's just that other things are more important to her right at this moment. Her emotional self is elsewhere, not thinking about her boyfriend, you, or the movies. So, if the answer to your silent question comes back to you a bit scrambled, try to discover the overall emotion. Ask: What is the nature of your friend's overriding feeling? Simultaneously, you stretch out an etheric hand and place it on her heart. That connects you to her emotionally, your sixth sense translates what it perceives, and you find out that she's worried about her mother who's been a bit unwell lately or whatever.

Now let's say that you have a reason to win someone over, for romantic or business reasons, or perhaps you just like that person and you want to be their friend. First, you do the obvious stuff like show up on time and be prepared for whatever is going to be happening. Like the business meeting, you've gone through it in your mind's eye, you've mentally placed yourself there ahead of time, you've seen it all going well, and you're ready. You're not plowing in, one shoe on and one off. If the situation is a romantic one, you've taken the time to put yourself into the best light, like you've taken a bath and you're looking good and feeling great.

Now, when you're with that special person, begin by really listening to them, become interested, and empathize with their inner needs, as well as with what they're saying. Ask silent questions. At the same time, join them on an inner level. Reach out to them etherically; reach into them and hold their heart in your hand. Imagine it beating in the palm of your hand. See if, etherically, you can feel its rhythm, its pulse. It can be a very beautiful and poignant moment. As you hold them close in this way, exude love and caring for them. The love transfers instantly. They feel good and their eyes light up ever so slightly—watch for that. They are not sure why they suddenly feel safe, good, and relaxed, but sooner or later, they intellectually or subconsciously associate that "feel-good" factor with your presence in their life.

If you are in close proximity to the individual—say, you're in a club dancing with them—see if you can hold their wrist or if can put your finger on their neck. You are trying to find their pulse, either through their wrist or the jugular vein. If you can get their pulse, go into your clear-mind mode and visualize yourself stepping out of your etheric and dropping back into theirs—reversing into their energy. Ask your heart to slow down to, or speed up to, the rhythm of their heart—which you are listening to via their pulse. Join your two hearts together so they beat as one, so to speak—similar to how I describe riding blindfolded, joining the pulse of the horse you're on. It doesn't matter if your heart isn't quite at the same rhythm; it's the etheric entering into their energy, joining them, that matters. It's a way of saying—on a cosmic level, anyway—"You and I are one." You'll be amazed by how well it works; people will really respond to this.

You can invent all sorts of other techniques and try them out, but always look for the inner way, the inner explanation in life—especially if there is no obvious external, intellectual explanation. So you have all your normal faculties and a few more—your extrasensory ones. Soon you know where everyone's going and when they'll get there. Perception makes you solid; it comes quickly once you settle yourself—very quickly.

Remember, you exercise your spiritual angelic self through relationships. That's how you discover yourself, that's how you express "spiritual action," and it's there that you discover the nature of yourself. It helps you get rid of the negative bits of self and enhance the positive, jolly-nice bits.

In the end, we are just tomorrow's angels inside today's bodies. When next you sit in the mall or at the park watching people, perhaps running through the exercises we've talked about, try to see people as angels. See beyond their gender, physical body, and characteristics. Instead, see if you can feel the opaque, oscillating angelic force field, momentarily trapped inside and around the mind-body mechanism of their life. If you look in that etheric way, a new perception opens up. Gone is the yin-yang of it all, and the battle of the sexes. Instead, walking past you, is an eternal, androgynous spirit, neither male nor female.

"Yingiddy-Yangiddy, up and down, take the bubble from root to crown."

Somewhere in that yin-yang balance is the androgynous-self. It holds the key to all knowing. I've stumbled on it from time to time, but I'd be deluding myself if I said I had found the key to it all. I have certainly had the key at times, but more often than not, I dropped it in the sludge of my own silliness. Then the light of God, like a warm summer's breeze, dried the sludge. And suddenly I saw the key once more—only to lose it in the mud of my ego/personality a little later.

Try this: Sit in front of a mirror in a darkened room; light a candle; and play some soft, sacred music—Gregorian chants work well. Stare at your eyes in the mirror. Start asking, "Who am I?" over and over. At first your mind will offer you the obvious by answering with your name. Keep asking the question over and over. Your mind doesn't actually know the answer. It may become uncomfortable, so it will flit about, trying to distract you. Keep asking the question in a voice that gradually descends to a whisper. Eventually the mind shrugs it off and goes silent. For only your deep, inner, spiritual feelings—those that hang in the pulse of your etheric field—know how to answer you.

If you drop to a meditative state while doing this exercise, you may see the shape of your face change as you gaze at your reflection. Don't panic, just watch. You'll see other faces laid over yours. They will start slowly, and then sometimes they gather speed. I've seen them pass through one-a-second, sixty-a-minute. It's quite awesome. Some say they're the faces of your previous incarnations; I can't say if that's right or not.

Some years ago, I had a really lovely, very spiritual person working for me as an editorial assistant, and she tried this mirror process at the office. The faces flashed through, and then she saw one that was covered in blood. She was convinced she'd suffered some terrible trauma in a past life. Maybe she had. The sight of the blood made her stop, which was a pity, as she might have seen the answer to it all if she'd been able to hang in there.

The faces are very mysterious. Some are beautiful. Maybe they are your past lives, or maybe they are the faces of people you've known in previous lives. But since they come from the question, *Who am I?*, you'd imagine that they are connected to you. Most likely it's your inner-self showing you that you are connected to much more than you realize, and that eventually we are all connected to everyone else.

The Grand Theory of Relationships

Scientists say that the universe started with a Big Bang. The Big Bang theory is very convincing, and it's been around a long time. The problem with the theory is that certain data contradicts it. When George Smoot and his team launched the COBE satellite to measure the background radiation of the cosmos, it found that the residue of the Big Bang is a radiation that has a temperature that is a few degrees above zero Kelvin. But what Smoot and his team also discovered was that there are ripples in that universal radiation. Now a Big Bang that starts from a singularity would expand out evenly in every direction, and so the ripples need to be accommodated if the theory is to hold water. Astrophysicists came up with Inflation Theory. Please be sure to know that I am not belittling their efforts, as even a hokey, third-rate physicist has a thousand times more brain power and knowledge than I would ever accumulate, but Inflation Theory is a bit of a botched job in my view.

What it says is that, in the minutest split second after the Big Bang, the expanding universe suddenly accelerated (inflation), momentarily going faster than light (Uh? Excuse me? Faster than light? Didn't you guys tell us that isn't possible?). Then, Inflation Theorists say that it stuttered back to normal, then it sped up again—and so on; a few times, very rapidly, all in a fraction of a second. That, they say, explains the ripples in the background radiation. Now they may be right, as the universe at that evolutionary moment just after the Big Bang was infinitely smaller than a pinhead.

But there is an alternative explanation, which isn't often mentioned. I offer it here, as it sounds spiritual, and it fits handily into my observations up the near-death tube—which gave me the impression that everything really is connected. Of course, it's natural for one to seek out data that backs one's ideas, but then again, I'm not holding myself up as an expert on the Big Bang or Inflation Theory; I just like to consider alternatives—especially one alternative that has been expressed by Hindu mystics and holy men for thousands of years—one that says everything is inside everything else.

It's the Grand Theory of Relationships, I suppose.

There are some cosmologists who say that the universe is immortal, that in fact it didn't begin with a bang. Instead, they say, it was born or emitted from a previous universe, much as a soap bubble might float up from a pile of suds. The bubble theory says that our universe was created in this way, and that other universes are or will be created from this one. So, in effect, each universe is the product of a previous one.

One of the mysteries of cosmology surrounds the question of matter. Is there enough matter in the universe to force it to collapse back on itself, via gravitation—the Big Crunch, as it is sometimes called—or will it expand forever?

CNI News (**http://www.cninews.com/**), an Internet newsletter I subscribe to sometimes, recently quoted a leading cosmologist, Andre Linde, who says that the Big Bang idea is all wrong. He claims that the known universe isn't the whole thing; that our universe "bubbled off" a previous universe, and it will, in turn, sprout other universes in a sequence that lasts, literally, forever.

Professor Linde, a Russian physicist based at Stanford University in California, explained his new idea at a recent meeting of the American Association for the Advancement of Science. Considered a leading architect of "new universe theories," Linde says that the problem with the Big Bang theory is that it can't explain observed phenomena. Among the biggest problems: The universe is not inflating uniformly as called for by the Big Bang. Some parts of the universe are newer than other parts, and the newer parts are inflating and expanding exponentially. They will eventually come to a stage similar, or perhaps dissimilar, to our observed part of the universe, Linde says.

Not only that, but as Linde sees it, the Big Bang theory cannot possibly account for all the visible matter in the known universe. By his reckoning, the Big Bang should not have produced even "the amount of particles necessary to make one journalist," let alone billions of galaxies.

The birthing of one universe from another sounds nice. It reflects our human condition, one human cell dividing to produce another human. Maybe the whole function of existence is for us to birth a further existence, so everything can progress ever further upwards. The Second Law of Thermodynamics, which requires everything to descend to a heat death, always sounded a bit grim to me. Birthing a new and upward spiral off a dying one seems a bit more hopeful.

And even if some of your relationships might have seemed to be failures at the time, each gave birth to a personal universe of more experiences, and that has helped you in the direction of an eventual reconciliation with self. So, in a way, relationships follow Professor Linde's theory, each one bubbling off the previous one. In the eternity of things, there aren't really any mistakes.

Intimacy, Vulnerability, and the Shadow Self

Of course, at a subtle energy level, a relationship has a built-in propensity not to last. Although its function is to accentuate love and one's inner spiritual self through interaction, the very act of bringing out the light and expressing it as love calls for a vulnerability that may cause problems. Most people are terrified of intimacy, so if your relationships survive, you can pat yourself on the back, but then again, they may only survive if each of you is prepared to deny and repress the shadow. Once the shadow comes out, your relationship may survive, and it may not. If it doesn't, you shouldn't take it personally or deem it a failure, as it has helped you discover yourself, even though the process might have involved a fair deal of aggravation.

We are all fragile. We have fears, antagonisms, hatred, and destructive tendencies. In social situations, we bury them to accommodate the rules of manners and politeness. But in the privacy of our relationship, much of the "stuffing down" of those feelings is suddenly released. That's why intimacy feels so vulnerable to many. Of course, most of those antagonisms and insecurities come from the programming we received from our family of origin and our upbringing, but they also come from our sense of insecurity, which is a natural part of the human journey. When you think about how many disasters you have to avoid on an average day just to make it through, it's not surprising that people are a little uptight.

You can so easily kid yourself that the social self you express to the outside world reflects the totality of who you are. It's easy to pretend to yourself what a good person you are, all sweetness and light and sugar and spice, blah diddy blah. Intimate relationships sooner or later throw us a "reality check." But you can't be too hard on yourself, for most of the fear, resentment, and anger was spoon-fed to you in your formative years. And the recipe for that concoction has been handed down for a thousand years or more. It's a miracle that we aren't all stark raving mad. The child mimics its parents' insecurities. Then it learns more dysfunction at school, where it is taught to compete. Having to constantly evaluate itself, it will soon envy and resent those who are more successful or more fortunate. It's a recipe for dysfunction.

Then there is all the subtle, insidious stuff that was projected upon you as a child. In a family where there are several children, you will find, more often than not, that one child silently agrees to harbor the shadow for the rest of the family. So, by silent contract, everybody projects their stuff onto that child. Child A is all sweetness and light, and Child B is bright and helpful. Child C is, for no obvious reason, a nightmare. Scream, rotate your head—spew green slime!

Child C is the brat, the troublemaker—the unreliable, moody one—the one the family can blame and project its shadow upon. We each create our shadow bogeymen in our families, our interpersonal relationships, and in our nations. Fascism and the rise of the Nazi party was the outcropping of a nation's shadow, the birthing of the pre-war Germany's shadow-self. If you look at the restriction, control, and emotional or physical violence that was so much a part of the German method of raising children, you can see how that might spill out at a later date.

Current-day Japan is fairly similar. Children are forced to perform at an early age. They are given endless restrictions, rules, and duties, and they have to subjugate their childlike tendencies to compete and study long hours—rather than playing, and being uninhibited, and discovering themselves. What's it for? So the kid can get a job as a clerk at Mitsubishi. What happiness might that bring him? I reckon that Japan will have to change, or all the restrictions of so many repressed individuals will spill over and bite the country on the bum.

When countries run out of energy, they act very much like ordinary people, looking for a scapegoat to accept their anger and disquietude. Notice how relationships change when you run out of energy. You may find that you try to place the blame on your partner. Once you see that in action, you'll be more aware of how each of you operates on energy dips. Each of you can then discuss what happens, and you can attempt to arrive at a more equitable method for handling energy deficits. If you have children, you can show them by example how you handle yourself in those sorts of situations. So then the children can learn to retreat to some quiet place to handle their discomfort, rather than punching out their brothers and sisters.

Expressed anger is destructive, yet repressed anger is only "delayed" destruction. It will leak out if not dealt with and discussed. You might want to have a family pow-wow from time to time, sitting round a campfire, each discussing how you feel—a place where injustices are aired and put right. Otherwise, the family's collective shadow builds as repressed anger, empowering the "collective brat" within—which sooner or later will come out and cause trouble until it is noticed and taken care of.

One of the techniques I have found useful, which you might consider, is to write down some of the darker elements or events in your life on a piece of paper. Then next time you're by a fire, light that piece of paper and release those aspects of self with a prayer, saying, "I return back to the God Force these darker aspects of myself that I am now coming to understand and process. I am now embracing my higher, Infinite Self. Please help me reconcile the light and the dark within me."

In the end, you're a mixture of both. Dark complements light and allows it to become special. If the dark comes out in an orderly way, especially in a family situation, you will see how creative your family members become, for, as I've said, creativity is the positive side of the shadow.

When I came off the road and entered into a bit of silence, I found music in my shadow. I can't sing for toffee, and I don't play any instruments, but I found I could hear music in my extrasensory perceptions. I could pick it up in my feelings, so I engaged the subtlety of that perception to make up for what I lacked in musical knowledge or my lack of a musical ear.

I have written a lot of books, so I've learned a bit about placing words. Through that, I found I could hang words off notes, even though I didn't know what the note was called or where it ought to be. I became a lyricist and made records with others who knew what they were doing. The first record I pulled together was called *Voice of the Feminine Spirit.* It featured a Norwegian soprano named Cecilia. It was made for the New Age market, and it was an instant success, selling over 150,000 copies—which in the New Age is close to miraculous.

Next, I wrote the lyrics for a New Age opera with the flute player, Tim Wheater. It's called *Heartland,* and it sounds a bit like New Age Wagner. And then I made four more albums, some of which are now out. So music and making records has given me a whole new place to play, and I've met some cool dudes and dudettes, and it's been heaps of fun. You never know what ideas and talents and opportunities lurk in the shadow once you start to look at it. Take the lid off and you'll see the crud. And under the crud, maybe there's a Grammy or an Oscar lurking, or a wonderful new form of creativity that may translate into a whole pile of money. Don't be scared of the shadow; it's a relief to resolve it and have it show you other aspects of itself.

Stepping into Free-Flow

To conclude this discussion on energy and relationships, I'd like to remind you that you gather power by being in control of the energy you have. Most people don't really have a need for external worldly power because they don't have a great need to influence other people. In fact, the more people you have to influence in life, the more you're burdening yourself with things you have to do. More often than not, having power over people is a tremendous misfortune, rather than a benefit.

The more you have to push and pull and maneuver people to get a job done, or you have to exert yourself to get them to do what you want, the more you burn yourself out. You go into struggle, which is the opposite of free-flow. Free-flow is the idea that the universe-at-large, your nature-self, and your energy, mixed with the God Force within you, will bring you everything that you'll ever really need. Things should come effortlessly in the fullness of time. The more people you're involved with, the more ego and mind you have to deal with. Sometimes having to deal with a lot of people is a setback. One should question carefully if one is too involved and overly sucked in to people and activity. Also, question whether in that involvement you're infringing on other people and changing their perspective. It's a powerful person who can walk through life and leave things as they are; even when he or she can see that by leaving people as they are, the situation might deteriorate before it gets better. But the purpose of life is to move through it effortlessly, consuming as little as possible, touching as little as possible, and walking silently through the gaps without really changing too much. The exception is, if people ask for help, then do what you can.

If you have to push and pull and strive and fight, you have to wonder, *Am I following the parabolas of energy that are the most productive for me, that have the most energy?* You need to engage the subtlety of your feelings to discover whether or not you're trying to put a square peg into a round hole. Looking toward the beauty and flow of things, you'll see a natural way. In any given situation, there is the path of least resistance, the one on which you don't have to fight to get what you want—one where you don't have to terrorize, manipulate, maneuver, control, or regulate to achieve your goals.

What you need is inner power, a personal charisma, a spiritual identity, and an extrasensory perception that makes you bigger than life, taking you beyond mundane things. How you garner that energy is through compassion, kindness, introspection, and solidity—and by understanding yourself as a spiritual being—one that is evolving quietly and gently through the human experience. In this way, you develop confidence, projecting silently out into the world.

The world has a rhythm, a destiny, and a karma. It is a collective; we are all inside the one global mind—each of us makes up a molecule of that mind. We don't have all the answers, so we are forced to move along one step at a time. The global mind and the individual evolutions that make up that global mind are entitled to make their own decisions. They are entitled to make the wrong decisions, for there is no right and wrong, really; there is only the infinite love of the God Force and the winding journey we all make, attempting to return to our celestial source.

In other words, we have plenty of time to work it out, and we are entitled to head up the wrong way, entitled to marry the wrong people, to get involved in the wrong deals, to eat the wrong foods, whatever. People are entitled to carve out their own destiny. The philosophy of non-infringement says that everybody is moving along according to the dictates of the ego-personality, or their inner Infinite Self, or a mixture of all of it. Where they are going is where they're supposed to be going, and one shouldn't be changing it.

Try this one: Next time your girlfriend is in the dress shop and she picks something that looks absolutely ghastly, say nothing. Just let her buy it. Now, if she asks you what you think, don't dissuade her; at most, suggest she try on a few more dresses before finally making up her mind. Try to let her act out her decisions without any influence from you.

The problem with our world is that we all infringe upon each other way too much. We haven't learned that control is old-fashioned, that consciousness has changed. If only we'd all back off a bit. If we all understood non-infringement, we'd have low taxes, safe neighborhoods, and the spirit of love and cooperation in our society and in our families. It will take time, but you can start the process right now. Focus on non-infringement. It becomes your teacher for a while, and it will show you things inside other things. It will show you aspects of compassion and infinity you may not have seen before.

The need to control others is a manifestation of insecurity. From that often flows infringement, then reaction. Then in the fear, one stiffens, and in the end you can't flow down the river of life. Sometimes you have to let go and become vulnerable. You have to flow and trust. To find yourself, you have to agree to lose yourself first. Odd, really, isn't it?

So you bring perception and the sixth sense to relationships by watching the flow of energy and reacting with positive action when needed—or by not reacting when negative energy is expressed—detaching and guarding your reserves of energy.

CHAPTER 13

26 DIMENSIONS OF THE ROTATING OCTAHEDRON AND THE ZERO POINT

I recently had a vision in which an acrobat was doing somersaults around a wall, one that was free standing. In the diagram below, you'll see that the acrobat was to the west of the wall. On the first somersault, he jumped from the west to the south, then he jumped to the east, then to the north and back to the west. And his last jump was all along the whole length of the wall from west to east. Five moves in all.

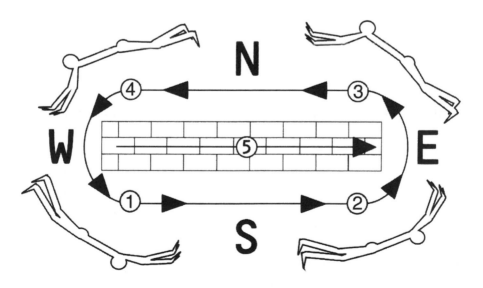

DIAGRAM #4: The acrobat somersaults around and along the wall.

I realized that another acrobat could have started from the north and gone the opposite way, jumping first to the east, then to the south, and then over to the west and back to the north. Then he could jump over the wall and end up at the south. Each acrobat could make five continuous maneuvers without going back on himself (backward in time), and without duplicating the jumps the other acrobat makes; as the two acrobats are, of course, going around in different directions.

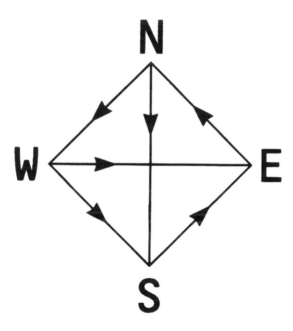

DIAGRAM #5: The acrobats' jumps describe a square and its diagonals.

I realized that the jumps around the wall describe a square and its diagonals. I came to the conclusion that the vision had to do with the previous one I'd had about the four forces of nature and the mysterious fifth force. Now, even if you're not mathematically inclined, you might want to follow along anyway, as the math involved will show you a symmetry that describes an interesting feature of the zero point, the gateway to other worlds that I discussed before.

Not long after the first vision, I had another. The corners of the square were assigned numbers. The south corner was given the number 60, the west 33, the north 80, and east was 170+ something. It all moved so fast that

I didn't quite get the last digit of the last number. I wondered what it meant, and what the last number might be. I started tinkering with the numbers, adding the three numbers that I was certain of; and I saw that south, west, and north added together come to 173 (60 + 33 + 80 = 173). I realized that 173 was the value assigned in my vision to the eastern point of the square. Now I had coordinates for my jumping acrobats.

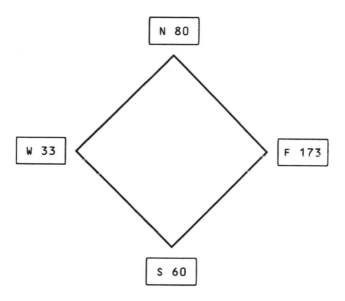

DIAGRAM #6: The coordinates I was given for the square.

I wondered what to do with the numbers that I'd been given; I added and subtracted them to see what they might mean. I went through various permutations, and eventually I came to one that looked promising. I subtracted east from north (80 -173) and got -93, and I then added south to west (60 + 33) and that came to +93. Adding north (80) to west (33) equals 113, and subtracting east from south (60 - 173) equals -113. Then I added north (80) to south (60) and got 140, and I subtracted west from east (173-33) and also got 140. You can see from Diagram #7 on the next page that to my amazement, there is a perfect plus-minus, mirrorlike symmetry between the opposite sides of the square once the various coordinates are subtracted or added together. And the two values for the diagonal are 140.

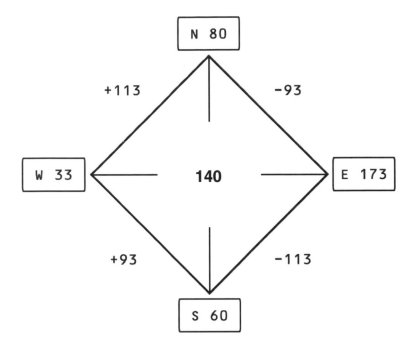

DIAGRAM #7: The strange plus-minus mirror symmetry of the square.

I became quite excited when I realized that the coordinates I had been given in the vision weren't arbitrary; they were there to tell me something. While pondering on it, I got a hunch to convert the 2-D square into a 3-D pyramid. I saw that if you mentally picked up the middle of the square where the diagonals cross at the 140 coordinate, it forms a pyramid with five points. The top of the pyramid I have marked "Apex A."

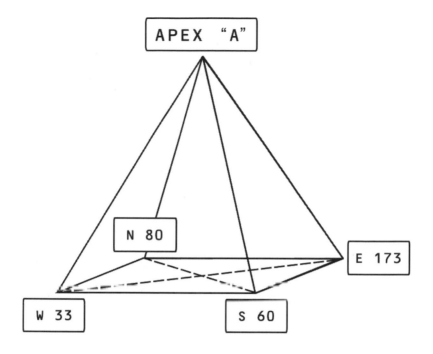

DIAGRAM #8: The 2-D square becomes a 3-D pyramid.

Now remember, one acrobat starts in the west and jumps first to the south and then continues around counterclockwise, arriving back at the west; and he then makes his final jump along the wall from west to east. And the other acrobat starts at the north, jumps to the east, and goes clockwise round the square, finishing up with a jump over the wall from north to south. So you have 10 (5 x 2) possible jumps or rotations. Of course, you could start the first acrobat at the east instead of the west, and have him jump counterclockwise, and the second acrobat could start at the south instead of the north. But that would not give you a different result; you would still only have ten jumps total. I realized that the acrobats can't jump backwards, as that would mean going backwards in time. So, for example, an acrobat can't jump from east to south and suddenly back to east.

I read Mishio Kaku's book *Hyperspace,* in which he talks about 10 dimensions of reality, and a rotation of those 10 dimensions in hyperspace, he says, describes a possible 26 dimensions. So I began thinking about the missing 16 rotations or dimensions in my vision of the square that had now become a pyramid. Remembering that I'd seen the spirit worlds as mirrored,

I suddenly realized that there had to be another pyramid on the bottom of the first one, its mirror image. So now I wound up with an octahedron—an eight-sided geometric shape made up of two pyramids that share the same floor or base (see Diagram #9). I marked the apex of the bottom pyramid "Apex B."

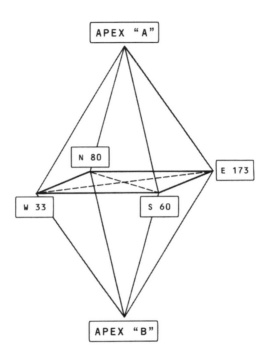

DIAGRAM #9: The second mirror pyramid creates an octahedron.

If the acrobats can make ten jumps around the wall, which now, of course, is the floor of the two pyramids, and those ten jumps occur in the top pyramid, then there would be the same number of rotations (jumps) in the bottom pyramid. So now we would have a total of 20 rotations or dimensions, for example. Now here is where the astounding beauty of this vision and its mathematics come into play. It's maybe a bit complicated for some to follow, but if you can endure it to the end, it will deliver you at the zero point, the gateway to the other worlds.

When the acrobat jumps from west to south (60), to east (173), to north (80), and back to west (33), and he then jumps along the wall (140) across the diagonal, which is now the diagonal of the square floor, he goes through rotations that total 486 (60 + 173 + 80 + 33 + 140 = 486).

And when the other acrobat jumps from north to east to south to west and back to north, he finishes with a fifth jump, along the north-south diagonal. Those moves also add up to 486. Remember that the two acrobats can perform five moves twice in the top pyramid (ten rotations), and they can do the same five moves twice in the bottom mirror pyramid. So there is a total of 20 jumps or rotations. So adding that up comes to 60 + 173 + 80 + 33 + 140 x 4 = 1944. Expressed more simply, it's 486 x 4 = 1944. The acrobats make 20 jumps for a 1944 total, and so you could say that 20 dimensions/rotations = 1944.

But we are still 6 rotations short of the 26 dimensions/rotations we're looking for. After pondering a while, I realized that if you convert/invert the two pyramids that make up the octahedron so they swap positions—basically you have to turn them inside out and outside in—you get six more dimensions. Before you start banging your head on the wall wondering what the hell I'm talking about, let me reassure you that there is a simple way of visualizing it.

You have to imagine that in Diagram #9, the point marked "west" travels along the diagonal of the pyramids' floor all the way over to east, taking all its connecting lines with it. And east travels all the way over to the west doing the same. So in effect, west and east swap positions, so the far left-hand part of the drawing of the pyramids swaps places with the far right-hand part.

Simultaneously, south travels to north along the diagonal, and north travels to south. They also take their connecting lines with them. So now you have four more moves or rotations. Adding those 4 moves to the 20 that we have already makes 24. But we're still looking for the last two moves, as we need to end up with 26.

Of course, what happens is, the two apexes that I have marked A and B also swap positions. Apex A travels down through the zero point in the center of the floor of the pyramids, all the way to B. And Apex B rises through the zero point where the diagonals cross to the former position of Apex A. Once that happens, all the points of the octahedron have changed positions with their opposites. That's what is meant by a conversion and an inversion. You'll notice how the outside of the top pyramid becomes the inside of the bottom one, and the inside walls of the bottom pyramid turn inside out to become the outside walls of the top one (see Diagram #10).

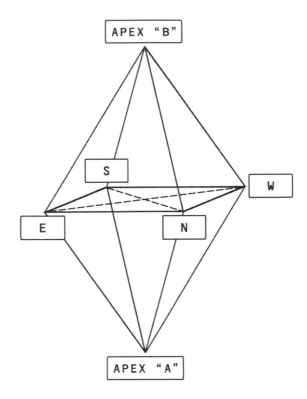

DIAGRAM #10: Both pyramids swap all their positions.

In such a rotation, the two pyramids act as mirror opposites of each other. It is a binary system, and it's a mirror image. When the octahedron is in its normal position with Apex A at the top and Apex B at the bottom, we could assign it the number one. And when all the points of the two pyramids collapse to the center of the floor (the zero point), the octahedron momentarily disappears into a singularity (0). It goes into a void, the zero state. So the first half of the conversion/inversion of the two pyramids is described as the ratio of 1:0.

When all the points then emerge from the zero point in the center of the floor and they complete the second half of their journey to the opposite positions, we could say that the octahedron is in its minus state (-1). The second half of the conversion/inversion starts with every point at the center of the floor at the singularity, the zero point (0); and the movement ends with Apex B at the top and Apex A now at the bottom. Of course, east has gone to west and south to north, etc. So the octahedron has flipped from a zero condition (0) to its mirror state -1, which is its binary opposite expressed as 0:-1.

You'll remember that I said that up the near-death tube there is a rotation, which causes a mirror twist as you pass it, so at the other end of the tube you would find yourself in an opposite mirror world. Well, that is what the two pyramids in Diagram #10 have just done. I also said that at the point of exiting from the body in an out-of-body experience, you black out, as I did walking through the forest when I flipped out of my body. I think that as one makes the transition out of the physical via death, or in a near-death experience, or in the OBE state, one passes through the zero point singularity, which is a void (0) in the middle of the pyramids' floor. Hence, the momentary blackout.

I came to think that the two pyramids of the octahedron, which convert and invert, describe our physical reality and its relationship to the mirrored spirit worlds. The rotating octahedron is a map of the journey up the near-death tube to the worlds beyond. I also discovered that, in fact, an octahedron with these particular coordinates would not exactly be a pyramid joined to another pyramid, as in the diagram. The shape of the octahedron would be a bit stretched out, with one long side in the direction of east (173). But it is easier to look at it as two pyramids for now, and it makes no difference to the calculations, as the coordinates are not a measure of distance. Rather, they are positions on a map—in the same way that one might use coordinates to express the position of Chicago in relation to Houston, L.A., and New York.

I wanted to see what the final mathematical total was for all the 26 rotations, so I tinkered with the figures once more, and something really astounding came to me.

In addition to the 20 jumps or rotations the acrobats make, you have to add the rotations that occur when the pyramids of the octahedron turn inside out and outside in. So west travels along the diagonal to east (140), and, of course, east goes to west (140); while north travels to south along the pyramid's floor (140), and south goes to north (140). Those four movements of 140 each come to 560 (140 x 4 = 560). So 560 has to be added to the previous total of 1944. Now we've got 2,504, and a total of 24 rotations so far.

Next, I had to work out what the value was for the journey that Apex A makes going to the position of Apex B. And that, of course, would have to be doubled as B also goes up to A's position. I discover that the value of the rotation as Apex A goes to the center of the floor is 50. Then it travels through the floor to the opposite position of Apex B. So the total journey for Apex A going to the position of Apex B is 100. Of course, Apex B does the same as it travels up to A. So we now add 100 twice (100 x 2 = 200) to the total, and we get a grand total of 2,704 (2,504 + 200 = 2,704).

Therefore 2,704 is our magic number, which in this case describes all the 26 rotations—the ones our two acrobats can make, and the rotation of the two pyramids converting/inverting as all their points change places. The square root of 2,704 is 52 (52 x 52 = 2,704). Since there are two pyramids, you have to divide the square root 52 by 2, and so you end up with 26.

So, 2,704 is the magic number of the octahedron in Diagrams #9 and #10. That describes 26 dimensions or rotations. After I saw the vision of the acrobat jumping around the wall, later on I was given the mathematical coordinates in the second vision. I came to see that the octahedron and the various numbers assigned to the points west, south, east, and north describe the potential 26 dimensions of hyperspace in which we humans find ourselves and the mirror worlds of spirit opposite us.

Remember, I said in chapter 2 that the subconscious is also in the mirror worlds. So you could say that we are in the first octahedron (Apex A up and Apex B down [Diagram #9]) when we are in our intellect, and we are in the other version (Apex B up and Apex A down [Diagram #10]) via our subconscious. So the relationship or rotation between the intellect and the subconscious is also a binary system 1:0 and its mirror opposite 0:–1.

One might make a leap of faith and say that the universe and its rotating 26 dimensions, and our human consciousness (the waking intellect plus the subconscious mind) are one and the same thing—meaning that reality and thought are one and the same. The paradox of quantum physics is that a particle only becomes real once you observe it. So there is an obvious link between the mind and reality at a quantum level, anyway. I'd guess that the mind and the solid particle are in, or they are part of, the same wave-field; possibly they are two versions of the same thing. Perhaps there is only consciousness in the universe, and the solidity of parts of our universe is a just an effect that occurs when energy flips into this dimension. So as the octahedron flips in and out of its two versions, it is moving through a solid version and a nonsolid version, back and forth. I find it very interesting that many UFO reports describe the crafts as solid, and radar returns seem to confirm that. Then suddenly the UFO flips to a different frequency, and it performs impossible feats, like dividing in two, which indicates a nonsolid state. It's also interesting that many witnesses report hearing a distinct hum as the craft fly by.

Pythagoras talked of the music of the spheres. He said that the universe is formed from numbers, numbers govern the way planets orbit, and musical notes also follow a mathematical sequences. That is perhaps why music induces an altered state of consciousness. We emotionally recognize an intrinsic mathematical formula within the structure of music that is very dear to us. It describes a cosmic order that is imbedded subliminally into our comprehension of things. Musical notes as numbers are parts of the symmetry of the inverting/converting reality in which we live. A note is a number. A mantra is a number. A prayer is a series of numbers. It's all part of one bloody marvelous all-encompassing simple formula. The square root of 2,704 divided by 2 comes to 26!

My pal, author Martin Wetherill, was driving along north of Sydney, from Dee Why to Manly. He was playing a cassette tape of Phillip Glass's soundtrack to the movie *Mishima.* He'd just come from a workout at a gym, so he was relaxed and slightly tired. The music put him into a euphoric state, and suddenly, with no volition of his own, his etheric detached from his body and rose up through the roof of the car. He found himself slightly behind the car at a height of about 20 feet, trailing behind it like a kite.

His first reaction was, *Isn't this fantastic,* but moments later he looked down and realized he was the man below driving the car. He went through an extraordinary moment of confusion and panic. He could not comprehend how he was hovering above the car and still driving it. He remembers quite clearly thinking, *If I'm up here, who is driving down there?* He had to force himself to reenter his body, fearing he might crash if he didn't. In fact, his mind/body was fully in control of the car, while Martin was temporarily in his other vehicle, the out-of-body one.

Martini, as his friends call him, says that without a doubt it was the music that flipped him out. There was some resonant frequency in the piece that his inner-self responded to. Jim Morrison sang, "Break on through to the other side." Maybe the Doors intuitively knew the secret code.

This idea of a hidden frequency takes us back via a long and circuitous route to one of the desires I have for this life, which is to discover the sacred hum. You'll remember I said that I think it's in F-sharp. I am sure the resonance of the hum flips you into your nonsolid state, the etheric state.

Meanwhile, we have the formula and coordinates that describe the rotation through the zero point to the mirror worlds. So perhaps now we can just use those coordinates to flip ourselves through the floor of the pyramids to experience those worlds. That would bring a technology and a new sophistication to the sixth sense not seen before. You can see why I tried to etherically turn myself inside out. I only tried it once and I messed it up, but I'm sure with a little modification, it might work very well. Meanwhile, if you need a boost in penetrating the zero point, I've put a special exercise with a couple of mirrors in the Appendix. It will help you visualize the zero point; it's easy to rig up, and it should help you to no end.

Once we have the exact sound of the hum, and once we discover how to use it, we'll add in the mathematical coordinates of the octahedron, and we'll be able to flip in and out of this reality with ease. Maybe it's just a matter of thinking about the numbers as one enters a trance state. Anyway, in time, we'll perfect the method, and we'll discover more and more about the other words, which will impact us. We'll see the God Force on a regular basis, and we'll also see the hellish worlds; and once people see those worlds even once, they will straighten up double quick.

So the answer to the troubles of the world could be just the simple sound of a hum on a cassette tape and a bit of mathematics, which flips one over to the spiritual mirror state. Suddenly violence, the rise of fascist sentiments, the threat of ecological disasters, and the other ominous portents of this age will melt into the woodwork. People will understand things in a different light, and we'll live to see the sixth sense triumph, as it establishes a real world order—a kind and spiritual one.

Onwards and upwards. Or perhaps I should say, inwards and outwards. And don't let the suckers grind you down.

'Bye for now—Stuart.

APPENDIX

THE L-SHAPED ROOM

Here's a technique I stumbled on while pondering the rotating octahedron. However, if you have not read and basically understood the rotation concept as the two pyramids move through 26 dimensions as described in the last chapter, then this upcoming process might be a bit confusing. You might want to go back and read chapter 13 before you try this technique:

Get two mirrors from the hardware store about 2.5 feet high and 1.5 feet wide, and mount them in a corner of a room so they're butted together at right angles. The long sides should be vertical. The mirrors show you the square floor of the two pyramids and the zero point. You'll see how in Diagram #12.

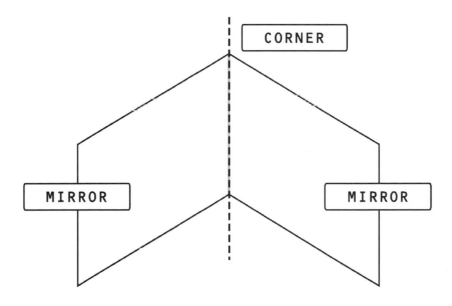

DIAGRAM #11: The mirrors butted together at right angles.

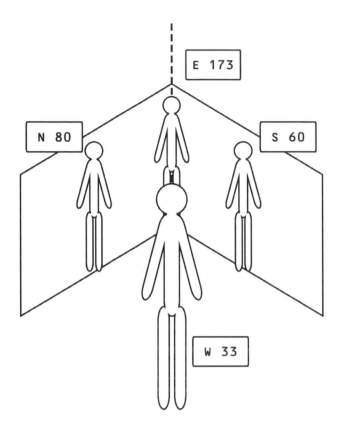

DIAGRAM #12: Sitting in front of the mirrors, looking at three reflections of you.

Sit about three feet away, facing the corner. To begin with, imagine you are at the west (33) point. The reason I've picked west rather than any of the other possible points is because my old teacher always said that there were 33 energies of man. He claimed that was the key to everything. He was a very irritating sort of bloke because he only gave bits of information, never the whole thing. But he knew things, bless him.

I'm not sure yet how the 33 energies of man ties into this octahedron thing, but it may help. Anyway, you have to pick one of the points—either north, south, west or east—so you might as well start with seeing yourself at the west. It certainly can't hurt.

Sitting three feet from the corner made by the two mirrors, there will be three reflections of your image. The one to your left is north (80). You may want to get a felt marker pen and mark 80 on the mirror beside that image. To your right is another image of you, and that is south (60)—mark that. Facing you is the third image in the mirror—it is east (173). Where the mirrors touch at right angles in the corner is the zero point on the pyramids' floor. You, of course, are sitting at west (33). So there are four of you—three reflections and the real you. That makes the square.

At first you might get slightly confused, as you might imagine that the zero point is in fact between you and the corner. In a way, it is. This is because your reflections are on two flat mirrors that are placed along the two 45° tangents that meet in the center of the square (see Diagram #12). But once you look into the mirrors and imagine a depth to your reflection facing you there, you'll see how the imagined depth then correctly places north, east, and south at the right distance from you. So the zero point then becomes the vertical line where the mirrors touch each other.

The important thing is that, when you're looking at the image directly in front of you, you are looking at east (173), which is beyond the zero point. So in a way you're looking at a spot that is beyond the near-death tube. Dim the lights, get a candle, and place it on the floor in front of you, and you'll see the candle reflected there. Now play your metronome or some sacred music, and get relaxed and deeply entranced. Open the chakras with the method I described before.

Next, you're going to want to walk through the zero point in your mind's eye. You do this by seeing yourself mentally twisting from your chair, through the zero point toward east (173), which is located, as I said, where the forward image of you is—the one that is directly facing you. Mentally visualize a twisting motion like an ice skater pirouetting, except you'll need to make two complete turns in your mind's eye. So you imagine yourself making two complete rotations between where you are sitting and the forward image of you that's in front of you at east (173) beyond the corner (0) where the two mirrors meet. I can't say I know why you have to twist twice, but that's what you do. There is a law in particle physics that describes the way certain particles spin, which follows the same double twist, so it may be a part of that law.

Anyway, imagine making two complete revolutions as you pass through the zero point with your mind. You are heading in your mind's eye toward the forward image of you that is facing you in the mirror.

Alternatively, you can see yourself tumbling forward as a gymnast might when doing a forward roll. If you mentally roll forward, make two complete rolls as well. The skater-type twist is a rotation around a vertical axis, and the forward roll is a rotation around a horizontal axis—either one is fine.

Going through the zero point toward east (173) is very interesting. You may find after a while that visions or impression come flooding in as you begin to penetrate the other worlds beyond the near-death tube. Perhaps you'll see your face change, as it is overlaid by many other faces, as I mentioned before. Sit and watch, and make a mental note of anything you see.

After you've tried going from west to east through zero, flip your mind and imagine that where you are now sitting has changed from west 33 to the top of the pyramid at Apex A (see Diagram #9 on page 206). Now you would be looking down from above at the zero point in the floor of the pyramids where the diagonals cross. Do the same twisting motion, and try to reach for Apex B, which, of course, is located in front of you beyond the corner where the two mirrors touch at the place where east 173 was in the previous exercise.

When looking from west to east, you are looking through the zero point along a horizontal plane, and when you imagine yourself looking from Apex A through the corner (0) to Apex B, it's the vertical plane.

The mirrors will help you a lot, as they show you the pathway to other worlds. Sometimes the experience is a bit eerie, especially when you're not used to it, but you have to hang in there and watch. After you've imagined yourself at west (33) and then at Apex A, try other things. See if you're prompted to make different moves or adjustments. Remember, it's the nature of the spiritual warrior to go where none has gone before.

Someone has to find the answers; it might as well be you. God bless.

BIBLIOGRAPHY

Chapter 1

About Time, by Paul Davies • Penguin Books • ISBN 0-670-84761-5

The Self-Aware Universe, by M. Goswami, R. Reed, and A. Goswami
J.P. Tarcher ISBN 0-671-71287-X

Shadows of the Mind, by Roger Penrose • Random House
ISBN 0-09-958211-2

Stephen Hawking's Universe, by David Filkin • BBC Books
ISBN 0-563-38301-1

Chapter 2

Hunting Down the Universe, by Michael Hawkins • Little, Brown and Company
ISBN 0-316-88333-6

The Roots of Consciousness, by Jeffrey Mishlove • Council Oak Books
ISBN 0-933031-70-X

Who's Afraid of Schrödinger's Cat?, by Ian Marshall and Danah Zohar
Bloomsbury Publishing • ISBN 0-7475-3192-7

Chapter 3

The Alchemy of the Heavens, by Ken Croswell • Oxford University Press
ISBN 0-19-286192-1

Companion to the Cosmos, by John R. Gribbin • Orion Books
ISBN 1-85799-891-X

The Fifth Miracle, by Paul Davies • The Penguin Press • ISBN 0-7139-9215-8

The Presence of the Past, by Rupert Sheldrake • Harper Collins
ISBN 0-00637-466-2

The Teachings of Don Juan: A Yaqui Way of Knowledge, by Carlos Castaneda
University of California Press • ISBN 0-52021-7578

Chapter 4

Holographic Repatterning (pamphlet), by Chlöe Wordsworth
HR Association of US • P.O. Box 6504, Scottsdale, AZ 85261-65054

The Secret Power of Music, by David Tame • Destiny Books
ISBN 0-89281-056-4

Skywatching, by David H. Levy • Harper Collins • ISBN 0-00-220028-7

Chapter 5

Alien Base, by Timothy Good • Random House • ISBN 0-7126-7812-3

The Biggest Secret, by David Icke • Bridge of Love Publications
ISBN 0-9526147-6-6

Man and His Symbols, by Carl Jung • Laureleaf • ISBN 0440-35-1839

Messengers of Deception, by Jacques Vallée • Ronin Publishing
ISBN 09-1590-4446

The Threat, by David M. Jacobs • Simon & Schuster • ISBN 0-684-84813-9

Chapter 6

Black Holes and Baby Universes, by Stephen Hawking • Bantam Books
ISBN 0-553-40663-9

The Fourth Dimension, by Rudy Rucker • Penguin Books • ISBN 0-14013-036-5

Journeys Out of the Body, by Robert A. Monroe • Main Street Books
ISBN 0-38500-8619

Chapter 10

The Last Hours of Ancient Sunlight, by Thom Hartmann • Mythical Books
ISBN 096-5572811

You Can Make a Difference, by Martin J. Wetherill and Bo Nielson
Business Artists Intl. • ISBN 0-646-30694-4

Chapter 12

The Cup of Destiny, by Trevor Ravenscroft • Samuel Weiser, Inc.
ISBN 0-87728-546-2

Chapter 13

Stalking the Wild Pendulum, by Itzhak Bentov • Inner Traditions
ISBN 089-281-2028

ABOUT THE AUTHOR

Author and lecturer **Stuart Wilde** is one of the real characters of the self-help, human-potential movement. His style is humorous, controversial, poignant, and transformational. He has written 14 books, including those that make up the very successful Taos Quintet, which are considered classics in their genre. They are: *Affirmations, The Force, Miracles, The Quickening, and The Trick to Money Is Having Some.* Stuart's books have been translated into 12 languages.

Stuart Wilde International Tour and Seminar Information
For information on Stuart's latest tour and seminar dates in the
USA and Canada, contact:

White Dove International
P.O. Box 1000
Taos, NM 87571
(505) 758-0500 (phone)
(505) 758-2265 (fax)
Stuart's Website: www.stuartwilde.com

OTHER HAY HOUSE TITLES OF RELATED INTEREST

Being: *How to Increase Your Awareness of Oneness,*
by Lee Coit

Chakra Clearing: *Awakening Your Spiritual Power to Know and Heal,*
by Doreen Virtue, Ph.D.

The Contact Has Begun: *The True Story of a
Journalist's Encounter with Alien Beings,* by Phillip H. Krapf

Interpreting Dreams A–Z, by Leon Nacson

The Meditation Book, by John Randolph Price

7 Paths to God: *The Ways of the Mystic*, by Joan Borysenko, Ph.D.

Sound Choices: *Using Music to Design the Environments
in Which You Live, Work, and Heal,* by Susan Mazer and Dallas Smith

What Color Is Your Personality? *Red, Orange, Yellow, Green . . .*
by Carol Ritberger, Ph.D.

NOTES

NOTES

NOTES

NOTES

We hope you enjoyed this Hay House book.
If you would like to receive a free catalog featuring additional
Hay House books and products, or if you would like information about
the Hay Foundation, please contact:

Hay House, Inc.
P.O. Box 5100
Carlsbad, CA 92018-5100

(760) 431-7695 or **(800) 654-5126**
(760) 431-6948 (fax) or **(800) 650-5115 (fax)**

Please visit the Hay House Website at: **www.hayhouse.com**